THE EUROPEAN UNDERSTANDING OF INDIA

General Editors of the Series

K. A. BALLHATCHET
P. J. MARSHALL
D. F. POCOCK

European attempts to understand India have been pursued in a variety of fields. Many of the books and articles that resulted are still of great historical importance. Not only do they provide valuable information about the India of the time; they are also of significance in the intellectual history of Europe. Each volume in the present series has been edited by a scholar who is concerned to elucidate both its Indian and its European relevance.

Essays on the Caste System
by Célestin Bouglé

Essays on the Caste System
by Célestin Bouglé

Translated with an introduction by

D. F. POCOCK

*Reader in Social Anthropology and Dean of
the School of African and Asian Studies
University of Sussex*

CAMBRIDGE
AT THE UNIVERSITY PRESS
1971

Published by the Syndics of the Cambridge University Press
Bentley House, 200 Euston Road, London NW1 2DB
American Branch: 32 East 57th Street, New York, N.Y.10022

© Cambridge University Press 1971

Library of Congress Catalogue Card Number: 79-154506

ISBN: 0 521 08093 2

Printed in Great Britain
at the University Printing House, Cambridge
(Brooke Crutchley, University Printer)

Contents

Preface to the English edition

The *Année Sociologique*, resuming its duties after the late war, paid tribute in the following words to Célestin Bouglé who had died in the tragic interim:

The name of Bouglé is...particularly linked with that of the *Année Sociologique* in which he was one of the earliest and most active collaborators. Born in 1870 at Saint-Brieuc, Bouglé was a Breton and possessed the two great qualities of his people: stubbornness and generosity. Drawn to sociology quite young, he published in 1896 a work on the social sciences in Germany (*Les sciences sociales en Allemagne*). He was pre-occupied above all by problems of structure and social justice and devoted his thesis, which he defended in 1899, to egalitarian ideas (*Idées égalitaires*), and was thus led, by the contrast, to a study of the caste system on which he published a memoir in the *Année Sociologique* in 1908. Three years later he brought out *La sociologie de Proudhon*, and, following up his interest in the great reformer, prepared an edition of his complete works. His lectures on the evolution of values (*L'evolution des valeurs*, 1922) constitute perhaps his richest and most developed work. Seized by an incurable illness, his smiling courage during his last years remains an unforgettable lesson for those who witnessed it. He died in January 1940.

...Bouglé is not to be found in his works alone. He was, in the fullest sense of the word, an animator. At the Ecole normale superieure of which he was Director from 1935 until his death but of which he had been deputy Director since 1927, he created a Centre for social documentation which, under his vigorous direction, became a fertile seed-bed of the social sciences. The majority of young French sociologists there acquired an interest in directing their energies along a path scarcely favoured by the public authorities and which might have seemed to many a blind alley. More a man of action than of the study, Bouglé was a militant apostle of sociology.[1]

This conventional obituary tells the English reader, whether he be a specialist in Indian affairs or a social scientist more than he is likely to have known about Célestin Bouglé. For all that he succeeded, finally, to Durkheim's chair at the Sorbonne, he has not in this country, nor I believe in France, that reputation as the great successor unassailably accorded to Durkheim's son-in-law, Marcel Mauss. As his obituarist indicates, Bouglé was dedicated

[1] *Année Sociologique*, 3rd series, 1940–8, pp. xii–xiii, Paris, 1949.

to political sociology and, one feels, this dedication sprang from a continuing belief that sociology was on the brink of demonstrating its practical utility in the service of liberal ideals.

There is nothing in Bouglé's career that might lead us to suppose that his *Essays on the caste system* had the importance for him that they have subsequently acquired. A careful scrutiny of the volumes of the Année, in which most of them appeared before the 1908 edition, does not reveal a hint of any interest in Indology on his part either before or after the completion of the task. Works dealing with the sub-continent were invariably handled by other reviewers.

Bouglé's concern with the Indian caste system is, then, not that of an Indian specialist but arose rather from methodological perfectionism. The bulk of the work was done while he was actively engaged with his thesis on egalitarian ideas and was undertaken as a comparative check to enable him to understand these ideas the better. It is an astonishing testimony to his energy and powers of synthesis that work which was essentially a side-line, a by-product of his major thesis, should continue to rank as a basic introductory work in its field. Bouglé was no sanskritist nor had he any first-hand experience of the Indian sub-continent and yet despite these apparent handicaps the *Essays* are unquestionably a work of sociological genius.

Why, the reader may well ask, has a work of 'sociological genius' had to wait more than fifty years to appear in the English language?[1] Apart from the chances that govern these things, we may still hazard a guess or two by way of answer. Two earlier authors in the French tradition had had their impact upon English thought about India. The famous Abbé Dubois was partially known to influential writers such as James Mill and John Wilson in the nineteenth century and Beauchamp presented the complete text to the English public in 1897.[2] Emile Senart, although certainly less known, published in *Les castes dans l'Inde* in 1896. Although this work had to wait thirty-four years before it was

[1] The present author translated the *Introduction* in *Contributions to Indian sociology*, edited by L. Dumont and D. Pocock, no. ii, pp. 7–30 (Mouton, 1958).

[2] Abbé J. A. Dubois, *Hindu manners, customs and ceremonies*, translated and edited by Henry K. Beauchamp, C.I.E., 3rd edition, 1906. See the editor's introduction for a brief history of Dubois's MSS.

translated,[1] one of the greatest living English authorities, Sir Herbert Risley, was quick to seize on the French original and to quote extensively from it in his *People of India* published in 1908.

Risley's *People of India* was almost the last production of that great tradition of administrator scholars who had long and extensive experience in the Indian Civil Service and had not found their arduous activity incompatible with scholarship. In the early twentieth century this tradition died and its last representative was J. H. Hutton whose *Caste in India* appeared in 1944 and contains only passing references to Bouglé. (Hutton's thought on these matters had not evolved significantly since 1931 when he formulated his views on caste for the Census of that year.) To note the differences in the relations between the thought of Senart and Risley on the one hand and of Hutton and Bouglé on the other is to see how English writing about India had changed since 1908. Risley had provided Bouglé with the volumes of the latest Census and would not have found Bouglé's interests or intellectual universe any more alien than he had found that of Senart. But, although Hutton wrote essentially from the premises of nineteenth century evolutionism and ethnography, this tradition was no longer vital in his hands.[2] Whereas the premise of social evolution had enabled the earlier exponents of the tradition to move towards bold syntheses of their facts, in Hutton's work we have only speculative palaeontology. Nesfield, Senart, Risley and Ibbetson couched their understanding of the essence of caste in the language of origins, for Hutton the supposed 'origins' which he lists are offered *as* the essence. No spirit could have been more opposed to Bouglé's synthesizing and global view of caste as a system.

Bouglé's work appeared when the tradition of the scholar administrator was on the wane but far too early for the revival of sociology in the form of British social anthropology after the First World War.[3] Although Bouglé was no stranger to the language of evolutionism, his concern with form and with system

---

[1] *Caste in India*, translated by Sir E. Denison Ross, C.I.E., 1930.

[2] 'Evolutionary social theory, and the positivist assumptions about the nature of science and of society which gave it vitality, died, in England, slowly and unspectacularly.' J. W. Burrow, *Evolution and society*, Cambridge, 1966, p. 260.

[3] *Ibid.*

brought him nearer to the British school of so-called function-
alism than any other surviving strain of anthropology in this
country at the time. But despite this, even when the view of
Malinowski and Radcliffe Brown had become the established
orthodoxy and the British student had come to hear of Durkheim,
Bouglé still remained neglected. Of this neglect the cause is
clear: the preoccupations of British social anthropology in the
years between the wars were with small scale, and, as it was
supposed, homogeneous 'primitive' societies. The great non-
European civilizations were too big, too complicated and so, in
short, nothing was done. Nothing was done effectively until after
the late war when India and Pakistan had achieved independence
and a new generation of British and American social anthropologists, trained for the most part by specialists in other areas,
turned their attention largely towards the new India. Since that
time, as Louis Dumont remarks, in his *Préface* to the fourth
edition of the *Essais*, 'We can affirm one remarkable fact: when
intensive field studies in this area gathered new impetus in 1945,
the partial translation of Bouglé in 1958 had a noticeable effect
upon the specialists: it concentrated attention upon castes as
constituting a system and helped to bring back into this system
the village network of the divisions of labour which had tended
to be left outside'.[1] More generally a historian of sociological
ideas could write: 'More than any other single study, this
[Bouglé's] essay [sic] laid the basis for the modern theory of
caste.'[2]

Bouglé's work was, then, almost entirely unknown to two
generations of British scholars and consequently to two generations of administrative officers. Equally, it did not constitute an
element in Indian thought about Indian society and had no impact upon what we may distinguish as the indigenous sociology.
This, to the extent that it did not derive uncritically from the
dharmasastra, lay split between the ethnography of the so-called
aborigines and a directionless manipulation of statistics: head
measuring on one hand and head counting on the other, either

[1] *Essais sur le régime des castes*, par C. Bouglé, préface de Louis Dumont 4e
edition, 1969, pp. viii–ix.
[2] D. Martindale, *The nature and types of sociological theory*, 1961, p. 265.

way alienated from the actualities, chronic and acute, of Indian society in the inter-war years.[1] The dialectic between thought and action is to be found rather in the writings of politicians, in the writings of Nehru and of Gandhi.

It would be foolish to argue that things would have been 'better' or even significantly different had Bouglé's thought been allowed to make its contribution. Certainly one would not wish for him what Beauchamp proudly claimed for Dubois's work that it had been received in India 'with universal approval and eulogy'. What one regrets is that given the propensity among academics of the period to accept all too readily the western version, Bouglé's conception of Indian civilization as a structured unity combined with an analytic approach resting on accepted facts might have been a healthy corrective to the growing emphasis upon diversity and academic palaeontology.

I have outlined elsewhere what I believe to be the contribution of Bouglé and that intellectual tradition which springs from him to the sociological consciousness of modern India.[2] The argument is briefly this: his presentation of the traditional unity of India permits us to see not only that the modern unity, still in process of creation, is flatly opposed to the traditional but also it prepares the ground for a rational strategy to assist in that creative process. To take a simple and gross example: however much the modern politician is obliged to temporize with caste belief and practice, the entire system *as such* stands opposed to the modern conception of the state however differently, and this is quite secondary, different political parties may choose to characterize it. And one must add, for fear of misunderstanding, there is no judgement of value involved here.

One can criticize Bouglé, of course. The most glaring gap in his account is the almost total lack of reference to caste in Muslim communities or to the Moghul period. More excusable perhaps

---

[1] Here one must make exception of G. S. Ghurye in whose varied intellectual history almost every strain is represented including a strong impulse towards a synthetic view of his own society in his own time. One cannot but feel however that the failure of this powerful and mercurial figure to achieve finally an intellectual integration is symptomatic of the period.

[2] 'Social anthropology: its contribution to planning', p. 271 ff. in *Crisis of Indian planning*, ed. Paul Streeten & Michael Lipton (Royal Institute of International Affairs, 1968).

is the failure to develop out of his discussion of Buddhism a treatment of what we call 'sect' in relation to caste.[1] Such negative criticisms, and minor details, relate to Bouglé's failure to incorporate material which was available to him. The more radical and positive criticism refers not to the man but to the work and relates it to a creative tradition which was able to correct its deficiencies.

In the work that follows the reader will note how determinedly Bouglé adheres to his definition of the caste system as expressed in the interrelation of three organizing principles: hierarchy, specialization and repulsion (or separation). It is because these three principles are found systematically related in India only that, he affirms, the caste system is found only in India or, to use his occasionally Platonic language, finds in India its fullest expression. The argument is conducted in synchronic or, better, achronic terms and the sudden movement into the diachronic comes as a jar to the mind. This, which can only be called a breakdown, a regression to an earlier mode of thought,[2] has been more fully discussed elsewhere and I need only sketch the argument here.[3]

Having established the nature and the uniqueness of the system Bouglé sets out to demonstrate from the beginning of Part I that any attempt to demonstrate what he calls the 'roots' of the system must fail if it does not take into account simultaneously the three characteristics that he has isolated. And yet, one comes to realise, in the very process of his critique in the ensuing chapters, he fails to do exactly that. His three characteristics are derived in turn from their 'roots' for all that the familial root of *separation* and the priestly root of *hierarchy* are, hypothetically, re-connected. Finally, Bouglé derives his system from 'the mysterious effects of sacrifice'. There is an irony here for later, Hocart, with first hand experience denied to Bouglé, was through his study of sacrifice to point to the basic formula

[1] On this see L. Dumont 'World renunciation in Indian religions', the Frazer Lecture of 1958 in *Contributions to Indian Sociology*, no. IV, 1960.

[2] I would stress the word *thought* here. Bouglé, in common with many contemporaries, often uses a diachronic *language* but I think it is only at this stage of his argument that he sets out to explain in terms of origins.

[3] The reader is referred to *Contributions to Indian Sociology*, no. II, pp. 31–44.

of the traditional caste system, the opposition of purity and impurity expressed by Dumont.[1]

Guided only by Brahmanical texts Bouglé was led to suppose that the Brahman was the sole sacrificiant. He could not have seen, as Hocart and others saw, the dependence of the Brahman's cult upon an inferior cult.[2] The pure priest depends upon the impure priest of inferior caste to perform the bloody act of killing without which his own sacrificial rite cannot proceed. For Bouglé the caste hierarchy was, so to speak, univocal and to be derived from a respect for the priesthood as, we may suppose, he saw the hierarchy of the Roman Church. He was in no position to seize upon the fact that the system derived from the polar opposition of purity and impurity, the simplest formula from which hierarchy, separation and the division of labour are derived.

Something must be said in conclusion about the history of Bouglé's text and its translation. He defended his thesis in 1899 and the Introduction and Part I of the present work appeared in the *Année Sociologique*, vol. IV, 1899–1900; later essays appeared in volume X and the essay on 'Race' had appeared in the *Grand Revue*, 1 April 1906. Durkheim's introductory letter in the first edition of the collection strikes a portentous note. The volume was to inaugurate an evolution in the life of the group: the years of research and bibliographic work were to bear fruit in a series of original works.

If his readers had no right to expect an original work in the strict sense, they surely must have expected that Durkheim would have chosen for his inaugural volume a work which had earned some considerable measure of his approval or that, if this was too much to expect, he would afterwards maintain silence. In fact the *Essays* were reviewed in volume XI of the *Année* by

[1] See *Contributions to Indian Sociology*, no. III. Dumont descends via Hocart from Bouglé. Dumont's comparison of *homo hierarchicus* and *homo aequalis* interestingly parallels Bouglé's juxtaposition of egalitarian and hierarchical ideas although the bibliographical sequence is reversed. See Louis Dumont, *Homo Hierarchicus*, Paris, 1966, references to Bouglé, pp. 7–9, 64–6, 268–9 and *passim*, references to Hocart, pp. 100 fn., 123 and *passim*.

[2] See for example M. N. Srinivas, *Religion and society among the Coorgs of South India*, 1952, pp. 186–99. The symbiosis emerges clearly from the author's description of a lengthy ritual.

Preface to the English edition

Durkheim and Renier. The reviewers gave a lengthy summary and conclude:

If we have remained at the level of generalities, it is because the author, wrongly in our opinion, has preferred to do so himself. He has presented them as a framework awaiting a content, as a perspective intended to direct enquiry, as provisional inductions. He has done so with such modesty that one scarcely dares to risk a criticism. But let us regret that he has not chosen to go more deeply himself into the problems which he has drawn to the attention of Indianists and sociologists and, for example, made a frontal attack upon the question of the roots of endogamy and the hierarchy of castes.

I leave this mystery for the historian of Durkheim and his circle.

The *Essays* were first published in 1908 in the *Travaux de l'Année Sociologique* series founded by Durkheim and, after his death, directed by Marcel Mauss. For the present translation I have used the second edition of 1927 which differs in only two particulars from the first edition: in the 1927 edition Durkheim's introductory notice was not reproduced and Lucien Herr, having died in the interim, the dedication was suitably modified.

The second edition repeats the misprints and slips contained in the first – 'murderer' for 'victim' is a typical instance. These I have corrected. The circumstances in which this work has been done and the unavailability of some originals have prevented me from checking all of Bouglé's references many of which are inadequate, some of which are simply wrong. I have expanded and implicitly corrected where I could and in this have been assisted by the fourth French edition. I have assumed that what is of interest is Bouglé's text; for this reason, and also because his bibliography is in many particulars outdated, I have relegated the original footnotes to the end of the book, leaving the translator's notes to appear as footnotes in this edition.

I am most grateful to Professor Louis Dumont for his advice on several points and for a list of some twenty-eight misprints. I acknowledge the swift and generous assistance of Marie-Louis Reiniche of the Centre d'Etudes Indienne and Dr Rodney Needham of Oxford in my pursuit of an elusive French collection of Maine's essays. I have to thank Peter Blindell at the University of Warwick for technical advice.

TO THE MEMORY

OF

LUCIEN HERR

Bibliothécaire à l'école normale supérieure

A TOKEN OF GRATITUDE AND AFFECTION

January 1927

To the readers of the *Année Sociologique**

The appearance of this volume marks a transformation in the organization of the *Année Sociologique* that should be explained.

In the ten volumes of the *Année* which have appeared so far, critical analyses and reports have occupied the greater part of the space. Circumstances imposed this bibliographical preponderance upon us. When we founded the *Année*, what we wanted to do was to react against the current love of generalization and facile constructs; we wanted to give the public and those young students who were being attracted to sociology, some sense of what social reality truly is, of its richness and complexity, in order to guide them away from the prevailing ideology. The most effective means to achieve this end would certainly have been to bring out annually works inspired by this spirit. This we certainly tried to do. Unfortunately, once one has left methodological controversy and philosophical disquisition behind in order to attack a definite object, the slightest sociological study is, by virtue of the variety and extent of data which it requires, a laborious work calling for a great deal of time. For this reason we could not, when we began, count upon the production of original works in numbers sufficient to have the required effect upon public opinion. Our contribution could, in such circumstances, continue to be both healthy and useful so long as it was modest. However, in taking as our prime task the annual analysis of works directed at historians of religion, law, morality, economic facts and at statisticians, demographers etc. we were able to achieve our goal by a different route. We could find the facts in these works, present them to our readers, try to classify them, show how they could be handled sociologically and even indicate what lessons were to be learnt from them. This indeed is what we tried to do. By a methodical grouping of the books and articles as we reported upon them, we achieved a natural classi-

---

* This editorial note by Durkheim appeared in the first but in no subsequent edition.

To the readers of the 'Année Sociologique'

fication of natural phenomena, the first to be attempted in such conditions. At the same time, in connection with the questions which we annually surveyed, many insights emerged which have subsequently entered into circulation.

But we certainly thought, and indeed we hoped, that this procedure in the *Année* would be no more permanent than the circumstances which imposed it upon us in the first place. We never lost sight of the fact that the best way of advancing a science is not to outline its scope, collect the material that it should use and pose problems but to confront some of these problems resolutely and attempt a solution. We believe we have now reached a stage at which we can, more explicitly than in the past, set ourselves to this part of the task; ten years of collection and research allow the collaborators in the *Année* to do so without excessive temerity. It seemed to us that, for the present at least, the proper format for an original sociological work was the book rather than the article; this is because in these matters, when almost everything has to be done from scratch, one must allow oneself some space if anything is to be achieved. This is why, instead of developing that section of the *Année Sociologique* which has hitherto been reserved for articles, we have thought it preferable to start a distinct series in which the works of regular collaborators in the *Année* might first appear. This series has no claim whatsoever to be an encyclopaedia, which anyhow we do not think to be a realistic aim at this time. We shall limit ourselves to particular questions bearing upon well-defined objects in the hope consequently of some precision in the results. These questions will, however, be sufficiently varied for the reader to be able to see that the basic ideas which inspire us are susceptible of application to all branches of sociology.[1] This is the series which we inaugurate today.

The *Année Sociologique* will not for all that disappear. However burdensome the task, we recoil from the responsibility for suspending a publication which has rendered, and still may, services which no one, we are happy to affirm, dreams of denying. All that is necessary is some modification in its plan and organization. First of all this series that we have founded makes unnecessary the articles that we have hitherto published annually.

To the readers of the ' Année Sociologique '

From another point of view we must, in order to have time to produce, alleviate somewhat the enormous bibliographic task that we have continued over ten years. The *Année*, while continuing a title that usage has made sacred, will not appear annually but cover slightly longer periods. The important thing is to go on giving a periodic survey of all those works which interest the different branches of sociology. It will, moreover, be easy to handle in one volume publications produced in a period exceeding the twelvemonth: we shall give less place to works of only secondary interest. Our readers themselves will benefit by this arrangement.

Such are the conditions in which we shall follow up the work that has been begun. We hope that the sympathy of the public, which up to the present has not failed us, will continue to support our efforts.

EMILE DURKHEIM

Preface to the First edition

It is not for nothing that I have entitled these collected studies on caste *Essays*. I know better than anyone to what extent they are incomplete. On more than one point the outline has been only sketched: the content is lacking.

My desire was not to imagine *a priori* but to research into the ins and outs of a system that was the most contrary to that which egalitarian ideas are establishing in the west. For this research it seemed at first that India provided the ideal field. Caste flourished freely there. Nowhere else can we find such clear oppositions between the elementary groups; nowhere is hereditary specialization more strict, nor hierarchy more respected.

Unfortunately, as soon as one tries to 'situate' these phenomena, describe their evolution, and define their relations with the life of the whole, one is stopped short. The combined efforts of so many illustrious Indianists have not yet been able to throw sufficient light upon the path taken by Hindu civilization. Too many landmarks are still lacking. It has often been said: this is a people without history, or at least without historians. A revealing lacuna, let us add. It tells us something not only about the mental orientation but also about the political destinies of India. Meanwhile one is too often faced with the impossibility of dating, localizing, of being specific. One works in a fog. Everybody is today agreed that the literary monuments of India – produced most often, at least in the early periods, by and for the Brahmans – tell us more about priestly ideals than about historical reality. As for epigraphic monuments – from which we can expect more objective information – their deciphering and classification is scarcely begun. An immense amount of preliminary work remains to be done, a work in which my incompetence, in particular my ignorance of Indian languages, forbids my participation. I can only wait for the results.

If, without waiting, I publish these *Essays* today it is, first of all, because the poverty of historical details does not make it

Preface to the first edition

entirely impossible to establish sociological inductions. What is of especial interest to us is not what passes away but what is repeated; institutions survive the flow of events. From this point of view it is not impossible to note even now a certain number of intelligible relations between the dominant system of collective practices which maintain the caste system and religious beliefs, juridical conceptions or economic practices – relations which appear to be more than the products of coincidence. They will perhaps allow us to test usefully certain current hypotheses – from historical materialism or the philosophy of races to more precise theories on the phases of law. The reader will judge for himself.

Finally, however provisional our inductions must be there is some advantage in formulating them at this time. They will at least serve to draw the attention of specialists to the kind of conclusions that depend upon their work. They will the better be able to see at what points support is lacking and in what quarter there would be interest in the products of their research. A sociological perspective can orientate historical inquiry. The frame attracts the content. In the expectation of firm replies – and to speed the time of their delivery – it is not a worthless task to pose the questions.

C.B.

The essence and reality of the caste system

Is the caste system* a universal phenomenon common to all civilizations or is it a unique phenomenon peculiar to India? What relation does this system have to analogous social forms such as guild, clan and class? In order to define the field of our research these questions must be answered at the outset.

DEFINITION OF THE CASTE SYSTEM

In his valuable observations upon *Hindu manners, customs and ceremonies*[1] the Abbé Dubois attempts to establish that a division into castes was common to the greater part of the ancient civilizations. In the same way Max Müller in his article on caste[2] tries to show the universality of ethnic differences, political oppositions and professional specializations upon which, according to him, the whole system rests.

The antipathy between Saxon and Celt, the distinction between nobility and gentry, the distance between the man who deals in gold and silver and the man who deals in boots and shoes, are still maintained, and would seem almost indispensable to the healthy growth of every society. Analogous implications are not lacking in more recent works. 'Another and even graver misconception', says W. Crooke, 'is to suppose that caste is peculiar to Hinduism and connected in some peculiarly intimate way with the Hindu faith.'[3] It is quite usual for travellers when describing Hindu customs to compare them with their European equivalents; they recall that there is no difference

---

* In the title and throughout I have translated Bouglé's 'le régime des castes' as 'the caste system'. Bouglé also refers on occasion to 'le système' without apparent shift in meaning. Nevertheless it should be borne in mind that *régime* connotes rule or sway.

in nature between the repugnance which the Brahman shows for the Pariah and the equal repugnance of a lord for a road-sweeper.[4]

Contrary to such opinions, Senart,[5] whose views more than those of any other contributed to a reassessment of the question, insists that caste is essentially a Hindu phenomenon; this idea is the pivot upon which his argument rests. In presenting the results of his research on the ethnography of Bengal, Risley offers further evidence for the originality of the sub-divisions in Hindu society.[6]

How can we decide between these contrary views? The choice naturally depends upon the way in which we define the system in question. Was the French revolution a socialist one? Are primitive societies egalitarian? The reply depends upon our ideas of 'revolution' and 'egalitarianism'. Without an agreed definition discussion can go on for ever. We are bound therefore to begin by constructing some idea of the caste system.

If we consider the current usage of the word, caste seems first of all to arouse the idea of hereditary specialization. The son of a blacksmith will be a blacksmith just as the son of a warrior will be a warrior. In the assigning of tasks no account is taken of expressed desires nor of manifest aptitudes but only of filiation. Race and occupation are bound together. None other than the son can continue the work of the father and the son cannot choose any other occupation than that of his father. Professions become the obligatory monopolies of families, to perform them is not merely a right but a duty imposed by birth upon the children. Such a spirit must reign in a society before we can say that that society is subject to the rule of caste.

But is this sufficient? It seems to us that in addition we must be able to recognize the existence of different levels in that society, the existence, in other words, of a hierarchy. The word caste makes us think not only of hereditarily appointed work but also of unequally divided rights. To say caste is not to say monopoly only but also privilege. By the fact of his birth one individual is bound to pay heavy taxes while another escapes them. In the eyes of justice this man is 'worth' a hundred pieces of gold and that one only fifty. The golden ring, the red robe and yellow girdle which are the dress of one are strictly forbidden to another. Personal 'status' for life is determined by the rank of the group to which one belongs. We are bound to say then that inequality is also the product of the caste system.

But another element also appears to us to call for definition. When we say that the spirit of caste reigns in a society, we mean that the different groups of which that society is composed, repel each other rather than attract, that each retires within itself, isolates itself, makes every effort to prevent its members from contracting alliances or even from entering into relations with neighbouring groups. A man refuses to seek a wife outside his traditional circle, he will moreover refuse any food not prepared by his fellows and regard the mere contact of 'strangers' as impure and degrading. Such is the man who obeys the 'spirit of caste'. Horror of misalliance, fear of impure contacts and repulsion for all those who are unrelated, such are the characteristic signs of this spirit. It seems to us that it is, as it were, designed to atomize the societies into which it penetrates; it divides them not merely into superimposed levels but into a multitude of opposed fragments; it brings each of their elementary groups face to face, separated by a mutual repulsion.

The spirit of caste unites these three tendencies, repulsion, hierarchy and hereditary specialization, and all three must be borne in mind if one wishes to give a complete definition of the caste system. We shall say that a society is subject to this system if it is divided into a large number of mutually opposed groups which are hereditarily specialized and hierarchically arranged – if, on principle, it tolerates neither the parvenu, nor miscegenation, nor a change of profession.

That this definition does no violence to the current use of the word may be seen from an examination of some other accepted definitions. For the most part they emphasize the relation between caste ideas and the idea of hereditary specialization. 'Caste', says Guizot, 'is essentially hereditary; it is the transmission of the same situation and potentialities from father to son. Where there is no heredity, there is no caste.'[7] According to Ampère three conditions are essential to the existence of a caste: 'to hold back from certain alien occupations, to prevent

9

any alliance with outsiders, to continue in the profession received from the ancestors'.[8]

In order to define the caste system the inequality of rights is frequently added to the discussion of hereditary occupation. According to James Mill:[9]

The classification and distribution of the members of a community into certain classes or orders, for the performance of certain functions, with the enjoyment of certain privileges, or the endurance of certain burdens, and the establishment of hereditary permanence in these orders, the son being ordained to perform the functions, to enjoy the privileges, or sustain the burdens of the father, and to marry only in his own tribe, without mixture of the classes, in regular succession, through all ages.

According to Burnouf 'three elements constitute caste: the division of functions, the hereditary transmission of these functions and hierarchy'.[10]

Others have proposed as essential to the system that spirit of division which we have noted as the third characteristic. According to Senart:

Caste is a circumscribed and separatist organism by nature. Caste and class do not correspond to each other either in their extent, their characteristics or in their inherent tendencies. Each of the castes which may belong to one class is clearly distinguished from its fellows; it isolates itself with a severity which is not impaired by any superior unity. Class serves political ambitions; caste obeys its narrow scruples, traditional custom and above all certain local influences, all of which ordinarily have no relation with class interests. Most important of all, caste is concerned to preserve its own integrity with a pre-occupation that effects even the most humble of its members.[11]

'From the social and political point of view', we read in an English report, 'caste is division, hatred, jealousy and distrust between neighbour.'[12]

The majority of these definitions have only one fault, their narrowness. They bring to the fore this or that aspect of the system to be defined whereas we must not lose sight of a single one. Only by keeping these three constituent elements of caste before our eyes can we see in which civilizations it has flourished and with what social forms it is associated.

Essence and reality of the system

If in our search for a caste system in historical reality we are guided by this integral definition we can see at a glance that easy as it is to perceive the scattered elements of the system it is less easy to find it complete and perfect in its entirety. If there are few civilizations into which one or other of its characteristic tendencies has not penetrated, there are also few in which all three united are to be seen flourishing freely.

It is for example clear that even in our contemporary western civilization, we can easily find certain traces of the caste spirit. Here also we may find the horror of misalliance and the fear of polluting contacts. Marriage statistics show that there are certain professions which inter-marry freely while there are many others which do so very rarely.[13] A number of customs show that the different 'worlds' do not like to mix and thus certain quarters of the city, certain cafés and certain schools are frequented exclusively by certain categories of the population.[14] It is difficult to contest that such distinctions correspond by and large to the degrees of a hierarchy. If the law does not admit the existence of class, the mores demonstrate it clearly: they are far from attributing the same coefficient of 'consideration' to the different categories of people and this consideration is translated, if not in declared privilege, in undeniable advantages.[15] Even hereditary specialization is far from having completely disappeared. One can always find villages in which the same industry has been practised for centuries;[16] the number of occupations monopolized by particular ethnic sections is still considerable;[17] finally the instances in which fathers transmit not only their fortunes to their sons but also their professions seem to be becoming more frequent.[18]

However numerous may be such indications no one would in fact maintain that a caste system dominates our civilization which in fact withdraws further from such a system at every step. If we analyse the judicial, political and economic reforms which have taken place in modern times we cannot fail to see that our society is obeying, more or less, slowly but surely, the exigence of egalitarian ideas.[19] Habits which recall the caste system, even

11

though they continue to exist in fact, are no longer consecrated by law. More and more are they being considered as survivals.

Does it then follow that we have only to return to our own middle ages to find the caste system? Certainly the further back in time we go the more clear-cut do social divisions appear. Between the superimposed levels of the past the differences are marked not only by custom but also by law; occupations are frequently monopolized by families. But we have only to remind ourselves of the sociological characteristics of the two powers which dominated the middle ages – the Church and the feudal nobility – in order to see that that condition of society is far from corresponding exactly to the system which we have defined.

It has frequently been said of the clergy that it constituted a caste. But as Guizot has correctly observed the expression is essentially wrong.[20] If the idea of heredity is inherent in the idea of caste, the word caste cannot be applied to the Christian Church since only celibates can be its functionaries. Where functions so far from being reserved by fathers for their sons are distributed among men who cannot be descended from their predecessors, and where co-optation replaces heredity, there may very well be a spirit of unity but that spirit is not the spirit of caste. In fact, by its methods of recruitment the clergy indirectly served ideas contrary to those upon which the caste system rests; a Church which can make a pontiff of a slave and elevate the son of a shepherd above kings, brought about that kind of social redemption which perhaps more than its dogmas, were lessons in equality.[21]

Similarly a great distance separates the feudal system from the caste system proper. First of all to the extent that the former followed the principle that 'the status of the land determines that of the landholder', it contradicts a principle of the caste system. By not determining the station of men by their birth it introduces upheavals in the hereditary hierarchy. In the course of twenty-four hours, simply because a battle or a contract has made him master of a town, a man may find that his position in the social scale has been raised. Let us add that when such a man is the holder of several fiefs his position becomes ambiguous; vassal to some, suzerain to others, his social rank is no longer clearly defined. Such a system does not approach a strict hierarchy.

From another point of view the divisive quality of feudalism prevented individuals from forming castes. Each lord lived on his own lands and governed on his own account a certain number of men who were solely dependent upon him; feudality was not built up of superimposed collectivities but rather by a 'collection of individual despotisms'.[22] In this way we may maintain without paradox that, just as the Church was, in certain ways, a school for equality, the feudal system was a school for independence. Its organization lent itself to individualism. It did not cut up society into mutually repelling compact bodies, it did not fragmentize it into castes.

Classical antiquity does not give us a precise picture of the system that we seek, any more than do our own middle ages. In the 'city', certainly, a strict hierarchy for long marked the different ranks. Without taking the slaves into account we know how many religious, judicial and political inequalities separated the plebian from the patrician. Hereditary specialization was not unknown; in Greek history we frequently hear of families of doctors or families of priests;[23] in Athens the names of four Ionian tribes were the names of professions.[24] Finally there is no doubt that the elementary groups which appear to have formed the city endeavoured not to become mixed; as long as possible the *genos*, faithful to the ancestor cult, isolated and retracted itself.

But it was precisely the destiny and, as it were, the mission of the ancient city to transcend all these tendencies. Hereditary specialization, in so far as it was ever the rule, became the exception there very swiftly.[25] Hierarchical organization never amounted to the superimposition of opposed groups. In fact to the extent that the city remained a collection of *gene*, the inferiors did not form separate groups: slaves or clients, they belonged to one family: they were of the same body as the Eupatrid.[26] Later when an independent *plebs* came into being it was not long content to be regarded as an inferior society. It imposed new divisions upon the city which, cutting across the old divisions, forced the citizens to mix. Agglomerated here by

13

demes and there according to their fortune or their arms, they could no longer remain grouped by clan. Progressively and as it were methodically isonomy, isegory and isotomy were achieved.* Reformers moved constantly to obliterate the traces left by the ancient divisions.

Thus since antiquity western civilization has rejected the system which we have defined.

We can best prove how difficult it is to discover this system in its pure condition, not by a general review of civilizations but by the examination of a distinctive case. The example of ancient Egypt is frequently offered as that of a society subject to the caste system: let us therefore try to find there hereditary specialization, strict hierarchy, and a clear cut opposition of groups.

If we rely upon the evidence of antiquity there seems to be no doubt in the matter. The Egyptians, Herodotus tells us, were divided into seven *gene*: priests, warriors, cowherds, swineherds, merchants, interpreters and pilots. Only the priests and the warriors enjoyed marks of distinction; special lands were reserved for them; they were exempt from all taxes. But like the rest of the population they were tied to the occupations of their ancestors. If one of the priests died he was replaced by his son. The warriors had no right to practise any other occupation than that of arms which was passed on from father to son.[27]

Diodorus is no less explicit. He recalls that the land was divided into three parts: that of the priests, that of the kings and that of the soldiers. As for the inferior orders (*syntagmata*), the shepherds, labourers and artisans, they were permitted neither to enter into public affairs nor to practise any occupation other than the traditional one of the family. Nor does Diodorus offer this as a custom merely, for he tells us that it was commanded by the laws.[28]

Modern discoveries tend at first sight to confirm this testimony of the past. The trilingual Rosetta decree tells us of the lands divided, as Herodotus said, into sacred, military and royal lands. Other documents such as the Canopos decree bear witness to the privileges reserved to the sacerdotal and warrior classes.[29] A

* Equality of political rights, equal rights of speech, equal rights of honour and privilege.

number of inscriptions also prove that there were veritable dynasties at every level of society. We have the coffins of thirty generations of priests attached to the Theban god Mentu:[30] almost all belonged to two or three families which married amongst themselves or took their wives from the priests of Ammon. One family of architects is known to have served the royal family for several centuries under the various Egyptian dynasties. All the contracts and documents of one family of Theban choachytes from the reign of Tabraka (680 B.C.) up to the Roman occupation are extant in the demotic: like their far-off ancestors the descendants were poor craftsmen. Facts of this nature have led Revillout to conclude that the classical view of Egypt was substantially correct and that the caste system prevailed there.[31]

Let us, however, look a little more closely. The division of labour does not appear to have been always and everywhere as clear as has been believed. Sacerdotal and military functions did not exclude each other. There survives the sarcophagus of a priest of the goddess Athor who, at the same time that he was priest, was a commander of infantry.[32] Specialization was not then absolute and the accumulation of professions was not forbidden. What then of the inheritance of professions? In fact we may say that the son of the high priest had the greatest opportunity of a place in the temple and that the son of the scribe in his turn took up work in the office. But if these facts, however numerous, prove that 'nepotism is as old as the pyramids'[33] they do not prove that the transmission of occupation from father to son was legally prescribed.[34]

We have, moreover, proof that a man was not tied to his father's occupation. Not only in the demotic period do we see the emergence of a sort of bourgeois class whose members do not seem to have any particular occupational affiliation, but also in the hieratic period the number of parvenus was considerable.[35] The famous Amten was the son of a poor scribe. Placed originally in an office of supplies he later became a crier and taxer of the colonists, then chief of the ushers and supervisor of all the king's flax; soon he is the head of a village, of a town, of a *nome* and finally is made Primate of the Western Gate. He died covered with honour, the possessor of many fiefs, having married his daughters well and placed his sons advantageously.[36] This example shows that the hierarchy was far from being petrified. The power of the king could over-throw the traditional order of things. We should further note that while it was the rule in the Egyptian feudal system for lands to be inherited, heredity was not enough for a noble to be recognized as such and a formal investiture by the Pharao was needed. By giving lands or charges the king could also create nobles.[37] Here we have facts indicating a social mobility incompatible with the rigidity of the caste system.

Let us add finally that the spirit of division and mutual opposition, which seems to us to be one of the constituent elements of the caste system, never appears to have dominated Egyptian society. We have no positive proof that systematic prohibitions for long isolated its elementary groups. On the contrary it has been rightly observed that in Egypt the administrative system very quickly effaced the spontaneous divisions of society. The exigencies of a common culture overcame there the hostilities of clans: the Nile, it has been said, demanded unity.[38] Whatever may be the reason it is certain that Egyptian civilization does not show us that invincible resistance to unification which characterizes the caste system. In our own western civilization such a system was prevented by the power of democracy; in Egyptian civilization a strong monarchy impeded its development.

The caste system in India

Does this system encounter analogous obstacles in India? Or on the contrary can we see the three essential tendencies freely at play there?

First of all we can nowhere find specialization pushed to such a degree as in India. Certainly the number of differentiated occupations is less than in our own contemporary society; but in order for a society to have ten thousand professions and to have seen them increase by more than four thousand in thirteen years that society must have a 'scientific' industry which alone is capable of multiplying and varying both the means and the needs of production.[39] So far as India was left to itself it did not see such progress.

But while her methods of production remained relatively simple she still divided the various tasks as far as was possible among different groups. We have only to think of the number of sub-groups of which each major occupational group is composed in order to appreciate this. Thus we may distinguish six merchant castes, three of scribes, forty of peasants, twenty-four of journeymen, nine of shepherds and hunters, fourteen of fishermen and sailors, twelve of various kinds of artisans, carpenters, blacksmiths, goldsmiths and potters, thirteen of weavers, thirteen of distillers, eleven of house servants.[40] No doubt these internal subdivisions do not all correspond to professional distinctions. But in many cases what distinguishes a caste from its fellows is that it abstains from certain procedures, does not use the same materials, does not manufacture the same products.

In Buddhist legends different castes are distinguished according to the instruments that they use or according to the fish that they catch.[41] In the matter of clothing those who make turbans will have nothing to do with those who make sashes. Amongst leather workers one caste makes shoes, another repairs them and yet another fashions leather flasks.[42] One may not see, we are told, the same man driving the plough as tends the beast. Among the Ghosi clans one looks after the cows and only sells milk; others buy milk and sell butter.[43] The Kumhars of Orissa are divided into Uria Kumhars who work standing at large urns and Kattya Kumhars who sit down at a wheel to make little pots. The coolie who carries a load on his head will refuse to carry it on his shoulders; he who uses a pole will not use a knapsack. Each of the house-servant castes has its own work and each energetically refuses to do the work of others.[44] From the top to the bottom of Hindu society the accumulation of function is forbidden in principle.

A change of function is no less forbidden. Work is divided once for all and each has his allotted task from his childhood. Heredity of occupation is the rule and has been since antiquity. It was this trait that struck the Muslim traveller who visited India in the ninth century.[45] 'In all these kingdoms...there are families of men of letters, of doctors, of craftsmen working on house-building and one never finds anyone in other families professing the same

17

occupation.' In the Jatakas which give us a glimpse of Hindu society in the sixth century the expression 'son of a caravan leader' signifies caravan leader; 'son of a blacksmith' signifies blacksmith, the families of potters and stone-masons are designated there, allusion is made to the streets and villages where certain hereditary specializations are localized.[46]

Strabo had already observed that each class in India has its particular occupation.[47] Even the names of castes, of which the greater part are the names of professions also, sufficiently prove the antiquity of specialization in Hindu society.[48]

No doubt there are many exceptions to the rule. It is not a question here of recent changes of profession which have inclined many of all castes to agriculture or to the administrative service:[49] these result from the disturbance of Hindu tradition by the English invasion. But at all times the Brahmans have kept all kinds of occupation open for themselves. So far from being confined to the study of sacred texts, we find some who are ploughmen, soldiers, tradesmen and cooks.[50] 'To fill one's belly one must play many parts', said one of them to the Abbé Dubois.[51]

Their superiority opens greater possibilities to them than the common run of mortality enjoy. This superiority implies purity and it is true that the concern to preserve purity excludes many kinds of activity. Does not the doctrine of *ahimsa*, which forbids the wounding of even the smallest living creature, forbid the priest to cut open the soil with a plough blade?[52] But faced with material necessities such prohibitions must be softened. Indeed the theory itself plays a part in this: the Brahmanic codes recognized the right of the Brahman to practise different occupations in times of distress. If Manu formally forbids him to traffic in liquor, perfumes, meat and wool, he permits him to engage in military service, agriculture, the care of herds, and a certain number of commercial enterprises.

In their turn the members of the other castes, which these same codes claim to tie to their traditional occupation, in fact and following the Brahman's example, take certain liberties with the rule. We have just observed that the names of castes are commonly those of ancient occupations. But let us also add that it is relatively rare today to find a caste practising the occupation which its name designates. The Atishbaz are indeed, as their names indicates, artificers and the N'Albauds farriers. But it is not the case that all the Chamars are tanners today, the Ahir shepherds, the Banjara porters, the Luniya salt-workers. The Baidya, according to their tradition, are a caste of doctors. But hardly a third of them practises medicine: many are teachers in schools, farmers, stewards.[53] Amongst the Sunris, traditionally distillers, one may find in some provinces, carpenters and tilers and elsewhere, grain merchants. If in Assam the Dom are fishermen, they are cultivators in Kashmir and masons in Kumaon.[54] The Kansari and Sankari are employed as domestic servants although in theory they belong among the commercial castes.[55] Among the Kaibartta of Bengal, while the Mechos have remained fishermen in accordance with their tradition, the Helos have turned to agriculture.[56] Generally today we can count many more cultivators and fewer herdsmen than there ought to be if the sacred divisions were respected.[57] The system of hereditary specialization in India allows them considerably more mobility than one would at first sight expect.[58]

But we should stress that this mobility is collective rather than individual. One will rarely see a young man leave the occupation of his ancestors in order to follow his road alone.[59] It is rather groups that leave the whole in order to take up some new profession; but within the detached group the rule is no less rigorously applied: the son continues to do the work of the father. Let us add that while, as we see, changes of occupation are not in fact rare, such changes remain in the eyes of the law illicit or scandalous. When we considered Egypt we pointed out that the fact does not prove the existence of the law. Although it was the son who most often succeeded to the occupation of the father it does not follow that hereditary specialization was the rule in Egyptian society. Here we may follow an analogous and inverse argument. Because the son in India does not invariably follow the occupation of the ancestors it does not follow that hereditary specialization was not the rule in Hindu society. This is a legitimate inference when we have established that a certain sanction was attached to a change of profession and that they did not take place without a certain degradation of social rank.

Introduction

We may be told that Brahmans, although exercising very different professions, remain universally respected. But first of all the peculiar position which they enjoy in Hindu society explains how they escape the general sanction: the Brahman is in a sense always above the law. Secondly it is not precisely the case that the Brahman is respected to the same degree in all situations: the respect given to a Pandit is quite different from the respect given to a cook. As for the mass of non-Brahman castes it is generally recognized that an admitted change of occupation, being a derogation of the norms essential to the social organization, carries with it a forfeit of status.[60] When the members of a caste change their profession they either hide the fact or try to justify it by some legend.[61] They feel themselves guilty of a general reproach.

Even when the change is the point of departure for a rise in the economic order, the changes themselves are not liked. Some Sunri have risen above their occupation of distilling and have become great merchants. They now call themselves Shaha and deny any connection with those who have held to the traditional occupation of the caste. Nevertheless these parvenus continue to be viewed in a dubious light. Conversely those who piously hold to the profession of their fathers, however low, however impure, derive honour from fidelity to tradition. In the Sakuntala the fisherman who is reproached with his cruelty to the fish, replies: 'Sir, do not admonish me, for we should never abandon the labour of our ancestors, however lowly it may be.' And no doubt it is in obedience to this same sentiment that many castes close their ranks and make desperate efforts before abandoning their traditional occupation under the pressure of want. We are told that 30 per cent of the weavers of West Bengal had to die before the remainder, ruined by English imports, could decide to look elsewhere for their daily bread:[62] to such an extent does adherence to the ancestral occupation impose itself as a duty upon the Hindu conscience.

In estimating the position of hereditary specialization in Hindu society we are bound to remember that this society is hierarchically organized. Nowhere may we observe distinctions more clearly cut, nowhere such extravagance of both respect and disdain.

Essence and reality of the system

Travellers have frequently painted the sad picture of Pariah life. Thus the Abbé Dubois:

Hardly anywhere are they allowed to cultivate the soil for their own benefit, but are obliged to hire themselves out to the other castes...Their masters may beat them at pleasure; the poor wretches having no right either to complain or to obtain redress...What chiefly disgusts other natives is the revolting nature of (their) food, they contend for carrion with dogs.

On the Malabar coast they are not even allowed to build huts. If a Nayar meets them he may kill them. On the other hand, see the account of the guru's entry:

They ride on a richly caparisoned elephant or in a superb palanquin. Many have an escort of cavalry, and are surrounded by guards...Bands of musicians playing all sorts of instruments precede them...along the route incense and other perfumes are burnt...new clothes are perpetually spread for him to pass over; triumphal arches...are erected.

A pinch of the cow-dung ash with which he marks his brow is an inestimable gift; his curse is petrifying, his blessing will save.[63]

Not all Brahmans lead this royal life but the greater part live at the expense of other castes. In principle the Brahman should live upon the alms of others. If you ask him for something he will reply: 'Get along with you', for he is made to receive and not to give.[64]

When one passes through a hamlet, says Jacquemont, one might believe that the Brahman caste is the most numerous for they remain indolently at home while others work.[65] Another traveller tells us of the ferryman of Benares who is sufficiently honoured if a Brahman deigns to employ his boat. Another says, speaking of the Brahmans, that they walk with an air of self-satisfaction and conscious superiority which is inimitable. It is not surprising, as the Abbé Dubois tells us, that they are superbly egotistic for are they not brought up to believe that all is owing to them and that they owe nothing?[66] Their absolute superiority is as uncontested as the absolute inferiority of the Pariahs.[67]

Between these two extremes the great multitude of castes are arranged in their different degrees, each one preoccupied to hold its rank and to preserve its prerogatives from usurpation.[68] In order to gauge rank different considerations enter into account:

purity of food, fidelity to the traditional occupation, abstention from forbidden foods.[69] Practically speaking the eminence or baseness of a caste is determined above all by the relations which it has with the Brahman caste. Will the Brahmans accept a gift of any sort whatever from a man of this caste? Will they without hesitation take a cup of water from his hand? Will they make difficulties? Will they refuse with horror?[70] Here is the true criterion of the dignity of a caste: the measure of its relative nobility is the Brahman's esteem.

If we consult the sacred codes we find these broad social divisions expressed with the precision of mathematical relations. We discover that the number of ceremonies practised, the total amount of fines imposed, even the rate of interest paid, varies with the rank of the castes and that in all circumstances the Brahman receives the maximum profit and suffers the minimum loss.[71]

No doubt, as we shall see we cannot trust the codes in matters of detail. The actual distinctions are far from being as strict as the ideal ones. At many points the hierarchy is uncertain.[72] The position of a caste varies in different regions and questions of precedence give rise to frequent disputes.[73] But these uncertainties leave the principle unquestioned; the very disputes and the fights to which they lead, prove to what a point the members of Hindu society are imbued with the idea that they ought to be hierarchically organized.

All observers have been struck by the fact that these specialized elements of Hindu society are not only superimposed but also mutually opposed and that the force which animates the whole system of the Hindu world is a force of repulsion which keeps the various bodies separate and drives each one to retire within itself.

The disgust which Europeans inspire in Hindus has frequently been noted. A traveller recounts that a Brahman with whom he was acquainted used to visit him very early in the morning: the Brahman preferred to see him before taking his bath so that he might then cleanse himself of the impurities which he had incurred. A Hindu with self-respect would die of thirst rather than drink from the cup which had been used by a 'Mleccha'.[74] But what is noteworthy is that the Hindus appear to feel something of the same repugnance in regard to each other; a proof that they are to a certain extent foreigners to each other. In Calcutta great difficulty was experienced over the establishment of a water system; how could people of different castes use the same tap? The contact of the Pariah inspires such horror that they are obliged, as their name implies, to carry warning bells which announce their presence.[75] On the Malabar coast there are people who are forced to go almost naked for fear that others may be touched by the billowing of their clothes.[76] The fear of an impure atmosphere is from all time one of the dominating traits of the Hindu soul.[77] The Jatakas are full of stories which bear witness to the disgust which has, in all ages, been inspired by contact with, or even sight of, the impure races. A Brahman discovers that he has been travelling with a Chandala: 'Damn you, candāla, raven of ill-omen; move out of the wind.' Two friends, the daughters of a Gahapati and a Purohit, are playing by the city gate. Two Chandala brothers come on the scene and the girls flee to wash their eyes.[78]

Undoubtedly not all races provoke an equal disgust. Nevertheless in the eyes of an orthodox Hindu any caste, other than his own, is in a sense impure. This sentiment of latent repulsion manifests itself clearly in certain circumstances.

For example, someone may not fear the contact of the man of another caste but nevertheless refuses to eat with him. It is above all from food that contamination is feared. It can only be eaten amongst caste-fellows: it should not even be touched by a stranger, whose glance is sometimes sufficient to pollute it.[79] If a Pariah so much as looks into a kitchen all the utensils should be broken.[80] Jacquemont recounts that one day at dinner time he almost spoilt his servant's meal. 'When the syce saw me coming he cried out in the most pitiable manner, "Sir, sir – I beg of you. Oh sir, take care. I am a Hindu, sir, a Hindu."' He goes on to say that in his escort of sepoys there were as many stoves, pots and fires as there were men. 'I don't know whether they are all of different castes, but there are not two who will eat together.'[81] In fact the Hindu isolates himself while eating in order to be sure of not contracting impurity. Among the Rajputs different families, even though they belong to the same caste, eat together only with difficulty.[82] Whence the saying 'For twelve Rajputs – thirteen cooks.' 'For three Kanauja Brahmans', another saying runs, 'you need thirty hearths.'[83] Scruples of this kind are naturally more lively in the high castes. But from the top to the bottom of the social scale, one encounters the same concern. In time of famine the Santal allowed themselves to die of hunger rather than touch food prepared by Brahmans.[84] He who eats food forbidden by his caste becomes an 'out-cast' an 'out-law'. Thus it has been possible to say that caste is primarily a matter of food.[85]

There is however one sphere in which the protectionism of caste raises yet higher barriers: more than a matter of food, caste is a 'matter of marriage'.[86] Marriage outside the caste is strictly forbidden: the caste is rigorously endogamous. We must add that this endogamy is coupled with an internal exogamy. While there is a wide circle within which a Hindu must find a wife there is a narrow circle within the first in which he may not marry. Many castes, in imitation of the Brahmans, divide themselves into *gotra*, the members of the same *gotra* may not intermarry. Sometimes the prohibition applies to the eponymous group composed of the descendants of the same ancestor, sometimes to a territorial group composed of the inhabitants of the same locality.[87] These rules of exogamy* are complex and vary according to the caste. What we have to bear in mind for the present is the rigour of the general rule which isolates castes and tends to keep them eternally closed to one another.

No doubt there are many exceptions to this rule also. The notions brought into being by the existence of hierarchy sometimes triumph over the feelings of mutual repulsion which otherwise separate castes. Many families seek husbands for their daughters in higher castes; 'hypergamy' then overcomes endogamy.[88] Certain Radhya of high rank are so sought after as grooms that they make marriage their profession: they keep registers in which they write the names of the women they have honoured by their union.[89] Even in high castes derogation of the rule of endogamy is not rare. According to Carnegy[90] the Rajputs

---

* The text here has 'endogamiques'.

of Oudh used to take their wives from the aborigines without any degradation of their descendants. In the same way it is habitual, according to Crooke, for Jats to seek out girls of low caste, pass them off as girls of their own blood, and marry them.

Even lacking such observations the analysis of (physical) anthropology* could prove that, despite the most strict prohibitions there have been innumerable mixtures of all kinds.[91] Nevertheless the fact remains that the only 'pure' marriage is that contracted between people of the same caste, that the public conscience, by the sanctions which it applies, manifests its concern to maintain this ideal and that, even more than a change of occupation, a marriage outside the caste carries with it a degradation of status; to such an extent is this separatist tendency inherent in Hindu society.

We could, moreover, measure the strength of this tendency by its results. The multiplicity of the groups into which Hindu society is divided is the best proof of the existence of a reciprocal repulsion between its elements.

Were we to confine ourselves to her sacred books, India would not appear to be so divided. According to Manu, there are four castes and 'there are not five'. This tradition has, up to the present day, dominated both historians and travellers. But it is precisely the value of this tradition that the recent work of indologists invites us to suspect. Criticizing the Brahmanic theory of caste, Senart has pointed out its waverings and incertitudes: on more than one point it masks and falsifies the reality more than it records it.[92] In the particular matter of the number of castes, the sacred codes, immediately after having affirmed that there are only four, implicitly recognize a considerable number. The 'theory of mixed castes' offers us, in fact, a certain number of degraded castes resulting from illicit unions between pure castes. But the theory is transparently a theory constructed after the event, to explain what could not be denied. It is an avowal of the multiplicity of castes whose names, professional or geographical, betray for the most part a very ancient

* Wherever Bouglé uses the term anthropology with or without a suffixed 'socio-' he has in mind the physical anthropology of his time that tried to effect correlations between physical measurements, race and culture.

origin.[93] Furthermore if, to test the veracity of the Brahmanic codes we consult the Buddhist literature, we certainly find the theory of four castes mentioned, but rather as a system for discussion than as a picture of the facts. Throughout the legends of the sixth century, Hindu society appears already divided into multiplicity of sections;[94] Sanskrit literature also shows the same multiplicity. Jolly, confirming Senart's view, cites more than forty names of *jāti* which could not be made to correspond to the four primitive *varna*.[95]

Contemporary observations tend to show that the theory of four castes, the *chaturvarna* has never been more than an ideal, blending a simplified and as it were shortened picture of the reality with a reiteration of frequently violated prescriptions. It would be useless to look at the castes of the present as the descendants of the four traditional castes; the Brahmans who had the monopoly of prayer and sacrifice, the Kshatriyas, warriors born, the Vaisyas destined to commerce, the Shudras created for the service of others.

The Brahmans as we see them today correspond best to the type described in the codes but again we must mark the differences. Not only do Brahmans exercise many more professions than the Brahmanic law ordains but in addition, and most important of all, so far from constituting one caste only, as might be believed from the sacred books, they are divided into a host of castes divided the one from the other.[96] As far as the other castes are concerned the gap is even more striking. There are the Rajputs who claim descent from the Kshatriyas, but first of all, apart from the fact that many of their pretensions are obviously untrue,[97] they also form a mass of families rather than one caste.[98] The occupations assigned by tradition for the Vaisya do not appear in fact to be reserved to one caste only, but are divided amongst very diverse castes.[99] Finally it is a waste of labour to look for the caste which would correspond to the Shudras.[100] This is why the census no longer uses these traditional names in order to distinguish the different categories of the population. One has only to look at present reality to realize that castes must be counted in their thousands. The Brahmanic theory tries in vain to conceal this essential multiplicity. The caste system has divided

Hindu society into a considerable number of small opposed societies.

To sum up on these points: hereditary specialization, hierarchical organization, reciprocal repulsion: as far as any social form can realize itself in its purity, the caste system is realized in India. At the very least it penetrates Hindu society to a level unknown elsewhere. It plays some part in other civilizations but in India it has invaded the whole. It is in this sense that we may speak of the caste system as a phenomenon peculiar to India.

Does this mean that the study of the system can only have a historical and not a sociological interest? Are we limited to the particular facts without being able to glimpse any general conclusion? Because caste is only seen at its maximum development in India are we forbidden *a priori* to disengage its essential properties from their contingent circumstances and to discern the influences which it might normally have upon economic, political and moral life: we do not think so.

First of all while it is true that the caste system is, in a manner of speaking, at its height in Hindu civilization and shows there a unique and incomparable development, let us not forget that the same system is found, more or less developed, in all or in nearly all civilizations. If one wished to discover the consequences of hereditary specialization one could, on many points, compare what happens in Egypt with what happens in India. For although in Egypt it does not appear to have been an absolute rule the transmission of occupation from father to son seems to have been at least a widespread usage. In the same way a parallel between the Hindu Brahmans and the Levites might teach us something about the causes or effects of the constitution of a sacerdotal caste. Even those societies finally committed to democracy would certainly furnish plenty of material for a study of the general properties of hierarchy. The most unified societies have in their earlier periods known and for long been aware of that spirit of repulsion which maintains the whole of Hindu society in a condition of practical division. We do not, then, lack the elements for comparison: Hindu caste is, in our eyes, no more than the synthesis of elements which are present everywhere; it shows us

27

the prolongation and, as it were, completion of lines sketched elsewhere, the unique dilation of universal tendencies.

Finally, to establish an induction, even more important than the superficial comparison of numerous instances, what could be more valuable than the searching analysis of the distinctive case?[101] It is fortunate for sociological curiosity that the caste system has triumphed in India over all the forces which elsewhere have thwarted or suppressed it, and that it has clearly imposed its form upon the whole of social life: in this way its distinctive properties are clearly manifest. Because it has realized itself as perfectly and as completely as possible in this civilization we are able to examine it, so to say, in its 'pure state', and the more clearly able to observe its characteristics. India is the favoured land of the caste system: for this reason the history of India is, in a way, a crucial experience for anyone who wishes to submit that system to a sociological study.

PART 1

The roots of the caste system

1

Caste specialization and the guild

In trying to see where in fact the caste system is found, we have tried not to lose sight of any one of the three characteristics that seemed to us necessary to its definition – hereditary specialization, hierarchy, and mutual repulsion.

It is most important if one wishes to throw light on the roots of this same system, not to forget a single one of these characteristics. How easy it is to reach fatally narrow conclusions by pursuing only one of them, we shall now show by a rapid examination of the most recent theories on the origins of caste.

For a long time people have been content with facile explanations on this topic. One had not far to seek it seemed. The roots of caste would surely be found in the souls of Brahmans. Their ambition explained everything.

The Hindu population was only fragmented, specialized, hierarchized in order to allow Brahmanism to exploit it. The ancient institutions of India appeared as the finest example of priestly machiavellism. Even today this way of seeing things is far from totally abandoned. The benefits which the Brahmans derive from the system are so obvious! Instinctively one applies the rule: *is fecit qui prodest*. One compares the Brahmans to the Jesuits.[1] 'The evil geniuses of the Hindu people.'[2] They have divided in order to rule. Brahmanism is the sun of India. It gave birth to the different bodies in the system which perform their evolutions around it; it is their origin and their end.

M. Senart has rightly pointed out that nowadays we have the right to challenge *a priori* explanations of this nature.[3] Quite legitimately they seem to us old fashioned. They are, one might say, contrary to the new spirit of social science. We must leave to the eighteenth century the 'artificialist' error, that only saw the results of the premeditation of priests in the majority of social institutions. The impartial study of institutions shows that those founded solely on charlatanism are rare and fragile. Above all when it is a matter of rules as complex and durable as those of the caste system, a deliberate invention is unlikely. To make the entire organization of Hindu society depend upon the will of Brahmans is to exaggerate the part played by voluntary creation in human societies.

It is, moreover, to exaggerate as M. Dahlmann points out, the power of religion over Hindu civilization.[4] It is very true that a religious concern is present everywhere in India, and not merely in theoretical speculations but in the slightest manifestations of practical activity. To the Hindu soul nothing is more important than sacrifice: it is through sacrifice that each day the life of the world is renewed, the universal order restored. But it is excessive to believe that all the energy of India has concentrated itself, from the start and forever, in the sacrificiant class, and that the people, lulled by their magic, have existed in a sort of passive lethargy, to be manipulated at will, lacking that sense of reality which makes races strong, and so incapable of independent thought and of virile action.[5] In fact the Hindu people, outside the Brahmanic circle, has given many demonstrations of the most fecund intellectual and material activity. While it may be true that the primitive law to which it is subordinated is pervasively religious, the epic period reveals the formation of a new law, less ritualistic and, if one dare say it, more laical: This is *dharma* as opposed to *rita*.[6] Already we find a large part of the sacred codes devoted to commercial interests. The existence of a voluminous body of commercial law is the sign of an active commerce just as the width of its bed testifies to the power of the river;[7] we have only to enumerate the rules in the Hindu codes which relate to finances, market regulation, the laws of the customs, loans on interest, inheritance[8] and we have proof enough that economic life in India was not as sterile as they suppose who believe that India has only existed in and for religion.

It is exactly this economic life that we must study if we wish to discover the forces which elaborated the skeleton of the Hindu organism. M. Dahlmann bids us connect the caste system with industrial evolution and see in the professional guilds the mothers of the castes and we shall then have gauged the impotence of the artificialist theory; we shall be able to demonstrate that the organization of the Hindu world is not the result of arbitrary and discontinuous transformations;[9] it will appear to us as the natural fruit of a continuous and spontaneous development.

Does not the great antiquity of occupational differentiation already prove the influence exercised by the division of industrial labour upon the whole of Hindu life? The Vedas refer to carpenters, wheelwrights, blacksmiths, goldsmiths, potters, ropemakers, curriers, etc.; as we come to the nearer antiquity the number of occupations that are distinguished, continues to increase.[10] From the epic period, the principal duty of the king becomes that of overseeing the distribution of tasks (*karmabheda*).[11] The codes and inscriptions mention an increasing number of constituted corporations.[12] Since Hindu industry operated no longer solely for princes but also for foreigners, and applied itself to export, we see the growth, principally in towns of veritable guilds having presidents, councils and their own law. They watch over the regulation of the markets, organize caravans, give their names to foundations and, in short, show every sign of a powerful vitality. We must go to medieval Germany to find a parallel efflorescence of guilds. The development of corporations never achieved either in Greece or Rome, that amplitude which it achieved in India. If the guild is not, as M. Doren[13] would have it, a purely Germanic phenomenon, we can say that it is essentially an 'indo-germanic' phenomenon.[14] Hindu corporations meet the same needs as the German corporations, and extend their sway yet more over society. It is they who give the social organization of India its distinctive form; it is under the pressure of industry that partitions multiply there: castes are only petrified guilds.[15]

The very hierarchy of castes offers moreover a striking confirmation of the hypothesis by proving that the entire system has received its particular orientation from industry. One has only, with Mr Nesfield,[16] to arrange the castes in their order of dignity and one can demonstrate that they are more or less high in the social scale accordingly as they are more or less high in the industrial scale. The lowest are those which preserve those kinds of activity only known to the primitive phases of human history: the castes of fishermen and hunters.[17] The agricultural castes are more honoured and those of the artisans honoured yet more. Those who practise the simplest skills, known before the age of metallurgy, such as basket-makers, potters and oil-pressers, occupy the inferior ranks; those who use worked metals have more prestige.[18] Thus it seems that the dignity of a caste is to be measured as much by the utility as by the difficulty of the occupations which it pursues.

The groups which have monopolized the most complicated modes of activity also enjoy the greatest consideration. The less 'primitive' an occupation is, the more is the practitioner respected. Each family of castes corresponds to one of the stations in that progress by which humanity has increased its power over things, and a caste is that much more esteemed in that the procedures which it employs were discovered later. One can then maintain that the degrees of the Hindu hierarchy correspond, in a general manner, to the phases of industrial evolution. 'The natural history of human industry provides the key to the gradation as to the formation of castes';[19] economic phenomena explain their superimposition as much as their specialization.

The study of India would thus provide an unexpected confirmation to those philosophies of history which tend to 'materialism': by presenting caste as a natural[20] and secular[21] institution derived from the guild; one would simultaneously have demonstrated that in that civilization which seems the most profoundly impregnated by religion, it is industry which has fashioned the dominant social form.

Certain facts might appear to throw doubt on this thesis. In order for the assimilation of castes to guilds to be exact, would it not be necessary that to each occupational distinction there corresponded a distinction of caste, and that there should be no other castes distinctions than occupational distinctions?

And, have we not seen that members of the same caste sometimes follow very different occupations?[22] Furthermore, if it is true that the adoption of a new profession often makes for the formation of a new caste,[23] many other causes have the same effect. If many castes bear the name of an occupation, many also have the name of a locality: proof that, from the highest antiquity, castes were opposed as much by 'country' as by 'occupation'.[24] In certain cases we even see a caste constitute itself under our eyes quite independently of any industrial influence. The worshippers of the same saint, the partisans of the same prophet sometimes unite in a tight, closed circle, which does not allow overlap with any other:[25] thus a caste is born from a sect and not from a corporation.

But, first of all, the fact that members of the same caste sometimes exercise different occupations does not suffice to shake the argument. We have seen that changes of occupation – frequent above all, moreover, in just those castes whose privileged position puts them above the common law – leave no less rigid the rule that each caste should have its occupation: the exceptions do not destroy the obligation. If then, even today, it remains in a general manner true that occupation involves caste, the hypothesis of an original connection between these two terms remains a licit one. The corporation could have been the root of the caste.

In the same way local or religious distinctions that make for the opposition of castes do not prove definitively that the distinction of occupations could not have engendered the matrix of the system. When a social form has dominated a civilization for a long time, it can happen that the most diverse associations, whatever may be their origin and their end, model themselves on this same form and imitate its constitution. Thus it is that religious associations, in Greece, imitate the constitution of the city;[26] similarly feudal forms recur in the organization of the communes. Perhaps an analogous phenomenon occurred in India? Could territorial contiguity or a community of belief have succeeded, here or there, in founding a caste if the specialization imposed by industry had not previously given the habit to Hindu society, and founded the typical mould into which these partial groupings could run?

But has the specialization required by industry the power to cast such a mould? Do we indeed find in the necessities of economic organization, the sufficient reason for the peculiar characteristics of the caste system? It is the answer to this question that decides between the partisans and the adversaries of the hypothesis.

In order to achieve a decisive answer, is it sufficient to look for those social phenomena which have determined the nature of these guilds with which castes have been compared?

This seems to be M. Senart's opinion.[27] He juxtaposes the two social forms and concludes that the ties by which they unite individuals are of very different qualities. 'Who could confuse the two institutions? The one, limited solely to artisans, enclosed within a prescribed form, circumscribed in its actions to economic functions created by interest or necessity; the other penetrating the entire social life, regulating the duties of all, flourishing and acting everywhere, governing even the most intimate areas of private life?'

The argument, thus presented, is to be approached with caution. He illegitimately limits the attributes of guilds and contracts their area of action. 'Unilateral' associations, confined to this or that particular function, are late and exceptional developments in history. In order that a group demand only a part of their total activity from its members and not claim to regulate more than one side of their lives leaving them free in everything else, society must have attained a high degree of complexity and the minds of its members a high degree of abstraction.[28] One of the tendencies of our own civilization is to multiply such unilateral associations at the expense of global associations; but this tendency is entirely recent.[29]

In fact the corporations of our middle ages are far from being purely economic groupings. Mr Ashley speaking of the first guilds of the English merchants says: 'The brotherhood, moreover, was unlike a modern society aiming at some particular material advantage, in that it entered into a great part of everyday life.'[30] It had very often its treasury for mutual assistance, its

chapel in the church transept, its feasts, its cult, its own jurisdiction. Its supervision was not limited solely to the quality of its
products but extended to the morals of the brotherhood. Similarly, according to M. Gierke,[31] the German guild was simultaneously a religious society, which paid for masses in honour of its
patron saint – a worldly society that gave feasts and banquets –
a mutual help society, which came to the aid of sick members or
those who were victims of theft or fire – a legal protection society
that proceeded against those who offended its members – and
finally a moral society with its own censors charged with main-
taining the respect for duties to comrades or the profession.

The guild's area of action was not then as limited as M. Senart
appears to believe. It is not as all pervading as that of caste, no
doubt: its prescriptions are not so far ramified. They are, nevertheless, sufficiently extensive to prove that an economic group is
capable of holding sway over morals and of linking men, not only
towards the achievement of a precise and determined end, but
'for life', and that in this sense industry can give birth to a
system analogous to that of caste.

But is it truly industry which is responsible for this prolifera-
tion of rules which approximates guilds to castes? Or is the root
of this elsewhere? If the guilds submitted even the private lives
of their members to a common discipline, if it embraced them in a
communal cult and occasionally united them around a common
table, this all derives less from the necessities of industry than
from the traditions which dominated all social organization in the
middle ages. It did not occur to anybody that one could form an
association without its own jurisdiction, without mutual assistance, without communal feasts, without a single 'patron'.[32] This
notion did not spring from the progress of industry. It is to be
explained rather by the persisting influence of religious ideas,
and perhaps by the ancient memory of the early practices of the
family. Has it not been maintained that the guilds of the middle
ages were modelled on the type of the old Roman corporations[33]
and these in their turn upon the type of the *gens*? 'A large
family', says M. Waltzing, 'no word better indicates the relations uniting the brotherhood,' and it is 'in the image of the
family' that the professional corporation instituted its cult, its

sacrifices, its communal meals, its burials. In this sense, even in the professional 'fraternities' we see once more the traces of the *gens* spirit.[34]

It is not the case that we have to think of an ancient tradition being revived, after centuries of sleep, in order to give birth to guilds and create them in every particular;[35] but when, in the progress of economic life, the need for guilds was felt, it is perhaps this tradition which determined the form of the required organ. Survivals of familial religion, not the exigencies of industry, would then be responsible for those traits which make the guild resemble the caste.

If then we find it difficult to explain the hold of the guild over its members by purely economic phenomena, it will *a fortiori* be that much more difficult when we come to caste which has, as we have seen, more widely ramified attributes. This impossibility becomes obvious if one tries to explain one by one, and as the result of an industrial evolution, the three characteristics which, in their synthesis, appear to us to provide the distinctive physiognomy of the caste system – hereditary specialization, strict hierarchy and mutual repulsion.

Hereditary specialization seems the most easily explained. The interests of industry clearly require not only that work should be divided between corporations but also that skills be preserved from generation to generation. If an occupation is relatively simple and calls for certain general aptitudes rather than particular training, this necessity will be less strongly felt. Thus, as Mr Nesfield points out,[36] the rules of hereditary specialization are normally more lax among the commercial occupations. But when we speak of industry – and above all an industry like Hindu industry: an entirely manual industry, and which makes up in dexterity what it lacks in machinery – nothing can be more precious than technical education. And only the father, in India, can give that. In the absence of manuals which would, anyhow, be singularly inadequate, only his advice can teach the secrets of the art, the workmanship, the turn of the hand. Comte has rightly observed: in all civilizations where a moral tradition is the sole preserver of ideas and practices, it is inevitable and indispensable that it is the father who transmits his occupation to the son.[37] In fact, wherever a literally 'manu-facturing' industry rather than a 'machino-facturing' industry holds sway, there, according to Mr Nesfield,[38] in Peru as in Egypt, in Abyssinia as in Greece, one can find the traces of an analogous organization.

However is it true in every case that the necessity for the division of labour and the transmission of procedures explain the form which this organization has taken in India? To show that it is necessary for the continuity of economic life, for the artisan to instruct his successor, this does not show that the son necessarily succeeds the father. If one still believed that habits developed in the exercise of an occupation, come to be printed on the organism and are thus transmitted as innate aptitudes, one could maintain that hereditary specialization serves the well-known interests of industry and shapes men expressly for a diversity of tasks. But no belief is more subject to caution than this. It receives daily some fresh contradiction.[39] If then it is useful for the artisan to have his apprentices, it is not indispensable that they be of his own rank.

No doubt it is entirely natural that the children a man has under his hand and whom he can constantly supervise, should be instructed in his art. This is why it so often happens, in fact, that the same profession passes from father to son in one family. But why is it that what is elsewhere only a tendency becomes, in India, an obligation? It is this which remains to be explained. However well proved it may be that hereditary specialization is useful to the progress of industry, could one say that a knowledge of this utility has elevated specialization as a duty in the Hindu soul? Would this not be to attribute to this latter all too compli-cated a view of the matter? Social rules are rarely explained by such calculations.[40] Perhaps, if we wish to find the most profound source of the rules which hold sway in India, we shall be driven back to beliefs of a religious order. We know that among many peoples certain objects are *tabu* for certain families: to touch them is a crime. Thus this or that task could be forbidden to some and prescribed for others. Perhaps the survival and the analogous extension of a like belief accounts for the distribution of occupa-tions in India. Thus a religious idea could have influenced its industrial organization.

At least, if we look for the reasons which determine the hierarchy of the groups which are thus specialized, the influence of religious ideas appears clearly enough. Mr Nesfield has tried to deduce from a universal sociological law, the order of respect in which occupations are held and from that the Hindu castes. The more recent the phase of industrial progress in which an occupation has emerged, the more delicate its procedures, the more important its products, in a word the more difficult and useful it is – the more highly is it regarded. And certainly considerations of this nature must have a certain weight on the relative evaluations which Hindu opinion makes among the different occupations: the lowest, according to them, are in fact, often, the most primitive, the most simple and the least productive. But how much more weighty are considerations of an altogether different nature!

And before all else, is the position of the Brahman, on the pinnacle, to be explained by 'the natural history of human industry'? Certainly, we do not say that the Brahman's occupation is, in Hindu eyes, unproductive. Quite the contrary for the Brahman makes rain and fine weather, creates sterility or abundance.[41] No skills are more useful than his prayers and sacrifices. But in what way can these skills be related to an advanced period of industrial progress? In what way are they linked with the coming of metallurgy which, according to Mr Nesfield, is a turning point for civilization? The prestige of the Brahmans does not allow of measurement by 'materialistic' criteria. And if it is true, as Mr Nesfield himself observes, that the nobility of a caste depends principally from its relations with the Brahmans, we can understand what havoc the ascendance of Brahmanism makes of the alternative theory.

But, indeed, how many of the known facts, prove that in determining the rank of a caste, considerations quite alien to industry enter into account. The Tagas and the Bhuindars are, we are told, more respected than other agriculturalists.[42] And is this because they use more elaborate techniques of cultivation? It is rather, without question, because they rigorously obey the law forbidding the remarriage of widows. Inversely, there are numerous examples of castes which have been degraded and eat forbidden foods.[43] Rightly we are reminded that those castes that

38

work with metal have a fairly high rank; but, it must be added, that if the Lohars, the ironsmiths, are inferior to the Sonars, who work in gold and silver, it is because iron is black, an inauspicious colour for the Hindus: gold and silver, on the contrary, are believed to be composed of the two most pure elements, water and fire.[44] Similarly if the fisherman castes are superior to the hunters it is because of the sacredness of water.[45] Yet more striking is the fact that the barbers, who often function as surgeons, certainly use metal instruments; nevertheless they are despised because their occupation obliges them to touch blood and hair. In the same way all those whose occupation requires them to work the skin of dead animals are irredeemably degraded.[46] The evaluation which the Hindus make of this or that caste depends then principally upon their ideas of what is sacred, permitted or forbidden, dignified or disgusting.

Social precedence is determined less by the usefulness or difficulty of occupations than by their relative purity and impurity. Mr Nesfield's work, valuable as it is, does not reveal those universal laws governing the gradation of occupations: rather he makes us conclude that there is no unique criterion for this gradation. Each civilization has its preferred manner of classifying occupations; and, no doubt its way of classifying best expresses its inner tendencies. In Hindu civilization it is religious beliefs above all, rather than economic tendencies, that fix the rank of each group.

The inadequacy of economic explanations is even more evident if we take into account the third aspect of the caste system as we have defined it. Can this repulsion which isolates groups and prevents them from intermarrying, eating together and sometimes from touching each other, be deduced from industrial necessities? These may be used to explain why a father passes on his skills to his son, but they cannot begin to explain why a man must not take a wife outside his own caste. How does the wife who bears his son affect the traditional occupation? The alien origin of the mother does not stop the child from being his son and continuing the art. Mr Nesfield, despairing of any explanation of the rules of endogamy* by his system, appears to conclude

* The text here has 'règles exogamiques'.

39

that they are the invention of Brahmans.[47] Surely this is to bring in by the backdoor what the caste-guild theory tries to eject from the front. It allows all too much to artifice and premeditation.

It is then insufficient for an understanding of the constituent characteristics of the caste system to compare caste with guild. If this comparison explains why functions are divided, it does not explain why they become hereditary. It does not throw light on the principles governing the superimposition of groups and finally it leaves utterly in the dark the reasons for their opposition.

2

The opposition of caste and family

The elementary groups of Hindu society are not only specialized but they also, in a sense, repel each other.

In the search for the origins of this mutual repulsion some have been led to compare the caste and the family. M. Senart above all, has followed up this comparison.[1]

M. Senart, even more than either Mr Nesfield or M. Dahlmann, is a partisan of a 'natural' explanation of the caste system. He condemns all theories which tend to present it as a recent invention. For him the germs of such numerous groups, separated by such rigorous rules must be sought in the very night of time, in the deepest past of Hindu history.

Does this mean to say that he would have us see castes already established in the Vedic period? Does the evidence of the Vedas allow us to deduce their existence? The question is still a controversial one. Some, with M. Zimmer, continue to believe that apart from the famous hymn in which the four classical castes are born from the limbs of Purusha – a hymn generally agreed to be later than the other Vedic hymns – nothing in the Vedas allows us to suppose that the Hindu population was and had been by then divided into hereditarily specialized groups. The term Vaisya referred to all free men, not to a group committed to a particular profession. Warlike activity was not the monopoly of the Kshatriyas. The term Brahman, finally, signified first sage, then poet; only later did it take on the sense of priest.[2]

Others, with M. Ludwig, maintain that by this stage the rituals were sufficiently elaborate to require the formation of a special sacerdotal class which might be expected to make a monopoly of sacrifice; side by side with this sacerdotal class an aristocracy developed which remained aloof from the common people – founded its privileges on heredity; thus not only was the conquering Aryan race opposed to the Dasyus but it was itself already subdivided into three superimposed groups.[3]

M. Senart takes up a novel position between these two arguments. He argues that if the facts invoked by M. Ludwig were correct, they still do not sufficiently demonstrate the existence of castes in the proper sense. He certainly admits, against M. Zimmer, that classes were in existence from Vedic times:[4] but classes are not castes. It seems to him likely that the Hindu population was at that time divided into groups analogous to the *pishtra* of Iran. But can a 'vague grouping' be assimilated to 'caste proper', necessarily more restricted, dedicated to a particular profession, united by common descent, enclosed within a body of particular regulations, governed by its own customs – an organism, finally, of its nature circumscribed, exclusive and separatist? Division into classes is a common phenomenon; the separation into castes an unique phenomenon. The first recognizes three or four enormous divisions in society; the latter divides it into an infinite number of rigorously closed tiny circles. One cannot then hope to find in the distinction of the Vedic *varna*, the origin of the caste system.[5]

The true prototypes of castes are not the *varna* but the *jāti*.[6] The chains which unite the members of the same caste were not forged from the scrap of those which united the representatives of the same class; they derive their links rather from those which united the descendants of the same lineage. Family circles alone were sufficiently narrow and numerous to give rise to the multiplicity of castes. The present exclusiveness of castes is but the ancient memory of the isolation of clans.

Truth to tell, the Vedas have less to say to us about the constitution of these clans and their relations than they have about the hierarchy of classes. We see that the Hindu population was divided into *visa* and in *jana*; following Zimmer, we can distinguish tribes, villages and families analogous to the social forms which are found among the Germans and the Slavs.[7] But we cannot grasp, sufficiently clearly, the constitution of these elementary groupings: we do not have sufficiently precise details about their organization, their customs, the prohibitions they imposed on social relations, to enable us to find the point of departure for caste rules.[8]

Is this a sound reason for abandoning the hypothesis? We have to recognize that Brahmanic literature by no means gives us an exact and complete picture of Hindu life. By other avenues of approach we have brought to light more than one institution, more than one belief which would have been buried forever, had we relied solely on the traditions of the Brahmans.[9] The silence of the Vedas is not sufficient, then, to prevent us looking for the root of the constituent rules of the caste system in the primitive forms of familial organization.

Analogies can satisfactorily supplement direct information. Let us, following M. Senart, look at the sisters, by race, of Hindu society, the ancient Aryan societies whose history is less clouded than hers.[10] Here we shall see, varying from place to place, the evolution of the ancient familial constitution unfold; and we shall discover that a number of traits in this constitution recall those which are so striking in the constitution of caste. In Rome as in Greece, it appears that the ancient Aryan family is essentially a religious association, a group of people of the same blood, met around a common hearth, participating in a common cult. It is the need to assure the continuity of this cult and its purity that underlies the greater part of the rules governing its members.

For example the meal produced from the sacred hearth is the external sign of familial community:[11] for this reason in the primitive period sharing a meal with a stranger was forbidden.[12] Even when this interdiction has been forgotten, descendants from the same lineage keep up the habit of reuniting to eat together in certain solemn circumstances: funeral feasts, the *perideipnon* of the Greeks, the Roman *silicernium* preserve the sacred significance of the family meal.[13]

Similarly we can recognize in their laws affecting marriage, the religious concern which penetrated the ancient familial organization. 'It was not only considerations of aristocratic pride but in the name of a sacred right that the patrician families, of pure race, remained faithful to the integrity of the ancient religion and rejected marriage alliance with the impurer plebeians, of mixed origin and devoid of family cults.'[14]

These prohibitions whose tendency was, even in the ancient city, to prevent 'strangers' mixing or even eating together, are they not the very ones which raise such high barriers between castes in India? Here this system of prescriptions has become stronger, as it were, aggravating itself, there on the contrary, it was to efface itself; but both here and there we find the same system, organized in the same spirit. In India the roots remain concealed, the foliage is luxuriant; among the peoples of classical antiquity, nearly all the leaves have fallen, the roots alone are prominent: but it is always the same tree, the Aryan tree. In India, according to Mr Ibbetson, the community of food is still the external sign, the solemn manifestation of the community of blood. And, in the final analysis, the endogamy of the Hindu caste rests upon the idea of the married couple as sacrificing upon the family altar of the hearth.[15]

It is possible, then, to recognize the impression of distinctively Aryan religious ideas on Hindu social organization: their influence explains quite naturally what could not be explained by the exigencies of industry. The distinctive customs of caste, the rules with which it surrounds connubium and commensality overlap 'exactly the domain of the ancient law of the *gens*'.[16] We are now in a position to see clearly: we can give a name to the ancestor of caste. It descends in direct line from the Aryan family.

What can we say of this theory?

It has been praised[17] for drawing attention to the multiplicity of castes which the Brahman theory veils over and for demonstrating the necessity for looking in India's most remote past for the seeds of this multiplicity of organisms so striking to the modern observer. But has the theory really demonstrated that caste is built upon the frame of the family and more precisely the frame of the Aryan family?

On this last point facts which contradict M. Senart are not lacking. For it certainly seems that the beliefs and customs which he represents as the monopoly of the Aryan people are, in reality, found among a number of other peoples.[18]

That certain objects are naturally sacred for certain people and that they must, therefore, inspire an ambiguous sentiment where respect is mixed with horror, and that such objects cannot consequently be touched without the greatest precautions, such ideas might seem strange to civilized people – they are common to nearly all primitive peoples. M. Senart speaks, somewhere of the 'Aryan scruples over purity' as if these scruples, which press so heavily on the Hindu caste, were not the lot of many races quite unrelated to the Hindu race. Among the Semites as among the Aryans, there are impure animals, whose blood contaminates, contact with which is forbidden especially to those who sacrifice.[19] And if one would seek the origin of such beliefs they must be related, according to Robertson Smith[20] to the *tabu* sentiment – a sentiment which would appear to be familiar to all known races.

But perhaps the more particular scruples, those which limit connubium and commensality, are distinctively Aryan?

M. Senart, in order to demonstrate that the Hindu caste descends in direct line from the Aryan family, reminds us that the communal meal, the essential sign of the community of caste is also, in the eyes of the Aryan peoples, the sacred symbol of kinship. But it was precisely his study of the Semitic peoples that led Robertson Smith to bring to light the importance of the 'sacrificial meal'. Among the Semites the sacrificial banquet is essentially a feast of kin. The sacred meal not only unites the faithful to God but unites them to each other: it gives them the same flesh and makes the same blood circulate in their veins. 'The act of eating and drinking with a man is the symbol and the confirmation of kinship, the proof that the two are linked by mutual social obligations.' This is so much so that it is sufficient to have shared food with a man to become in a sense his brother.[21] To this extent the Semites, together with the Aryans, make a close relation between commensality and fraternity. Caste prescriptions governing food may be drawn from the common stock of primitive ideas; they in no way demonstrate the existence of a specially Aryan stock.

Are the rules governing marriage any more significant? Can we say, for example, that only tribes of the Aryan race practised endogamy which still today separates castes, while exogamy prevails in the majority of other races?

Certainly, the observers of primitive societies tell us mostly about rules of exogamy. But here it is a matter of not being taken in by the antithesis. It is a mistake to classify peoples as 'exogamous' and 'endogamous'. For exogamy is almost always found accompanied by a correlated endogamy. That is to say that marriage rules simultaneously mark out a narrow circle within which a man may not take a wife and a wider one within which he can. M. Durkheim, discussing current theories on the origin of exogamy[22] observes that 'exogamy does not mean marrying a foreigner. Generally men find their wives in a clan of the same tribe or the same confederation. Clans thus allied consider each other as kin. . . If marriage is exogamous for the totemic groups (primary or secondary clans) it is generally endogamous in relation to the political society (the tribe).'

No doubt in many instances we are told which groups cannot intermarry without being told at the same time which groups can. But it is probable that in most cases more detailed information will reveal a wider circle of endogamy enclosing the smaller exogamic circles. Even those forms of marriage which seem contrary to endogamic practice can be accommodated by it. Marriage 'by capture' seems to imply that men can marry any foreign woman snatched from an enemy tribe. But if a tribe always goes to the same tribes to capture wives, this is surely the beginning of an endogamous practice? In fact, sometimes where the ceremonies following marriage by capture are better known, we can ascertain that a man does not believe that he can licitly marry a woman simply because he has captured her.[23] Before marrying her, he has her adopted by his tribe: proof that even where this form of abduction is practised, the concern for endogamy is present in force. Endogamy, then, is much more general than we once thought. Like Hindu castes, many tribes of very diverse races are endogamous while their sections are exogamous. Hindu scruples over marriage have nothing which necessarily demonstrates an Aryan descent for caste.

The thesis would only be defensible if it could be proved on the one hand that a particular family organization was alone able to give rise to caste and on the other that this organization was only found among the Aryan peoples. We shall be told, perhaps, that

patriarchy and the ancestor cult is, par excellence, an **Aryan**
social form, and that the Aryan peoples never knew matriarchy,
which is so often found, united with totemism, among Semitic
peoples.[24] But first of all it would be possible to find traces of
matriarchy among peoples of the Aryan race. And even then one
cannot see why the fact that a people has passed through the
phase of matriarchal organization should prevent them from
reaching the caste system. In order for this system to come into
being all that is necessary is the survival and the predominance of
the sentiment of kinship which is the cement of primitive groups.
But whether these groups were originally composed of families
in which the children belonged to the father, or of families where
children bore the mother's name, is of little importance.

We shall say as much of totemism. M. Senart discovers traces
of totemism in the Hindu world which are 'astonishing'.[25] Does
this mean to say that a people who have been subject to totemism
are unable to form endogamous groups like castes? It has been
established that, on the contrary, adherents of totemism, like
certain Australian tribes, do, if they practise clan exogamy, also
practise tribal endogamy.[26] There is no reason, then, why Hindu
castes may not have totemic hordes among their ancestors. And
if we make this point it is not an attempt to demonstrate the
universality of totemism, but simply to draw attention to the fact
that the division of the Hindus into castes in no way proves that
they were subject in the formative period of their present social
organization, to distinctively Aryan beliefs.

Ethnographers are, then, right in supposing that the early
Aryan castes no doubt much resembled those non-Aryan tribes
which today still live on the frontiers of Hinduism.[27] Already it
has been shown for a number of inventions or institutions that the
part played by the Aryan conquerors has been exaggerated, and
that India did not have to await their coming to compose books
and produce doctors any more than to cultivate the soil or found
villages.[28] Similarly it had not to wait for them before it could
know these scruples about purity or these rules of endogamy
which in their persistence and exaggeration constitute the distinctive originality of its castes. It is not that we claim that the
autochthonous people imposed this social organization upon its

invaders. We note, simply, that it was the monopoly of neither. When they first met it is probable that both Aryans and aborigines were divided into tribes; their collision no doubt redoubled the intensity of that repulsion against the foreigner that each of these primitive groups already carried in germ. But we cannot say that this spirit of division and mutual opposition, which was to penetrate the entire organization of India, was brought to it by one race rather than another. Almost always when one is trying to construct the history of an institution, one begins by thinking of it as the apanage of one race. But also, almost always, as the research proceeds, that particular race is dispossessed: one realizes that the institution is more common than one had supposed. Thus we have known for a long time that *wergeld* is not peculiar to the Germans;[29] today we see that the domestic community is found among non-Aryan as much as among Aryan peoples.[30] Similarly, in the matter of caste we must be on our guard against the 'Aryan mirage'. In order to explain those practices which to this day fragment the Hindus, it is not necessary to think of them as the direct consequences of a distinctively Aryan belief; they are the survivals and, as it were, extraordinary petrifications of very general religious customs.[31]

M. Senart rightly warns us against 'over-comprehensive' theories.[32] Rightly he hopes that historical relations and precise causal links will replace vague affiliations. But we must not allow this concern for precision to mask the generality of customs. Those which forbid marriage, communion and sometimes contact between different groups are too widespread for us to accept that Aryan influence alone imposed them upon the Hindus. We can, then, only accept the hypothesis by widening it: if it is true that caste derives from the family, there is no proof that it could only have derived from the Aryan family.

And, nevertheless, once we admit that caste derives from the family we must be clear what we mean; we must not understand the term family in the narrow, precise sense in which it is ordinarily used. It would be a mistake to take it as proven that all the members of a caste are descended from one ancestor and are really consanguinous. All that has been demonstrated is that the sentiment of kinship prevailed in the organization of caste. But to say kinship is not necessarily to say consanguinity. In primitive thought kinship often seems to derive from membership of the same cult, or from the simple identity of names, or even from simply living in the same place.[33] It is quite possible that the members of a caste could have belonged, in reality, to different lineages. And we should go so far as to look amongst large and composite groupings of kin if we wish to form some idea of the group which generated a caste rather than among the small and simple groupings of consanguines. In this way it is easier to escape certain objections which would have to be met if we wished to derive caste immediately from the family *stricto sensu*.

For a long time it has been noted, for example, that the cult of the ancestors seems alien to caste; we see members of a caste worshipping the tools of their profession, we do not see them sacrificing to an eponymous hero:[34] and this is strange if a caste is only the prolongation of a family. M. Senart could, no doubt, reply that in default of the cult of an eponymous hero, the memories or the legends of castes prove that the greater part of them have a clear notion of their genealogical cohesion; or yet that this cult may have gradually faded away in a caste after having served, nevertheless, as its creative spark.[35] But surely the absence of this cult seems more natural if we envisage a caste as a synthesis of several lineages rather than as the prolongation of a single one?

There is a more serious objection to this latter way of conceiving the relation of caste and family.

M. Dahlmann, discussing M. Senart's theory, radically opposes caste and *gens*.[36] M. Senart maintains that caste rules overlap 'exactly the whole domain of the ancient law of the *gens*'; but in fact we find the two in contradiction on an important point. Caste, it has been said, is about marriage: it is marriage laws which above all separate castes forever. The caste understanding of these laws is quite different from that of the *gens*. The *gens* forbids its members to intermarry; the caste requires them to do so. The one is as rigorously exogamous as the other is endogamous. The spirit of caste could not then be born of the spirit of the family.

This is too easy a triumph. M. Senart has not forgotten *gens* exogamy. He reminds us of Plutarch's evidence that in the old times, the Romans never married women of their own blood.[37] He sees, therefore, that memories of the *gens* may very well explain the internal exogamy of caste, which, for example, forbids marriage between members of the same *gotrā*; but they cannot explain its endogamy. Necessarily one must admit that caste is the union of several *gentes* rather than the prolongation of one *gens*. If, nevertheless, M. Senart maintains that caste is modelled on the familial organization, he admits also that this organization has given their form not only to the primary groups which are families in the proper sense, but to the composite groups, secondary or tertiary, formed by the union of several families, the clans and tribes. The clan and the tribe, whatever names they may take in different countries, are only enlargements of the family[38] 'they copy its organization while extending it'. Caste is then endogamous in the image of these large groups of kin – clans or tribes; it is not endogamous in the image of small groups of consanguines – families in the strict sense.

Are these larger groups really an enlargement of a primary group – the family? Or should we rather believe that the family, properly speaking, has, by detaching itself from the mass, become progressively more specific? Or again, are we to find the true germ of caste in a 'tertiary' group or a 'secondary' group – that is in the tribe or in the clan? We should like to have more precise ideas on these points. But the different types of primitive societies are not yet, it seems to us, defined and classified with sufficient clarity to allow us to reach a decision. All that seems to us as established is that a spirit, common to all these societies, has survived in caste and that religious scruples of all kinds which make them repel each other naturally explain those which still today isolate the castes of India.

3

The hierarchy of castes and the priesthood

The dominance of ancient familial exclusivism explains why castes refuse to merge: it remains to be explained why we find them ranged in tiers.

For to say opposition is not to say superimposition. A society can be divided up into closed sections without these sections becoming hierarchized. No doubt it is difficult for co-existing social bodies to remain at exactly the same level, as it is difficult for them to maintain the same attributes: from the moment that a certain life in common unites them, they cannot fail in the long run to range themselves, however vaguely, and at the same time to specialize. Thus even where the primitive opposition of clans holds, it is not rare for a hierarchy to merge. Among the Scots we see that certain clans are subordinate to others.[1] Among the Israelites there were some generally despised tribes; others, like Ephraim enjoyed a peculiar esteem.[2] But how far are these rough outlines from the masterly architecture which ranges the multiplicity of Hindu castes in a sacred order!

The key-stone of the whole edifice is, as we have seen, the universally recognized primacy of the Brahman caste. However diverse the castes may be and however closed the one to the other, a common respect for the Brahman orients them in the same direction, and weighs upon all their customs. We have seen that the greater part of these customs can be explained by a sentiment of common kinship; it is remarkable that, strong as this sentiment may be, it must give way in front of the sublimity of the Brahmans: for them the closed circle of kin opens. Not

51

only do they preside over the majority of family ceremonies – even the poorest Hindus would not marry or rear their children without their help[3] – but also, in certain cases, they are, so to speak, substituted for kin. Thus the practice of the funerary feast, offered to the spirits of the ancestors, is widespread in India as in many other countries; but in India it is the Brahmans who sit down in the ancestors' place. The family banquet is served with their permission, under their auspices, in their honour; they are deemed to represent the ancestors and eat in their name.[4] Similarly in the event of murder, compensation was originally paid, in India as elsewhere, to the family of the murdered man;* but in the end it comes to the Brahman.[5] On more than one point, we see the Brahman's prestige override the unquestionably powerful memory of the first familial groupings. And, further, we know that if these groupings are ranged in tiers, the measure for this is the extent to which they are close to or far from the priestly class. The uncontested superiority of this class is then one of the constituent principles of social organization in India; it has even been said that it is the most sure characteristic of Hinduism.[6]

Certainly the priestly class possesses a privileged position everywhere, and often holds the highest rank. But it is rare to find it dominating without contradiction and by its own unsupported powers. More often it has to deal with a secular power; sometimes it allies itself with this; sometimes it joins combat; but its presence constitutes a limitation upon the extension of priestly prerogatives and more often gradually reduces priestly influence. Among the *gene* discerned by Herodotus in Egypt, the priestly body was named first: its privileges are not subject to discussion, its lands are reserved and it is not touched by common levies. The corporations of the temples form a society which is juxtaposed to rather than blended into civil society. But the prince supervises the government of the temples and puts his creatures at their head. These states within the state continued to be dominated by the royal power.[7] Similarly, powerful as they were in the middle ages the powers spiritual never succeeded in subordinating the powers temporal; in the final count it

---

* The text here has 'la famille du meurtrier'.

was the kings who gained most in the period of Catholic theocracy.

In the Brahman theocracy on the contrary, the priests stand alone on the summit.[8]

But, as might be supposed, not without battles. The sacred literature preserves the memory of Kshatriya power and the obstacles that it threw in the path of Brahmanic power. Even the way in which Brahman pre-eminence is asserted proves that it was not admitted without discussion.[9] The epics recall the violence to Brahmans of evil kings such as Vena or Nahusha. If the story of Parasurama is to be believed, the rivalry of the two classes was marked by bloody wars.[10] The Upanishads, at all events, bear witness that their respective functions were not always as strictly specialized as Brahmanic theory would have us believe. There we see Kshatriyas rivalling the Brahmans in knowledge and even becoming their preceptors.[11] Elsewhere, sons of kings, like Visvamitra, become Brahmans by the power of their austerities. All these legends testify that it took time for the ranks to be clearly settled and for their attributes to be defined. But the balance of privilege was to weigh down unambiguously in favour of the Brahmans.

There is no question that they ever took temporal power into their hands. Born for religious functions, Brahmans could not directly exercise political functions. Similarly, the Brahman caste could not accumulate riches, as priestly classes often do; it possessed nothing of its own. 'The instruments of sacrifice are its only weapons,[12] but with these arms it subordinates the whole Hindu world. The *purohita*, the chaplain, grows up at the king's side and soon surpasses him, and that simply because he monopolizes the religious offices. It is the priest who consecrates the king and presents him to the people, saying "Here is your king, oh people; the king of the Brahmans is Soma." '[13] He measures out and dispenses all social dignities. Even the *rāja* owes his prestige less to his material power than to his fidelity to those rites the Brahman guards. Their power is the more uncontested in that it is entirely spiritual; they have avoided those hazards which the priestly class has the most frequently met once it tries to increase its strength by arrogating temporal power.[14] One might say that they have no part in government and yet are obeyed by all; they possess nothing and yet have all.

How can we explain this amazing power?

Its development has, no doubt, been encouraged by the absence of a political organization worthy of the name. There is in India, M. Senart notes, no rudiment of the state.[15] India, adds M. Sylvain Lévi, has always lacked a central history. It is not that it has not known great empires. But it seems as though they have passed over Hindu civilization without penetrating its depths. Even the historians who, in our own time, draw our attention to India's great unifiers add that their achievements were never more than ephemeral and superficial.[16] The division of society into castes prevented the formation of national unities;[17] thus the priestly class had a free hand. Its domination could spread and encounter no obstacle.

It would be a great error to suppose that the priestly caste was able to achieve what others had not achieved and to oppose it, as a duly organized body against an inorganic mass. In reality, the Brahman bodies lacked unity as much as the others. It is by failing to recognize this feature that some have sought deceptive comparisons. We have seen, for example, that the Brahmans have been compared with the Jesuits: as if all the Brahmans, wrapping the Hindu world in a permanent conspiracy, followed one will in the interests of 'the Order'. But the Brahman caste, or rather the Brahman castes, have never constituted anything resembling an Order. One cannot even say that they amount to what we call the clergy. Not one of the social forms to which we are accustomed by a great organized and centralized religion like Catholicism is to be found in Brahmanism. It does not even know the rudimentary organization known to the Druids: the nomination of a high priest, elected or chosen by lot and the convocation of an annual council. No more do we see Brahmans gathering in monasteries, uniting to submit to a common discipline, as do Buddhist monks. Brahmans are priests without a Church; no one has a mandate to be heard, none a pontiff to venerate; by definition they are equal, precisely because they derive their dignity from birth alone.

Burnouf, imagining the reply of a Brahman to someone who spoke of ordination, makes him argue thus:[18]

It is the masculine principle which has made me what I am: my father was a Brahman and so, therefore, am I. I could no more wish to cease being one than I am able to do so, for this is the law of my nature, a law laid upon me even before I was born, in the womb of a Brahman mother where a Brahman father sowed that seed from which I sprang. To be a priest I have no need of outside assistance... When Manu enunciated those laws which govern the functions of castes, did he not establish the superiority of the Brahman over the other three orders? But he did not say that one Brahman should be superior to another: for as he created us from his mouth Brahma gave the function of composing hymns and celebrating sacrifice to us all. Our first fathers transmitted to their sons that power which we have received from them; and since the generation of one Brahman is in everything like that of another, we cannot understand how one priest can command another and impose a faith upon him of which he is neither the first author nor the unique interpreter.

The caste system, in dividing men according to birth, points in principle the equality of Brahmans; this is naturally incompatible with the hierarchical organization of a clergy. The strength of the priests in India does not derive from any power of organization. Could it, rather, derive from the rigour and the precision of the ideology they hold in trust? Since their power is not explained by their discipline, can their dogmatism explain it? It is most unlikely when we consider how close the relations are between the dogmas of religion and the social organization. 'Where there is no hierarchy', writes Zeller, 'all dogma, thought of as a general rule of faith, is from the outset impossible, for no organ exists to formulate and support it.'[19] Where religion does not find a unified society, nor clergy, congregations nor councils, it would be astonishing if belief were systematically coordinated and forever established, *ne varietur*. Burnouf also tells us that the independence of doctrines is a natural result of the caste system.[20] And indeed what is remarkable about Brahmanism is its flexibility rather than its rigidity. 'It is a receptive religion and in no way intolerant. Everything comes in and nothing goes out.' Its pantheism opens easily to all the inventions of polytheism: gods of all sorts find room in it by becoming the *avatāra* of traditional gods.[21] This is so much so that from the moment we try to define the true religion of the Hindus in dogmatic terms, we are acutely embarrassed; we note that it lacks an orthodoxy, that it is defined by its rites rather than its dogmas, by practices rather than ideas, and that finally, respect for the Brahman united with observance of caste custom, is the essence of Hinduism. As a religion without a Church, we can say that Brahmanism is a religion without dogma.

From this we understand the discussions which have arisen concerning the 'missionary' or 'non-missionary' character of Brahmanic religion.[22] The idea that there existed a religious truth valid for the whole world, and that this had to be propagated as much as possible, appears to have been alien to the Brahman's mind.[23] He would prefer to accept that each race has its gods. His religion is in essence closed to the *mleccha*. And nevertheless one should not think, remarks Lyall, that Brahmanism lacked its proselytes. Perhaps no contemporary religion has more conversions to its credit. But conversion to Brahmanism is not adhesion to a precise dogma. If a Brahman converts an aboriginal tribe, this does not mean that he overthrows their beliefs, but rather that he teaches them to respect caste custom and himself above all.[24] It is by making himself worshipped that the Brahman conquers souls. The great article of faith which he promulgates is the sacrosanct nature of the born-priest.

From this characteristic of the Brahman race springs all the vitality of their religion. If they continue to dominate the mass of the Hindu population from so great a height and impress even the aborigines they owe it not to a social discipline, nor to doctrinal rigour but solely to the prestige of their blood. The Brahman is of a special species; he has by birth virtues that no other can acquire; on this notion rests the power of the Brahman caste.

It is true that if we accepted as literal some pronouncements in Brahmanic texts we should believe that the dignity of the Brahman was the reward of learning and virtue rather than the privilege of blood.[25] 'Why ask for the name of thy father or thy mother? Thy father is the wisdom of the Vedas.'[26] The true Brahman 'is he who has understood'.[27] Indeed the sacred codes submit the young Brahman to a long novitiate; he must devote many years to understanding, from the venerated lips of his *guru*, the knowledge of the Vedas. But this initiation, necessary as it is, is not sufficient in itself; nothing takes the place of the gift of race. One is born a Brahman, and cannot become one. *Nascitur, non fit.* The texts which would have us believe the contrary are no more than 'a device to glorify the supposed virtue and knowledge of the priests and in no way involves forgetfulness of the rights conferred by birth alone.'[28] The pivot of the Hindu world is the respect for these rights, by belief in the peculiar virtues of Brahmanic blood.

How is it that the whole of India, for so many centuries has been fascinated by this special prestige?

In part the very origins of Hindu civilization explain the lofty idea it holds of the qualities of race. It represents itself as the product of a superior race supplementing with its riches those refinements denied to inferior barbarians. The Vedic hymns testify not only to the invaders' rage against those they fought, but also, and above all, to their contempt for those they conquered. The moral differences between the Arya and the Dasyu are as striking as the physical ones. What a gulf is there between the fair skinned, fine featured Aryan, scrupulously observing religious laws and the black, flat nosed Dasyu, who eats what comes to hand and offers no milk to the gods![29] In the latter portrait we are to recognize the present day aborigine and in the former the high-caste Hindu. And from these some have gone on to elaborate a theory according to which the caste hierarchy in India would correspond exactly to a racial superimposition. Risley, after having measured more than 6,000 natives of Bengal arrives at the following conclusion: 'It is scarcely an exaggeration to lay down as a law of the organization of caste in India that a man's social rank varies in inverse ratio to the width of his nose.'[*][30] M. Senart has already impeached the likelihood of such correlations.[31] More recent anthropometric data, published subsequently, allow us to demonstrate from the figures themselves that Mr Risley's thesis rests upon a manifest exaggeration.[32] This does not make it less likely that social and moral differences

* Risley's word was 'paradox' not exaggeration. In his *People of India*, 1908, he prefaced his remarks with the following qualification: 'In those parts of India where there is an appreciable strain of Dravidian blood it is scarcely a paradox', etc.

originally corresponded to clearly marked physical differences; the memory of this fundamental ethnic opposition has, no doubt, contributed to the particular preoccupations of Hindu opinion.[33] In fact, interbreeding between the descendants of the two races must have grown: this has not affected the ideal that the purity of the superior race must be saved. The Brahmans being thought of as respecting this ideal the most and most strictly obeying the laws of endogamy, it is natural that they should also be regarded as the most faithful specimens of the Aryan type: thus the particular prestige of Brahmanic blood came first of all and in part from the general prestige of Aryan blood.

Purity is lost, however, in other ways apart from mis-alliance. It is quite sufficient, as we have seen, to share a meal with certain people, to ingest certain foods, even to touch certain objects to find oneself in a state of pollution. Therefore, it is not only their obedience to the laws governing marriage that gives respect to the Brahmans: it is also the care they take in abstaining from forbidden foods and shunning contaminated people or things. The more a caste sets itself to respect the laws which safeguard purity, the more it is esteemed. It is, then, quite natural that they should be most respected of all who have made a speciality of the rigorous observance of these laws. 'The Brahmans strive most to keep up appearances of outward and inward purity' writes the Abbé Dubois. 'It is chiefly to the scrupulous observance of such customs that the Brahmans owe the predominance of their illustrious caste'.[34] They consecrate their entire lives to the full and complete realization of that ideal which every caste, with more or less success, only partially realizes. Is it surprising that, in the eyes of the Hindu multitude, they, the descendants of a race that has controlled itself so scrupulously over so many centuries, should represent and, in a manner, incarnate that ideal?[35]

At every point if we wish to understand the most decisive reason for the prestige of their blood, we have to take into account the nature of the function reserved to them alone. The warrior class also claims to be of the Aryan race; it also preserves its purity jealously. Nevertheless, it steps back before the priestly class for the latter is the 'guardian of the sacrifice'. And there, without a doubt, lies the deep source of its privileges.

To understand this we have to call to mind primitive ideas about the nature of sacrifice and the qualities of the sacrificer. We know that sacrifice, which has for its end the creation of communication between men and gods invests those who perform it with a particular character: the sacrificer becomes a 'sacred' being in himself: at once to be worshipped and dreaded.[36] He possesses this character most fully, no doubt, at the moment of sacrifice, but it is not immediately lost thereafter. The ceremonies which ordinarily accompany the 'coming out' from the sacrifice show that it is not always easy to divest himself of the special quality which he has contracted there. No doubt it is a sense of this difficulty which has led people to specialize the function of sacrificer.

With our modern ideas we tend to explain this specialization solely by the growing complication of rites. And certainly it must become more and more difficult to accomplish all those operations that are needed to act upon the will of the gods, without a technical education.[37] Only the practitioners, truly 'doctors of sacrifice', surveying the whole infinite complexity of manipulations and recitations, can restore the mechanism 'as one articulates one limb with another, or as one laces up pieces of leather.'[38]

But quite apart from these material necessities, moral sentiments, in response to primitive ideas which are found all over, require the specialization of the sacrificer.[39] For when he enters that bark which carries him from the profane to the sacred world, he deals with ambiguous or fluid forces, at once the most dangerous and the most beneficial of all. And from them he is charged with a particular kind of electricity[40] (it is a comparison that authoritatively imposes itself on all who study the elementary forms of religion). They themselves are more or less *tabu*. They remain 'consecrated'.[41]

The habit of sacrifice gives, then, a sort of second nature to the sacrificer. This makes him participate in the essence of these gods that he puts in communication with men. However slight may be this commingling of the divine and the human natures, the sacred character of the officiant attaches to his person not only for his whole life, it is transmitted after his death to his descendants; having passed 'into his blood', it becomes a property of his race.

Thus is explained the virtue of the Brahmanic blood. It is natural that a people which, more than any other, has magnified the action of sacrifice upon the order of the world[42] should also imbue the reaction of the sacrifice upon the sacrificer with particular significance. He who speaks to the gods seems a god himself: he who lights the sacred fire becomes *āgneya*, participates in the nature of fire. In these ideas underlying the infinite superiority of the Brahmans and so the very hierarchy of Hindu castes, we recognize once more primitive ideas, only carried to their highest power.

We refuse, and rightly, to attribute the creation of the caste system to the interested calculations, artifices and conspiracies of Brahmans: it was born and grew, rather, from the concurrence of spontaneous and collective tendencies. It is a mistaken fear to think that we can exaggerate the control that religion exercises over the Hindu soul. These tendencies are subject, for the most part, to the influence of ancient religious practices. It has proved useless to attempt to explain by the perfecting of industrial procedures what could only be explained by the survival of rites. It was difficult enough to account for hereditary specialization solely by industrial exigencies. *A fortiori* it was not possible to find in this area the principle of caste opposition or superimposition. It is the habit of the closed cult of the first familial groups that prevented castes from mingling: it is the respect for the mysterious effects of sacrifice which finally subordinated them to the caste of priests. The sociological examination of India so far from providing confirmation to the 'materialist' philosophy of history, tends more to confirm what, at any rate, the most recent sociological researches show: the preponderant role of religion in the initial organization of societies.[43]

It is important to remind ourselves that if the caste system as we have defined it only bears all its fruits in India its roots do not grow only in Hindu soil. The ideas which generate it are not peculiar to the Hindu people: one cannot even maintain, as we have seen, that they are an apanage of the Aryan race: their general features are a part of the common patrimony of primitive peoples.[44] The most complex and unified societies of today have also passed under the rule of clans: in their past we find small juxtaposed groups at once internally unified and externally separated by one and the same religion.

It is simply that for the majority of these civilized societies, this was an entirely transitory phase. Primitive religion comes up against new powers which cut down its attributes and overcome its scruples; greater political unities englobe the first familial groupings and, bit by bit, absorb them; the ancient barriers, breached first at one point and then at another, are finally thrown down forever.

Hindu civilization has refused with an extraordinary resistance, this unifying and levelling force; not one political unity has succeeded in overcoming the mutual opposition of the primitive groups; the requirements of primitive religion have continued to govern the whole social organization without question; they have even given their form to groups created by industry and of economic origin. Thus a sort of arrested sociological development characterizes Hindu civilization. India has prolonged, indefinitely, a phase that other civilizations have only passed through – or rather, she, like the others has developed the primitive principles but in an inverse direction to the general one. Where other civilizations have unified, mobilized and levelled she has divided, specialized and hierarchized. That is why we are able to see in India, clearly outlined and as it were crystallized, a system of which elsewhere we can discern no more than the vaguest features.

PART 2

The vitality of the system

1

Caste and the Buddhist revolution

We have defined the principal characteristics of the caste system. We have established that they are found more clearly marked in India than anywhere else. We have, finally, indicated the origins of the present system. It might now seem that before we can gauge its influence on Hindu civilization, we must follow its evolution step by step.

This task has been attempted. Some scholars have pointed out that at a certain period, for example, contacts between groups are more strictly forbidden, occupations more jealously guarded, hierarchy more respected: they have tried to establish the period at which the system ossified.[1] Others tell us of a progressive crumbling; they show us how, as a result of various influences, the primitive groups disintegrate and return to dust.[2] Thus in different ways people have tried to pinpoint the phases of the life of caste.

Such attempts are undoubtedly premature in the present state of Indian history. Whether it be the fault of the all-powerful religious preoccupation or the impotence of its political organizations, it is the case that India has no historians. 'The Chinese had their annals as the Greeks have Herodotus, as the Jews have the bible. India has nothing.'[3] She gives us as few as possible precise, dated documents upon her own past. Only at the cost of great effort and by the most indirect methods have European scholars today been able to establish a few landmarks amidst this obscurity. In such conditions how could we determine the curve of the evolution of caste with any certitude?

But, happily, for our purposes, this is not the most important task. What does a civilization owe to a particular social form? This is the question we now wish to answer. The enquiry is sufficiently justified if it is established that the social form in question 'dominates' in the civilization, which is not difficult to show when we are dealing with the caste system in India. If the phases of its existence are unknown, proofs of its vitality abound. At every point where a shaft of light penetrates the shadows of India's past, we see those same traditions at work which almost everywhere else function no more: they continue to divide the mass into closed, specialized and superimposed groups. On whichever side we turn our eyes, everything reminds us of the dominance of the same institution which, in a manner, supplements all the others. It naturalizes only those forces which can serve it. And, as it only allows those customs to enter which can be bent to its convenience, so it only allows those ideas to develop which are most apt to support, and so justify, its dominance.

We do not have to be prepared for that kind of monotony that the early researchers into the history of Hindu civilization led us to expect. At the time when Sumner Maine attracted the attention of sociologists to the phenomena which he had observed *de visu*, and noted the instructive analogies between certain aspects of India's present and our own past, it was the fashion to oppose the progressive mobility of the occident to the hieratic immobility of the orient.

But as the veils obscuring their history are lifted we see that oriental societies are also capable of mobility and metamorphoses. In India, in particular, however rare and vacillating the lights may be that reveal the path of civilization there, the most recent historians believe that they can discern an evolution whose major periods recall our own.[4] They recognize an antiquity, middle ages, a renaissance and a classical age. They have noted the appearance of social forms analogous to those which have succeeded each other in the occident. The Rajput in his castle-fort, with his vassals whose swords defend him, his serfs whose ploughs support him, is surely the distant brother of our barons? Akbar, giving audience to the members of his court nobility and corresponding with his provincial governors, comes before us like another Louis XIV. Thus India has known petty feudal seignories as well as great administrative monarchies.

But the same historians recognize that these forms have only rested on the surface of India, they have not thrust deep roots into the very soul of the people, they have not one jot altered the share of sun and shadow assigned to each, nor radically altered the social status of the majority. Akbar's central administration was minutely organized but it could no more succeed than Asoka in unifying Hindu society. This society has not been able to resist the great managers of men; it has supported them all; but we can say that it has not acknowledged one of them. The sole, intimate, ever present authority that regulates every detail of Hindu life, is precisely that which keeps the Hindus apart from each other, and forbids them to weld themselves into a nation: the authority of caste. As this has prevented them from uniting against the force of empires, it has prevented them from being united by the force of empires. As they have never established cities worthy of the name, they have never created associated vigorous provinces.

Where so divisive and dislocating a power holds sway, is it possible to establish truly feudal institutions? Feudal society, as has often been said, is 'territorially based'. It presupposes that all the inhabitants of the same place, however different their origins may be, are grouped around a common sovereign. Caste must work against just such local groupings and the superior authority of the Brahman, deriving from sources quite other than the possession of land, must decentralize the whole system and limit the normal consequences of the Rajput baron's authority. This, no doubt, is why the feudal system has not, any more than the monarchic system, changed the depths of Hindu society. The caste system allows all regimes to pass over its head: it alone remains. And like the tenacious jungle, its vegetation rapidly swallows up once more the few cleared patches: it is as though Hindu soil belongs to it from all eternity and forever.

But perhaps where politics have miscarried, religion has succeeded? All observers are agreed on this: caste is basically a religious institution. It rests upon scruples about purity which have been so consecrated by long traditions as to become quasi-instinctive. But if we find that these traditions are questioned and that changes occur not only in the superficial, imposed constraints but also in the system of private belief which is like a frame for the soul of the masses, cannot the caste system in its turn also be shaken?

In religious matters also we must not be deceived by the apparent immobility of India. Sir Alfred Lyall, taking a theological inventory of a province in our own time, has been able to find, in their full vigour, the majority of known kinds of belief, from fetishism to the cult of heroes.[5] Under our eyes new divinities emerge, and we have every reason to believe that thus they have been emerging all the time. In this way and behind the traditional facade of Brahmanism, innovations have never ceased proliferating. The Hindu pantheon is like the king's palace which becomes a caravanserai in the Persian parable: the dome is always the same, but never the inhabitants.

But this same mobility of belief was incapable of profoundly modifying the foundations of the social system. The reason is easily discovered when we remember what the religious feelings of the faithful, among the Hindus, adhere to above all and on which point their born-masters, the Brahmans, hold them hypnotized. As a religion without a Church, so we can say that Brahmanism is a religion without dogma. It is its very suppleness, plasticity, its inorganic nature that gives it not only a preserving, but also a conquering power. A priest by birth, the 'superman' of Brahman caste worries himself little with the theological preferences of his flock. What is important for him is that they still regard him as their regular intermediary between humanity and the celestial powers (whatever the form these may assume in imagination); that they respect in practice the superiority of his race and the whole system which assures this superiority: which is to say precisely the caste system. Hinduism is defined more by the observance of caste rules than by fidelity to some precise dogma. This is why at the very heart of the flux of beliefs, traditional scruples remain, and preserve their dominance. Religious innovations do not touch the consecrated customs. Sects can multiply without wearing down caste.

Yet, among so many sects, are there none to give the signal for revolt against these tyrannical customs, to lift the standard against the Brahman's privilege, to proclaim the idea of equality in the very midst of that civilization which seems the most fundamentally opposed to it? And indeed, Hinduism has seen the rise of its protestants, its intransigent reformers. Lapsed Brahmans like Bāsāra, inspired Muslims like Kabir, low caste prophets like Ramdas the tanner or Dadu the cotton carder – all in their different ways, have tried to emancipate the voluntary slaves, reunite the enemy brothers.[6] This one would abolish all distinctions between men, even those of dress. Another translates the sacred texts into the vernacular – preaches the vanity of outward observances. Nearly all in principle reject the authority of the Brahman and deny that he is the sole necessary intermediary between gods and men.

But first of all in the majority of cases, the ancient prestige of the born-sacrificers survives theoretical debates. It is not uncommon to find, after some generations, that Brahmans once again monopolize the sacred offices in sects that were originally the most anti-Brahmanic. Were not Brahmans able to insinuate themselves and find employment even among the Jains?[7] And again, even when it has effectively dispensed with the Brahman, the sect effects no great change in the traditional order: the celibate, the ascetic and the inspired members live in a sense, at the edge of as well as at the expense of the society. The lay members continue to believe themselves obliged not only to follow the occupation of their fathers but also to marry in the circle where their fathers married; the law of endogamy is not infringed.

Elsewhere the division into sects quite simply reproduces in their broad lines the division of society: thus in the sect of the Vallabhacharyas, which in theory excludes no one, we find rich merchants more than any other: among the Sanyasis, *a fortiori* among the Kharta-Bajas or the Paltu-Dasis, the common folk dominate.[8] In other instances it is true that people of all castes mix in an egalitarian sect, but between the group thus formed and other groups, communication is cut and soon mixing is no longer possible; in its attempt to gather together all who revolt against the caste system, the sect succeeds only in finishing up as yet one more caste.[9] Thus sometimes the reformer's ploughshare slides into the existing furrow; sometimes he ploughs a new furrow, but it only parallels those that exist already; he does not succeed in cutting across them to plough new transverse furrows that would obliterate the traditional distinctions.

Just as very diverse political regimes have failed to overcome it, so also religious innovations which seemed most to contradict it have failed to uproot the caste system. We have taken account of the relative diversity of ideas as of the relative mobility of Hindu institutions. But this diversity and this mobility remain only superficial phenomena; they in no way touch the profound unity which this system maintains. The proof lies in the unparalleled authority with which it weighs on India. All that can serve it prospers there. All that could hurt it, perishes.

One great historic fact, it must be admitted, seems to stand in opposition to this general affirmation; this is the existence of Buddhism. To validate our thesis it is important to pay special attention to this fact and understand its significance.

We have just affirmed that in the moral atmosphere generated by the caste system, ideas which are hostile to the system, and in particular egalitarian ideas, cannot survive. And nevertheless in this very atmosphere we have seen the 'Lotus of the Good Law' spread itself for all to see. 'Is it not' asks Burnouf 'a sort of axiom of oriental history that the Buddha's mission was to lift the tomb-stone that weighed upon the Hindu conscience?' Michelet celebrates the movement which the Buddha began as the 'abolition of castes which emancipated four hundred million men and founded the greatest church on earth'.[10] Like Luther against the papacy, the son of the Sākyas fought against the Brahmans, foot to foot. Like Jesus he opposed and substituted for the Pharisaism of ritual, the private cult of pity; like him, said Taine 'he preferred the small and the poor'.[11] Max Müller shows us thieves and bankrupts, brigands, beggars, cripples, slaves, prostitutes and road sweepers thronging around the Buddha.* He adds: 'The evil spirit of caste seems to have vanished.'[12] There was, then, a

---

* In the original: 'Max Müller ne nous montre-t-il pas, *comme dans le Christ aux cent florins*', etc. The sense is clear enough. The reference is to a pictorial representation that I have been unable to trace.

Buddhist revolution, elder sister to the reforms and the revolutions of the west. And the inspiration which breathed over the land of castes, five or six centuries before the Christian era, was already the inspiration of equality.

What are we to think of this objection?

We could turn it by pointing out that if Buddhism did indeed rouse up an egalitarian protest in India, it finally paid with its life, shall we say, for this paradoxical audacity. It was aimed against the evil spirit of caste, some conclude, but finally this spirit struck it to the earth. We must add to the proofs which the system gives us of its vitality, the flight of the Buddhist religion which it succeeded in expelling from its kingdom. And we know, in fact, that if the Buddhist religion has won, and continues to win throughout the Far East millions of followers, it has, on the contrary, lost the greatest number in the land of its origin. It has produced a vigorous swarm, but its first hive is almost abandoned. Mystery still enshrouds, however, this disappearance of Hindu Buddhism. It certainly seems that to understand it we must reject the first explanation that comes to mind: there is no trace of a systematic persecution which might have driven the Buddhists away. And this, perhaps, less because the Hindu soul, as has been often said, has no place for dogmatic intolerance than because Hindu society always lacked that degree of political unity without which it is difficult to organize a major persecution.[13] This leaves the field open to hypotheses; it allows us in particular to suppose, what is not unlikely, that if Buddhism progressively withdrew in the face of the returning offensive of Brahmanic tyranny, it is because there was a congenital incompatibility between its spirit and the most inward tendencies of Hindu civilization, between the egalitarian theories of the one and the anti-egalitarian instincts of the other.

But it must be admitted that it is difficult to find positive proof for this hypothesis. Not one fact allows us to think that if many Hindus abandoned Buddhism it was because caste scruples prevented them from staying with it. Moreover, Buddhism prospered too long and in diverse areas of India and even in those from which it has completely disappeared today, has left too many monuments, durable proofs of its fecundity, for one to suppose that there is some kind of vital antagonism between its genius and that of Hinduism.

We are obliged to look in quite another direction for the clue to the enigma. And perhaps this might be found more easily if one directs one's attention less to what opposes the general tendencies of India and the particular tendency of Buddhism, and more to that which relates them and makes them converge. We are told that Buddhism is anti-Hindu because it is egalitarian. But perhaps it would be possible to show that, properly speaking, it was not egalitarian precisely because it remained Hindu. Perhaps we must methodically resist the promptings of analogy, and insist that there is no kind of relation between the social revolutions which renewed the occident and the 'Buddhist revolution'.

At first sight it might seem difficult to maintain, without paradox, that Buddhism was not imbued with egalitarianism. The history of the 'Enlightened One', the practices of his community, the doctrines of his law, all seem to confirm the impressions of the first European commentators.

One remembers how, when the Buddha had exposed the roots of universal sorrow and found, in the overcoming of desire through understanding, the way to final deliverance, Māra, the tempter appears for the last time before him. Through his power the Evil One offers the Buddha the immediate peace of Nirvana on one condition: he must abandon the world to its misery and the cycle of rebirth. But pity ever wakeful in the heart of the Buddha is stronger than the thirst for eternal rest. He refuses to abandon men before he has endowed them with his viaticum, the viaticum that gives deliverance from the torment of life. He returns to the earth to preach his laws 'the law of grace for all', which all without exception and whatever their condition here below, can benefit by, – here is an egalitarian proselytism as far as one could ask from the haughty exclusivism of the Brahman.

When the Buddhist community is organized, it does not forget this lesson. When the Chandala maiden, coming from the fountain, charitably warns him of her impure caste, Ananda, servant of Sākyamuni, replies: 'My sister, I do not ask you for your caste or for your family: I ask you for water, if you will give me some!' And Sākyamuni received the amazed Chandala among his disciples.[14] Thereafter the Buddhist monasteries profess not to close the door to anyone on grounds of social inferiority and the only hierarchy which is recognized within them is that of seniority, personal merit, age or acquired learning. And thus in the heart of the monastery we can say that castes blend and are lost to sight.

Just as, oh disciples, the great rivers, every one of them, the Ganga, the Jumna, the Asi, the Sarayu and the Mahi, once they reach the mighty Ocean, lose their old names, their ancient race, and only bear one name, that of the mighty Ocean, thus, oh disciples, the members of the four castes, nobles and Brahmans, Vaishyas and Sudras, once, following the rule and the doctrine preached by the Perfect One, they say farewell to their house to lead a wandering life, lose their old name and their ancient race and only bear one name, that of ascetic followers of the son of the Sākyas.[15]

Nor are theories lacking, besides, whether illustrated by stories or not, to justify this practice and to rebut Brahmanic claims. Triganku, the Chandala king, turns against them the same sort of arguments that we find in Europe in the egalitarian hymns of peasant risings.

Between a Brahman and man of another caste there is not the same difference as between stone and gold, between shadows and light. The Brahman is born neither of the air nor of the wind, he did not split the earth to appear in the light of day as the fire that escapes from the Aranī wood.* The Brahman is born from the womb of a woman, just like a Chandala. Why then should the one be noble and the other vile?

It is not only the Brahman's privilege which is directly disputed. In a more general manner attempts are made to attenuate the differences which Brahmanic tradition makes between high and low castes. Historical and entirely human explanations are substituted for the mythical explanation that would have each class spring from one part of the divinity.[16]

'We wish to appoint one, who, on our behalf, will reprimand those who deserve reprimand. In return we are willing to give him part of our rice.' Thus men spoke when the first thefts made them understand the need for a public authority; and this was the origin of royalty. By analogous conventions the origin of priesthood was explained. This is proof of an already positive and

---

* Wood of the *Ficus religiosa* or *Premna spinosa* used for kindling fire by friction.

critical spirit, well suited to shake the sacred traditions which are the pillars of the system.

Let us, nevertheless, look closer: we shall see that the spirit of the Buddhist reform is far from having that intransigent combativeness which we tend to give it when we look at it through our own revolutions. We shall not be surprised that, finally, it leaves the essential parts of the caste structure intact.

Is it, first of all, true that Buddhism 'went to the people' and took pride in addressing the humble? The general tone of its preaching should suffice to warn us: it is not easy to believe that this was, in preference, addressed to the 'poor in spirit'. The Buddha no doubt spoke the popular language of eastern Hindustan, but his sermons retain the marks of scholasticism.[17] When with any number of distinctions he shows how forms spring from ignorance, and from forms cognition – from cognition the name and (bodily) form, from these the six domains: contact, sensation, thirst, attachment, existence, birth and so all the sorrow of the world – to be able to follow him one needs a subtle intellect, well trained in traditional dialectics. He himself said, moreover: 'For humanity acting in the hurly burly of the world, which lives in the hurly burly of the world and finds its pleasure there, the law of causality, the chain of cause and effect is a difficult thing to grasp' and again 'The doctrine is for the man of understanding, not for the fool'.

And indeed, these are cultivated folk, scions of noble families (*kulaputtā*) that the Banares sermon speaks of and that we see gathered around the Perfect One. M. Oldenberg identifies among them nobles like Rahoula, young Brahmans like Sariputta, sons of leading members of the bourgeoisie like Yasa.[18] Despite the story of Ananda, not a single Chandala is mentioned. Even among the lay followers, princes and nobles, rich and highly placed people preponderate over those of little substance. And if we add that when the previous existences of the Buddha are spoken of, the tradition is careful not to place him in an inferior caste, but always in the ranks of the Kshatriyas, we cannot avoid the impression that Buddhism was first of all a sect for nobles, one of these schools of Kshatriyas which occur from the most remote days of Hindu antiquity, with a theology – as the epics and the Upanishads bear witness – opposed to the Brahmanic theology.

And certainly, Buddhism, more than any other sect, must have appeared formidable to the Brahmans: it tended to make them superfluous by limiting at once the part of theology in the strict sense and of the place of rituals and without trying to resolve the ultimate mysteries – a wounded man does not debate with the doctor who stanches his wounds* – it offers those wounded by life the means of saving themselves by their own efforts. It is clear that the Buddhist community worked to undermine the Brahman's clientele: the conflict of interests is undeniable. But, as M. Senart says, what was there in a squabble between clerics which could ruin the entire caste system?[19] The observation made with reference to small reformist sects remains true of Buddhism. Those that it gathers into a community it at the same time, in a sense, abstracts from social life. The vow of mendicancy and the vow of chastity which it imposes on them turns them away simultaneously from the work of reproduction and the tasks of production. The rules of hereditary specialization as well as those relating to endogamous marriage no longer have any relevance for them; but they continue to weigh upon the faithful outside, upon the lay folk whose sons swell the community's ranks and whose labour supports it. These go on working for their living or choosing a wife, taking care not to transgress the sacred limits: converted to the Buddhist faith they may be but they are still encircled by the Brahmanic organization.

From this one can see how far the Buddhists were from reconstructing the edifice of Hindu society according to new plans: if they worked at replacing the roof, they never gave a thought to changing the foundations.

We can see how careful they were not to trouble the established order or bring down on their heads the powers of this world, when we remember the restrictions governing admission to their

---

* This refers to the famous discussion of 'unprofitable questions', Sutta 63 of the Majjhima-Nikaya. No more than a wounded man enquires after the caste of his attacker before he will allow the arrow to be removed, will the seeker require assurance concerning life, death and the great hereafter before he submits himself to the way of the Buddha.

monasteries. Their admirers are heady with lyricism as they would have us see the homeless, the thief and the slave wrapped in the yellow robes of the Buddhist monk. In fact, the monastery was closed, in principle, not only to the infirm and incurable, not only to criminals, but to absconding debtors, slaves and minors, to all those who might be claimed by an outsider and whose presence risked sparking off, for whatever reason it might be, a conflict between the community and the age.[20]

To retire from the age, to no longer participate in any way in the illusions of creatures who let themselves be dragged along by the wheel of life; this was the secret idea of the Buddhist Church; we encounter no difficulty in understanding how ill-suited was such an ideal to the promotion of true social reform.[21] It lifts no standard of revolt: it sounds rather the signal for flight. Let us not talk of reconstructing the edifice of the divided classes, this would be to build clouds upon clouds. The main business is to escape the cycle of rebirths, not to install oneself in the life of the present. And thus the essential pessimism of Buddhism sterilized the germs of egalitarian reform which its proselytism seemed to carry.

What does this amount to if not that this kind of political neurasthenia, this incapacity to react and reform belongs precisely to the diffuse philosophy in the Hindu atmosphere, which Buddhism allowed to infect it? It is often said: Hindu thought rests on the absolute. Under the meditation of its philosophers, divinities are united and transformed and finally dissolved in the unique Being, as moving clouds after their indefinite metamorphoses return to the ocean. From this point of view all that changes and passes, all that lives and dies seems unworthy of human attachment.

Movement is only another name for evil. The individual *ātman* must find refuge and lose itself in the bosom of the universal and immobile *ātman* which alone is above the world's sorrow: 'Outside of that', says the Vedanta, 'there is only affliction.' Sankhya philosophy, similarly, would have the soul take the strength to immobilize itself, to withdraw to the banks of the river, to hold itself apart from material becoming, repeating: 'I am not that.' The same antithesis between Being and Becoming is the foundation of Buddhist pessimism. In fact the doctrine manifesting what we can call its positive and practical tendency in the very midst of the current of traditional ideas, is not slow to think of absolute Being in itself, to give it a name and divinize it: to pronounce a verdict of universal detachment it is sufficient to affirm universal mobility.

The Buddha is not only a man weeping over old age, sickness and death: he is also and above all a philosopher who has only disdain for the eternally ephemeral.[22] A Sutra tells us that when rays of light, springing from the smile of Sākya, appear in the sky, these words are heard: 'That is passing, that is misery, that is empty. That is lacking in substance' – 'Oh religious', we read elsewhere 'everything which is compound is perishable. It is not durable. One cannot rely upon it with confidence. Its condition is change: such that we should not have thought for what is compound nor take pleasure therein!'

In a word Buddhism retains and reinforces that in Hindu thought which turns away from life. Certainly we should not represent Buddhist law, as for long has been done, as a funeral urn, an inexhaustible flask of despair. There is a joy peculiar to Buddhism which shines in the faces of priests and people and whose light has impressed European pilgrims. The most recent commentators on the Doctrine make us see that one falsifies its character by presenting it as a philosophy of the void.[23] Perhaps, as Max Müller thought, that Nirvana to which it leads, is the highest achievement of existence rather than its suppression, the clearest light and not the deepest shadow.[24] But at all events the prospect of this final peace pacifies the philosophers here below, protects them from ascetic extravagances and communicates to those whose senses are still 'a perfect joy that even the gods envy'.[25] It is no less true that this superior joy, foretaste of liberation, is only found by turning away from the world, by refusing to pay it the slightest attention, to assist it with a single effort: in this sense no doctrine has better justified social abstentionism.

Can we see in this renunciation of terrestrial effort simply the normal consequence of the principles around which Hindu speculation gravitates? Charles Renouvier, the founder of personalism, shows how pessimism is the eternal and constantly reborn product of philosophies of emanation: they take away from the individual all motive for action upon the world and simultaneously, all veritable reality.[26] But we must suppose that not only the natural but also the social context must have some significance if Indian thought has taken this turn, and has preferred, by a sort of instinct which has never belied itself, doctrines which justify detachment and inaction. It has repeatedly been said that in India nature and society conspire to crush the individual. Think in particular, said Taine, in how tight a circle of obligations caste encloses him and immobilizes him for life and you will understand 'that desire for final deliverance which, like a passionate and continuous cry, rings from this pit of desolation'.[27] In this way the caste system, because it has deprived India of the sense of active hope, is itself responsible for the inertia that Buddhism displays in the matter of social reform, however egalitarian its doctrines may be.

In addition we can understand why the very idea of these reforms did not come easily to Buddhism and why it did not feel the need for them. It is not only its distaste for life but the belief, which it shares with all India, in the transmigration of the soul from life to life. One could affirm, in fact, that what the Hindu fears above all is not death but rather not dying, to be condemned to be reborn in various forms, each one the fatal retribution of his works.

Manu decrees that the thief of grain is reborn as a rat, the stealer of linen as a frog and the adulterer as a consumptive. Thus the world is full of souls enjoying their rewards, suffering their punishments. Its hierarchy is the expression of a secret justice. The form in which I lodge today was prepared for me by my earlier acts. What I am is the fruit of what I have done. 'My works are my property, my heritage, the womb that carries me and the race to which I belong.' Such is the theory of *karma* to which Buddhism also allowed considerable room.[28]

It has been pointed out that there is, at first sight, some kind of contradiction between this theory and the theory of the *ātman* adopted by a certain number of Buddhist schools of thought.[29]

For does not Buddhism represent the self as a simple compound unity, quite superficial and transitory, analogous to the unity of a chariot? And is not its doctrine rather more 'apersonal' than atheistic? How then can an individuality, which is, after all, a nullity, subsist through change and pass from body to body 'as an ape swings from branch to branch', until it finally reaches liberation and loses the memory of all existence 'as a snake sloughs off its wrinkled skin'? But, without postulating the persistence of an identity having the attributes of personality, can we not allow of a sort of transmission of the effects of action from one life to another? The fire which consumes the forest leaps from tree to tree: according to the properties of what it has burned it grows or diminishes, is pure or impure, brilliant or fuliginous. This might be an image of the *karma* which passes from *ātman* to *ātman*. However, if these two ideas are difficult to reconcile nevertheless the belief in transmigration persists at the heart of Buddhism, this no doubt simply proves the power of traditional opinions upon the minds of the philosophers. And here again we cannot but admire how the obsessions of that opinion, directly or indirectly, served the interests of the caste system.

Michelet is gravely mistaken when, effusively rejoicing in the Hindu's respect for our 'lower brothers', he conjectures that the theory of transmigration, to the extent that it binds and in a sense mingles the worlds of men and animals, must be hostile to that spirit of distinction and opposition which maintains caste. 'The caste of beasts is abolished', he cries, commenting on Rama's embrace of the monkey Hanuman 'how could anything remain of the caste of humans?' Much more shrewdly M. Pillon observes that one has reason to fear that a doctrine which will not distinguish the human and the animal kingdoms, will set a low price on human personality and the value of individual merit. Is it not likely to go on, exactly because it ignores the distinctions drawn by nature and reason, to accept that the distinction between Brahman and Sudra is as legitimate and natural as the distinction between man and beast? There is nothing more baneful than these vague pantheistic comparisons with the idea of the equal rights of reasonable beings.

But independently of these dangerous confusions, it is chiefly by its positive arguments, its explanation of present ills that the theory of transmigration shores up the caste system; if a radical pessimism atrophies 'the instinct of revolt' in men's hearts, this fatalism extirpates even the sense that the present may be injust. Nobody has deduced the consequences of this kind of sterilization better than M. Pillon:

By discounting the notion of immortality, the law of transmigration discounts at the same time the idea of merit and demerit, of punishment and reward. There is no longer distinction between the fact and the right, between what is real and what is ideal, between physical fatality and moral order. Physical ill is thought of not only as a necessary consequence, but as the certain expression and infallible sign of moral ill, to such an extent that the two inseparable ideas end by composing a single one: At the end of the proposition: *All demerit necessarily brings on grief*, the following is attached: *All grief necessarily brings demerit, a sin, and necessarily punishment and expiation.* From this point all reality is accepted on the conscience, every fact becomes an expression of justice and must be so respected, all sorrow and all suffering, without one knowing how and why, is merited by him who endures it. Brahmanism is led to this monstrous position that it holds as legitimate an expiation unaccompanied by consciousness or memory of the sin which is expiated! Thus the conscience becomes the accomplice of all natural and social fatalities; it will no longer object to anything, will not protest against anything, will not revolt against anything. The law of transmigration consecrates, immobilizes, renders eternal the inequality of conditions and the division of society into castes.[30]

It is not astonishing then that the Buddhist reform, having accommodated transmigration, should have adapted itself to the system which this philosophy legitimizes. M. Barth points out that, in fact, Buddhism not only did not destroy caste where it was dominant but probably imported it to those areas where it had not hitherto existed and had stayed at the frontiers – the Dekkan, Ceylon and the Sunda Isles. Now we can understand the profound reasons for this persisting solidarity. Despite its opposition to Brahmanic privilege, Buddhism had not the strength, it had not even the intention, to renew the social forms of India, because it never ceased to draw on the same fund of ideas by which India lives. It never let flow a stream of entirely new ideas: it also drank the powerful and troubled waters of traditional emanatism, this Lethe of the Orient which pours out for the living who drink it, disdain for the injustices of life.

It is then true that the 'dominants' of Hindu civilization remain forever in harmony with the requirements of the caste system. That first impression that we derived from the resistance which the system offered not only to a diversity of political institutions but also to a multiplicity of religious innovations, has only been confirmed as, gradually, we have come to understand better and more closely analysed the nature of the 'Buddhist exception'.

2

Caste under British administration

We said that the ancient history of India disappears and is lost in the mist; its recent history on the contrary is floodlit. While Hindu idealism disdained to leave monuments to the acts and achievements of men, British realism has, on the contrary, paid every attention to the slightest movements in the population it governs. Every decade the growth of population, its distribution, the gains or the losses of languages and religions, the decline or the progress of various institutions – all is noted by the diligent Civil Service in an admirable collection of statistics and reports.[1]

This collection contains, in particular, a mass of information upon the current development of caste. It is worthwhile recalling, at this point, the chief results: this latest information on the system we are studying will no doubt throw an interesting light on its past and at the same time provide us with another opportunity to gauge its vitality. If up to a certain point it is able to resist even British civilization, it will furnish a final proof, and by no means the least striking, of the grip it exercises over Hindu civilization.

Frankly, the Englishman has never claimed, indeed he has frequently disclaimed any attempt to modify this civilization. He represents himself neither as a conqueror in the proper sense nor as a missionary. He preferred to respect the indigenous ways and customs, beliefs and laws. His motto has been administration with a minimum of government. He has declared his ambition limited to assuring men that minimum of security and justice indispensable for their earning a livelihood.

But to realise this plan the British have quietly disembarked a whole new civilization with arms and luggage upon the sacred soil of the Vedas. Few arms in fact but a great deal of luggage; all the paraphernalia of European inventions and institutions, ideas incarnate in things, dressed in the tangible form of factory and school, post office and locomotive, which as they change the external scene are capable, slowly but surely, of stirring the very depths of the soul.

It is easy to understand this: the introduction of British civilization has multiplied, fatally for the members of different castes, such occasions as they have for contact and for using the same instruments at the cost of traditional repulsion. We have already mentioned how when the government wanted to install a water system in Bombay there was a great outcry at first:* pure and impure, twice-born and Sudra were to drink at the same taps! But an adroit panchayat resolved the difficulties by decreeing that the tax raised by the British administration for this canalization could be regarded as a reparation; it would redeem the sins to which this sharing of taps would expose them. This is but one example of the concessions of all sorts and adjustments to the times to which the spirit of caste is daily driven. Simply the use of what Kipling's Kim calls 'the te-rain', weakens the power of this spirit. The railway levels as it unites. Material mobility prepares for social and moral mobility. Individuals now more easily lifted out and detached from their original milieux, have less difficulty in freeing themselves from traditions which oppress and separate them.

Moreover Britain reaches out to touch the Hindu soul not only by indirect means and by upsetting its experience but also more directly by the changes which it imposes upon its very circumstances. The exercise of a certain number of traditional caste-linked crafts has been made impossible by the increasing import of manufactured goods from the metropolis. Thus many weavers, after desperate resistance, have had to turn to agriculture. Elsewhere the ancestral occupation is dropped for the sake of a job in a newly opened factory. Finally the administration itself offers unexpected openings: one can become an agent, clerk, tax collector or superintendent: a number of Brahmans are policemen and wear, with no sense of scandal – what would their ancestors have said – leather belts. Nor, in principle, is indi-

* The earlier reference (above p. 23) was, correctly, to Calcutta.

genous ambition limited to the level of lower functionaries: *a priori* there is nothing to prevent a Hindu of the lowest caste, if he can only successfully pass the required test of competitive examination, from climbing the ladder of the Civil Service to a directive position.

From this we see that it is not merely occupations which change, but the very social situations: together with specialization the traditional hierarchy can be overturned. A type unknown to ancient India, it would seem – the self-made man – appears on the scene. If a member of a low caste finds himself, as the result of an open examination, invested with some of the civil power, respect cannot but be disoriented from its traditional directions. The effects of these shifts in value are felt even in the matter of marriage: parvenus and young graduates, it is said, are now highly sought in certain quarters, even though the purity of their genealogies leaves much to be desired.

The three supporting columns of the caste system – hereditary specialization, the sacred hierarchy, mutual repulsion – are more or less directly undermined by British administration. It must be added that it seems on the way to giving the peoples of India what the caste system has always denied them: a principle of cohesion and a motive for unity. To put the weight of a single and ever present power upon their shoulders is to suggest the idea of a common enemy which they had hitherto lacked. As gradually they understand so they experience a sense of being exploited in common and so the desire to unite and resist. Their national self develops in opposition to alien domination. The Hindu motherland is born at the feet of the British state, in order to rise up against it.[2] In this way, as much by indirectly weakening primitive divisions as by providing a positive principle of superior unification, one can say that Britain – whether it intends the one or the other – is leading India along the levelled roads of occidental progress.

Nevertheless we should be sadly mistaken if we suppose that the 'Europeanization' of India is an accomplished fact. One can easily measure how slowly the transformation is being accomplished, if indeed it is ever to be totally accomplished, when we move from *a priori* conjecture to objective evidence. One has but to dip at random into the decennial collections of which we spoke, to find that the handmaids of disunion, the Parcae of India, are ever at their work. The same passion for distinctions, the same fear of mixing, and of being degraded by mixing, animate these social micro-organisms, these castes, and drive them to infinite subdivisions instead of agglomerations.

We saw that British civilization at more than one point, has broken the ancient chain that binds occupation and blood. But we must not suppose that the fatal result of this rupture is the dissolution of caste. Often as not it has for its effect the formation of a new caste. Marriage relations soon cease between those families which have fearlessly abandoned the ancestral vocation and those which have piously preserved it: the circle within which a man can look for a wife, the endogamic circle, is only the more jealously confined.

This is not to say that professional limits coincide at every point with the limits of caste. Recently it was supposed that this was so – as we have seen – and it was hoped to prove conse-quently that castes were petrified guilds.[3] The necessities, tradi-tions and evolution of industry were to explain the way in which castes are specialized, ranked and mutually opposed. This theory seems to have been decisively abandoned by observers today.[4] To maintain it we should be able to count as many castes as there are occupations. But all the evidence tells us that in many cases the practitioners of the same occupation come from diverse castes, while the members of the same caste are divided into several occupations. In the one caste of Vanis, for example, the investi-gator in Bombay Province has recorded 25 per cent in commerce, 39 per cent in catering, 10 per cent in cloth and clothes making, 3 per cent agriculture, 2 per cent employees of the administra-tion. Inversely in the Central Provinces one finds forty-one castes of agriculturalists, eleven of weavers, seven of fishermen. This is proof sufficient that the link between occupational specialization and marriage prohibitions is fairly loose. It is no less true, despite these facts, that the dominant opinion still holds that members of the same caste *should* preserve the occupation of their common ancestors; and this is enough to enable us to understand why changes of occupation such as we observe today, can, in more than one case, serve as pretexts for division in a caste.[5]

For this to happen it is not essential that one section of a caste change its occupational habits and look out for other employment: it is quite sufficient if it adopts some new manner or forsakes some ancient usage. A habit of neglecting a certain detail of the sacrificial ceremony brought about the degradation by several ranks of certain sections of Brahmans or Kshatriyas. Inversely the Awadhia Kurmis, in Bihar, have risen above the common Kurmis thanks to the zeal with which they have forbidden widow remarriage.

Elsewhere it is change of belief that determines the subdivision: in other words, sects end up by forming castes. This has happened to the Atiths and Gosains of Bengal and the Bishnois of the Central Provinces.[6] This phenomenon is all the more remarkable in that quite often, and as we have seen, these sects appear to be egalitarian in principle.[7] They set out protesting against the divisions which caste scruples, supported by Brahmanism, impose on the Hindus. But today as in the past the genius of caste is the stronger: it makes those very groups which initially rose up against it accept its system of interdictions.

In addition, without change of custom or belief, a simple migration can result in the creation of castes. Relations slacken between the group which has emigrated and that which has stayed at home. People no longer know each other: marriage contracts between the groups become less and less easy. Thus when the Khedawal Brahmans of Gujarat settled in Damoh, the home group made difficulties over giving its daughters to them.[8] A native explains that in such cases it becomes difficult for a member of the caste who comes asking for a wife to prove his identity and the purity of his genealogy. By the very fact that he comes from afar, he is suspect. The fear of possible misalliance ends up by producing a ban on all alliance between the two separated segments.

Furthermore it is the case that the emigrants find wives on the spot in an inferior caste, if not from an aboriginal tribe, and that this mixing of bloods lowers the status of their descendants, which normally brings about the formation of a new group. Such for example was the origin of the Shagirdpeshas, born from the union of immigrant Kayasths with the servant castes of Orissa.[9]

As on more than one point, observation has here confirmed the theories formulated in *The Laws of Manu*. These claim to explain the multiplicity of castes, which one must distinguish from the four classical Varnas, as the products of illegitimate unions between superiors and inferiors. It is a forced explanation amounting to puerile invention if one uses it to account for the origin of all castes. But we have to admit that in the past a certain number owe their origin to misalliances of this sort since the fact is reproduced under our very eyes today.

We must add to the various groups which have multiplied those formed by Hindu neophytes. As we have seen, people have often asked, whether Hinduism can be classified among the proselytizing religions. Can, one wonders, these born-priests, the Brahmans, isolated in their pride of blood, have anything of the missionary in them? In fact, as Sir Alfred Lyall has rightly pointed out, no great religion can perhaps, at this very time, credit more conversions to its account. The semi-barbarian hordes that live on the frontiers of Hinduism have nothing nearer to their hearts than incorporation within its ranks. They burn to exchange their savage independence for a superior dignity: and for this elevation they have need of the Brahman's help. And he, little concerned to overthrow their traditional beliefs teaches them to respect above all his own superiority and the rules of caste. Thus we see converted tribes like the Doms of Bihar, the Gujars of the Punjab, the Kolis of Bombay – more or less profoundly Hinduized besides, some preserving their name and even their totemic customs, others striving to make themselves unrecognizable by total reform[10] – observers watch them form, little by little, more new castes, rising unequally in the hierarchy.

We can get some idea of the multiplicity and variety of groupings brought about by these different principles of division by taking up Mr Risley's imagined hypothesis applied to areas with which we are familiar. Let us think of that multitude of people in our own country called Smith,* and imagine them subordinated to the rules and imbued with the spirit of Hindu

* Smith is Risley's original. Bouglé substituted Dupuy for the French public.

civilization. They would then think of themselves as the descendants of an eponymous ancestor to whom legend would attribute some characteristic and distinguished feat. In principle, marriage within this great family would be legitimate, any male Smith could marry any female Smith. In fact this liberty would soon be found to have its qualifications, and this for the most diverse reasons or under the most trivial of pretexts. Divisions would develop between Smiths and Smythes, between Conservative Smiths and Labour Smiths, the Smiths of Oxford and the Smiths of Sussex, the brewing Smiths and the baking Smiths, the fishing Smiths and the hunting Smiths, the teetotal Smiths and the Smiths who drink, etc. All these sections of the Smiths would finally repel each other: they would disallow intermarriage, or even commensality. And no doubt there would be different degrees of repulsion which would be translated in their turn into various practices. One Smith might prefer death rather than eat 'at the same dish'. Others might find no difficulty provided the food was prepared without water. Thus they could drink chocolate made with milk but not tea and above all not tea served in porcelain. If this analogy gives us a precise impression, if indeed the divisive principles and the characteristic practices of castes are so infinitely various, we can understand how one of our observers can exclaim in vexation: 'The caste system is an amorphous collection of anomalies and anachronisms, calculated to embarrass the most expert enquirer, and discourage the most enthusiastic researcher.'

There is a real question as to whether the groups which we see forming under our eyes properly merit the name caste. The majority of inquirers call them sub-castes: sections which have the same origin and which preserve the same name continue to be united by a vague sense of kinship even though such pretexts as we have discussed justify a schism. An ideal and indefinable link continues between them. It is still true that this link weakens as the separated groups, each in its own way, grow in social importance and independence. The sub-castes of today are the castes of tomorrow.[11] In any case these are the groups which directly define and immediately determine individual obligations. If, for example, we want to know the status of a particular Brahman, it is not enough to find out that he belongs to the Panch Gaur category, nor even that amongst the Panch Gaurs he is a Kanauja and amongst the Kanauja a Jighotia. What is important to know is that he is a Bundelkhandi Jighotia. He can only marry within this local section. He has to respect its distinctive ways and customs above all. From it he derives his prestige and his place in the social hierarchy.

We can understand how difficult it is, in the midst of such mobile multiplicity, to discern the outlines of this hierarchy. The groups we deal with are not of the same nature: if some are of the crystallized guild type, others as we have seen, are petrified sects, these owe their origin to mixtures of blood, those to the conversion of tribes. How can one establish the respective places of such heterogeneous elements on one scale of respect? We should add that if physical difference is sufficient to divide a caste, changes of location also mark, most often, change of situation, ascent or descent: the Minas are singularly more highly thought of in Alwar, for example, than they are in Marwar.[12] As we move from north to south or east to west we can frequently observe sudden leaps in the prestige of one and the same caste. Here we experience that lack of unity which is so often noted in Hindu civilization. Everything which makes for the existence of nations is absent in the masses which it has collected together but not unified; they do not even have a public opinion to which they might appeal and so settle questions of precedence.

Nevertheless, if there is one point on which the populations of India seem prepared to agree, it is precisely about this system which keeps them divided. It has often been said that patriotism is totally lacking in India; but the belief that there are and that there should be castes, and that it is a sin for a man to try to upset the whole order by leaving the path his fathers trod – surely this is a substitute for the feeling of patriotism throughout India? And no doubt each man is on principle proud of his caste and professes that he would not wish to diminish it by comparison with any other. But only bring these Hindus of diverse castes together and inevitably they must admit what certain traditional practices proclaim and which no one has the power to refute: that there are superior castes universally revered or envied, and inferior castes, universally despised. In this way, at least within the same province it is possible to derive a sort of official scale of caste dignity from public opinion. This is precisely what British investigators have tried to do since the last census. Their attempt has not been unaccompanied by some protests, nor without setting off some quarrels. The Rathors telegraph to ensure that they are not classified with the Telis. The Khatris draw up a long memorandum to prove their right to the title of Kshatriya.[13] But for the majority we can say that they recognize themselves in the results of the inquiry and subscribe to the gradations proposed there.

It is remarkable that in their broad lines, the hierarchies which have been obtained in this way coincide with the hierarchy consecrated by Brahmanic tradition. The Brahman's prestige is still the magnetic centre of the system from which emanate the lines of force coordinating the mass of castes. The esteem in which the Brahman holds it is the measure of a caste's dignity. And when there is indecision in the matter, one looks to the way in which it is treated by the born-priest. At the very lowest level by common consent and without question are placed the impure castes, those that have no right to enter the temples, whose slightest touch pollutes, whole glance contaminates all food. But when it is a matter of classifying castes which are intermediary between this excess of indignity and the excess of honour that Brahmans enjoy one is most often reduced, even today, to asking whether the Brahman would or would not accept food at the hands of their members – whether they would accept food cooked with water or only food cooked without water. Criteria of this kind always decide precedence; their operation under our very eyes is proof of the power with which the classical traditions of Brahmanism are imposed on public opinion.

It is not that Hindu society is frozen – the investigators warn us here – in a sort of sacred immobility. We can easily discover incessant movement which is not limited only to the creation of new divisions, but also here to an elevation, there to a fall. Sometimes it is a growth in its social power, whether economic or political, which finally raises the level of a caste. Another will climb in rank on religious grounds by demonstrating greater austerity, greater exactitude in ceremonial matters, greater strictness in observing prohibitions. But what is striking is that in either case every group that moves upwards justifies itself by appealing to the best known tradition. In India even ambition seems always to incline towards the past, bent upon finding there those titles which alone confer respect. From this we have a crop of justificatory legends.[14] The Khatis, for example, claim to be descended from a Kshatriya woman, the sole survivor of a massacre; she was sheltered by a Brahman who was obliged to eat with her. The Purads have taken as their ancestor a Brahman who lost his sacred thread while crossing a river.[15] Here are proofs of the vitality of the sacred codes: if they cannot arrest social movement, they force it to take account of them. Social opinion allows you to transgress the traditional order on condition that you demonstrate that the order has been perverted; and from that point you only violate the law in order to respect it the better.

In this way we can say of Manu's theories that if they do not exactly reflect the realities of Hindu society, they have succeeded to a great extent in impressing their form upon it.[16] They are triumphant as 'idea-forces'. They provide for public opinion the frames into which it will henceforth instinctively be inclined to classify groups of all sorts. A fine example of this kind of obsession is furnished by the Lingayat sect – a sect which was anti-Brahmanic in principle and which declared war upon the caste system: Today its members protest when official statistics lump them together as one group. They ask to be distinguished according to the classical formula, as Brahmans, Kshatriyas, Vaisyas and Sudras.[17] Even better, among Hindu convicts, on the islands where criminals of all castes are thrown together, an analogous preoccupation comes to light; a classification of the same order is developing. To such an extent then is it true that the peoples of India stay firmly attached, even in our own day, to the prohibitions that separate them and the hierarchy that rears them in ranks.

For, we are here in the presence of two forces that pull in different directions. If the individual groups, each isolated in its pride, tend to repel each other continually, they are none the less attracted, each one, towards a single summit. This attraction can come to terms with repulsion and produce complex phenomena. The sense that there are superiors and inferiors even acts against that matrimonial protectionism which is the rule for even the lowest castes; and instead of endogamy pure and simple 'hypergamy' results.

We said that a group obeys the rule of endogamy when its sons are forbidden to take a wife outside the group. Endogamy, properly speaking, ceases to exist and hypergamy comes when, for two given groups, one superior and the other inferior, the superior agrees to marry the girls of the inferior but not to give its own daughters in marriage. Recent research has directed attention to this phenomenon and to its social consequences.

It is not only a matter of those professional husbands that are found throughout India, cynical Brahmans who exploit the prestige of their blood and successively give their hand to the daughters of any low-caste that wishes to ennoble itself. For it is by no means rare to find regular hypergamy established between the sub-castes that we have discussed. Thus we find that among the Rarhi-Brahmans of Bengal, hierarchically divided into Kulins, Siddha-Srotriyas, Sadhya-Srotriyas and Kashta-Srotriyas, the Kulin can take a wife in his own group and in the two highest groups of Srotriyas: the Siddha-Srotriya in his group and in the Sadhya-Srotriya group but the choice for Sadhya-Srotriyas and the Kashta-Srotriyas is limited to their respective groups.[18] Marathas of the Kadam, Bande, Powar or Nimbalker families, the reigning families of the great days of Maratha power refuse their daughters to inferior caste-fellows. Pods who have received an English education and have become clerks or doctors, agree to marry the daughters of Pods who have remained agriculturalists or fishermen; but reciprocity is no longer allowed. Moreover one can foresee a time when this distinguished class of Pods will reject an alliance with the rustic Pods not only for their daughters but also for their sons. Their numbers having increased, they will be self-sufficient. They will have passed from hypergamy to endogamy.

Were such developments perhaps the rule in ancient Indian history? We can suppose that the colonizing Aryans did not bring a sufficient number of women of their own race to India. Like nearly all conquering-colonizers they must have taken the daughters of the aborigines without giving daughters in exchange. Thus distinct groups would have been formed which would have been more or less high in the hierarchy according to the proportion of Aryan blood they could boast. Let us now imagine, with Mr Risley, that in the desire to distinguish themselves, to preserve or increase their prestige, to avoid the degradation consequent upon the continuance of such mixings, such superior groups, now moreover, sufficiently rich in women, finally close their doors; let us imagine that this example is followed, as so often happens, gradually down and down, to the lowest castes. We can understand from this the genesis of endogamous prohibitions. Once more India's present gives us the key to its past.[19]

Whatever truth may be in these hypotheses there is a certain number of institutions and characteristic practices of Hindu society which continue to develop under our eyes and which can no doubt be explained by the consequences of hypergamy; we refer to the ban on widow remarriage and the precautions taken to marry children at a very early age.

Why are people so often, and more and more, opposed to the remarriage of widows? The Brahmans have a ready explanation. The widow must remain a widow in order to perform the annual *srāddha*, the ceremony which ensures repose to the spirit of her departed husband. In addition, when she was married for the first time the husband received by a sort of special manumission from her father, the ownership of his wife: how could a second marriage conformable with the rites take place when the owner who alone can transmit his property is no longer there? However, it is likely that utilitarian reasons are hidden behind these religious ones.[20] We can well understand that a family is not in a hurry to remarry a widow; first of all they would have to pay another dowry; further the new husband would, contrary to the interest of the group, carry off those goods which the woman shared with her first husband. Finally, and above all, in a very general way, all the families of the caste have a common interest in forbidding the remarriage of widows: as one Hindu put it, these experienced women might enter into disloyal competition with the young girls whom it is difficult enough to get married as it is.

Here we see the repressive influence of hypergamy; we cannot doubt that it tends to increase the number of 'old maids' in the superior groups. If young Kulin Brahmans can take wives indiscriminately from inferior sections as well as their own, it is clear that the young girls in the latter will find fewer suitors: just to the extent that the area of choice is widened for the masculine members of a group to that extent the chances of being chosen diminish for the female members. Thus we can understand the ease with which the collective instinct accepts all the reasons which tend to the exclusion of widows from an already crowded marriage market.

The same preoccupations, perhaps, explain the practice of child marriage. It is said to be a convenient practice for the family: it saves them the domestic difficulties and scandals which their daughters' misconduct might provoke and all sorts of conflict in which they would be involved were the girls to have a hand in the choice of their own husbands. But surely, much more important, the disquiet with which a father sees the number of suitors diminishing around him must be a much more important motive in driving him to betroth his child as soon as possible. It is a disgrace, it is almost a sin to keep a maid of twenty years old in the family: to marry off his daughters as soon as opportunity offers, even in their infancy, is the surest safeguard against such opprobrium.[21]

It is obvious that hypergamy alone cannot be solely responsible for the extension of these practices. It is only at the heart of superior groups, amongst such as are able to indulge themselves or who believe themselves obliged to refuse their daughters to others, that the number of possible grooms is limited. Restrictive or preventative measures such as the ban on widow remarriage or the practice of child marriage are not vital necessities for inferior groups whose daughters may be sought for by young men of higher rank as well as by those of their own standing. But the instinct for imitation is as powerful as the instinct for the preservation of groups. And is it not a law that the inferior in one way or another takes on the ways of the superior, even when these are not directly useful? The prestige of the twice-born castes and the desire to approximate to, by imitating them, explains why it is that daily we see the practices in question multiply and enlarge their circles of influence. In fact we could cite more than one caste that has improved its status thanks to its eagerness to marry its children, or better, thanks to the severity with which it forbids the remarriage of its widows. Of all those social ascents which take place under our eyes none are less disputed than those which have taken the path of respect for tradition, a concern for purity and orthodoxy.

Such instances of 'progress' sufficiently prove that western progress is far from having triumphed once and for all over Hindu tradition. Contrary to what might be supposed, the latter is well able, in its own turn, to protect its native tendencies, by using the very instruments that an alien administration has provided for it.

Who would have suspected that the railway would make for the consolidation and at the same time the expansion of Hinduism? Nevertheless this is what Mr Risley would have us suspect. He points out that low castes are more than ever tending to adopt the ways and customs of high castes in which the Brahmanic ideal is as it were, incarnate. In recent years, he assures us, one could maintain that this ideal, so far from having lost ground, has gained it thanks to the very ways and means of communication. The population travels more, pilgrimages are more easily organized and the influence of the orthodox élite spreads wider and wider. 'The railway, which has often been represented as the destroyer of caste prejudice, has extended enormously the area in which these prejudices reign.'[22] The 'te-rain' in the service of caste: what has become of our predictions about the egalitarian virtues of the locomotive?

Thus India in its own way recalls what Japan has violently taught us.[23] The ancient civilizations of the east learn to use all the apparatus of European civilization, but it is to defend themselves: if they change their bodies it is to protect their souls.

PART 3

The effects

1

Race

What influence does the caste system exercise upon the distribution of races in Hindu society?

This question must be answered first. Indeed, according to some theories a reply to this question is *sufficient*: it holds the secret of India's destiny. There is no need to search further. The tendencies of a society only express its ethnic aptitudes and the way in which these are used. In this way anthropology renders sociology superfluous.

Certainly the guiding thesis of the philosophy of races – so much used and abused in the nineteenth century – seems to have been decisively abandoned. Civilizations are no longer represented as the specific creations of distinct races. We have been obliged to take account of the fact that in all societies, the crucibles of civilizations, too many elements are amalgamated. There is not a nation which under anthropological analysis does not soon reveal its essential heterogeneity.

But where the 'philosophy of races' loses ground, 'anthroposociology' sets up new claims. Far from ignoring ethnic heterogenity, it takes that as its point of departure. It sets out, by the use of precise measurements, to reveal the different superimposed racial layers in societies. It proposes to bring to light those physical differences of which mental diversity and social inequality are merely the logical consequences.

The pity of it is that here, once more, history holds the cards. She shuffles and deals out a mixed hand of elements which, if anthroposociology is to verify its hypotheses, should be kept isolated.

How is progress to be defined if not as the shrinking of moral as well as of material distances? That way not only does it gather together in one place, often far from their countries of origin, people of different races, it also urges them to an incessant intermingling. Like the frontiers of provinces, the barriers of class are progressively lowered in the hearts of nations. There is no longer the same horror of misalliance. With democracy, the time of what Gobineau called 'panmixie', of universal cross-breeding, of general impurity has come. Thus our own societies, instead of presenting us with two or three neatly defined types, readily distinguished and classified, so that we could easily track their destiny and compare their distinctive qualities, only offer us collections of almost indiscernible hybrid types, literally 'insignificant'. All the proclamations of anthroposociology conclude with the same cry of alarm. 'Interesting types are disappearing before our eyes: mixtures and crosses increase in disastrous proportions.'[1]

But perhaps Hindu society has preserved for anthroposociology exactly that area for research which our own societies have denied it. There, civilization is not drunk with egalitarianism. On the contrary India is fed on anti-egalitarian ideas. And since India is the homeland of castes it will no doubt prove the paradise of the anthroposociologists.

Indeed they have often praised the prescriptions of Brahmanic wisdom as conforming with the healthy requirements of 'racial culture'.

In the matter of food, the quasi-vegetarian diet which Brahmanism imposes proves that it was aware of the physiological effects of climate, which does not allow too strong a diet. Its marriage prohibitions are yet more prudent. They take precaution to eliminate the infirm for fear that individual degeneracies might otherwise propagate and change the purity of types. Even more, they have understood that if for the sake of purity of type one can only allow unions between people of the same blood, nevertheless unions between close kin also threaten degeneration of the race. And this is why rules of exogamy wisely come in to complement and correct rules of endogamy. Two circles limit the individual's choice: he may not marry outside the larger nor equally within the smaller; he must marry inside his caste but not inside his family. Thus the advantages of consanguinous marriages are preserved and all their disadvantages avoided. The whole system has been admirably contrived indeed. Might we not think that Manu has anticipated Darwin? Anthropology can proclaim the Hindus a 'model people'.[2] Like good selective breeders they have taken care not to mix their races.

Certainly, in many other places as well, we have seen the confrontation of races. Is not history, in reality, an incessant 'war of the races'? But nearly everywhere oppositions give way in the long run; none is too strong. The most blood-spattered history ends, like a comedy, in a marriage. Thus the conquerors are most often absorbed by the conquered, the Lombards by the Italians, the Greeks of Alexandria by the Egyptians, the Normans by the French. In India, the original antipathies, no doubt kept warm by the different colours of the races involved, have had a longer life. They have given birth to indestructible institutions and secreted the social forms which still dominate India today. Born out of these primitive repulsions, the caste system has maintained them through thirty centuries for the delight of the anthropologists.[3]

Nowhere else is a population so clearly divided in more exclusive, closed groups, none more hostile to misalliance exist.* Therefore in India, above all, primitive ethnic types have had the greatest chance to preserve their distinctiveness, each in its own rank. Furthermore, nowhere else have occupations been more rigorously separated nor hereditary specializations more carefully maintained. Therefore in India, as nowhere else, one must expect to find agreement of social function and natural faculties. Here at least we are free from that spirit which throws down and levels: blood is no more mixed here than functions are exchanged.

Here, consequently, those secret harmonies will be revealed, that join different bodily forms to different dispositions of the mind and predestine men with bodies made in this way or that to

---

* Bouglé uses the term 'formariage' a feudal term referring to the marriage of a serf outside his station or outside his seignory.

play this or that social role. The fact that India has been divided by the caste system since the most ancient times, and that races there are not only hierarchized, but strictly enclosed and specialized, will no doubt enable us to verify the guiding hypotheses of anthroposociology: it will demonstrate constant relations between physical, social and mental differences.

From the outset travellers in India, more than anywhere else, have been struck by the great diversity of types they have encountered. Were they to go by the succession of physiognomies they encounter, they might believe themselves transported now to Greece, now Africa and now the Far East. Jacquemont tells us of his astonishment when he visited the Anglo-Indian college at Calcutta. Forty young natives were gathered there: 'More than half had handsome faces, nearly all very fine hands. Draped rather than covered in thick but soft muslin, many of them by the natural elegance of pose and gesture, reminded me of Greek statues.'[4] Colonel Dalton reports his surprise when among the Kurmis and Goalas he found boys and girls who by the refinement of their features, the harmony of their forms and clarity of complexion might favourably compare with the shepherds of Arcady. Often, beneath the tatters of the fakir or beneath the uniform of a sepoy, one seems to recognize a man of one's own people, an 'aryan brother'.[5] But, turn now to the agricultural Oraons of Chota Nagpur:[6] the nose is no longer straight nor thin; the brow is not developed, but low and narrow, hidden below half-crinkly hair; the jaw protrudes, the lips are thick. You feel an immense difference between yourself and these misshapen and squalid creatures. Climb up among the Murmis of Nepal[7] and you are no less at a loss: narrow heads, short noses, prominent cheek bones, eyes oblique, yet another new human. Thus you get the impression that India is indeed, as has been said, a museum of races in which the most varied specimens co-exist without for all that mixing.

Longer acquaintance with the Hindu world might make you think, from the evidence of your eyes, that these various types are not merely juxtaposed but also superimposed, and that the ethnic distinctions correspond to so many social distinctions. You could easily see that the same occupations are carried on by men of the same type, and different occupations by men of different types; and thus you would come to recognize the weaver, the grain merchant, the banker, the warrior and the priest not only from their dress and manner but also from their stature, conformation and physiognomy. In some European countries one can also derive occupation from race; but what is the exception amongst us is the rule in India. We are assured that for the experienced eye the physique of the majority of Hindus clearly indicates their caste.[8] It is, we might say, written on their faces.

But can these impressions be verified and made more precise? According to Mr Johnston it is sufficient to classify individuals by their colour.[9] One can then see that colour differences correspond to differences of social situation. It is simply a matter then of taking literally the ancient Sanskrit word *varna* which denotes caste and signifies colour. Hindu society is essentially polychromatic and the notation of social distinctions within it are so many racial differences. A story in the Mahabharata classifies men as white, red, yellow and black according to their qualities and occupations. We are told that observation confirms the legend. The Brahmans are remarkable for the paleness of their skin, while the skin of the warrior Rajputs veers towards red. Among agriculturalists, among the Kochs of Bengal or the Savaras of Madras, one finds mostly a Mongol type with yellow skin while, in the artisan classes the black Dravidian type predominates. The methodical comparison of the dominant skin colours in the various Hindu classes thus confirms our first intuitions.

It was however left for Mr Risley's 'monumental' statistics to provide a striking verification.[10] Questions of colour are always open to discussion: in the discrimination of shades there is always a personal coefficient which it is difficult to eliminate. But if we know how to use the anthropometrician's 'bag of tricks', if with compass or square rule we measure everything about man that can be measured, if we work out his cephalic indices, nasal, nasomolar, vertico-zygomatic, vertico-molar, vertico-cephalic, vertico-frontal, we shall end up at last with 'objective' results, perhaps.

As a result of subjecting 5,505 Bengalis to these measurements, Mr Risley distinguished two dominant types in contemporary Hindu society. And these are precisely the two types whose opposition is the original characteristic of primitive Hindu society. Let us recall the insults hurled by the Vedic Aryans at the Dasyus. The conquering race, proud of its white skin, straight nose and symmetrical appearance mocks the indigenous tribes as 'black-skins' 'no noses' and 'squash faces', as it drives them before it. One could not have hoped, says Mr Risley, for a more valuable anthropometric description. Our measurements of the living enable us to distinguish, beyond any doubt, the grandchild of the aborigine here and there the grandchild of the conqueror. To such an extent have the Aryan type and the Dravidian type maintained their differences and kept their distance. They continue to perform different functions and from figures it can be proved that the higher a man is in the social scale, the more he approaches the first type – the lower he is, the more he approaches the second type.

In this area the comparison of cephalic indices is misleading. It would have been nice to demonstrate that the superior are always and everywhere distinguished from the inferior by a greater dolichocephality. India will not allow us this gratification. Is this because the inferior race in India is closely related to the negro who, as we know, are unfortunately very dolichocephalic? The fact remains that, according to Mr Flower's observations, cranial proportions throughout India are very nearly constant. The Mongol element, which is brachycephalic has, no doubt, here and there, raised the average of the index by lessening the proportion of dolichocephalics examined. But according to Mr Risley the intervention of this element is negligible in the constitution of castes. Since the two constitute elements of Hindu society, Dravidian and Aryan, are almost equally dolichocephalic even though they belong to quite different biological varieties, it is not surprising that our cephalometric reward is slight.

Happily the revelations of the nasal index assure us rich compensation. They not only enable us to distinguish radically Dravidians and Aryans by showing us that the former have noses as broad as negroes and the latter noses as fine as Parisians, but also, unexpectedly, they mark the degrees of the Hindu hierarchy. Mr Risley affirms that social superiority in Hindu society is proportional to the fineness of the nose. He proves this in two ways.

The small societies which compose Hindu society are for the most part exogamous as well as endogamous; this means that their members are forbidden to take a wife within certain defined circles. But these circles are defined in different ways. A man recognizes a woman that he may not marry, sometimes from the fact that she respects the same totem as himself, sometimes because she lives in the same place as himself, sometimes from the fact that she is descended, or is believed to be descended from the same ancestor: exogamy can be 'totemic', 'territorial' or 'eponymous'. It is an established fact that these different modes of exogamy do not belong to the same moral level. Some are, we might say, more distinguished than others. Totemic exogamy demonstrates a state of inferior civilization and eponymous exogamy a superior state. If now we measure members of these diverse societies we find the smaller number of platyrrhines among those who practise eponymous exogamy just as we find the greater number among those who practise totemic exogamy. Which proves that fineness of nose is an index of superiority.

But one can make a more decisive experiment. Take at random a certain number of people in Bihar province and classify them according to their traditional social values. Above the Kols, the Korwas and the Mundas which are not castes but still semi-savage tribes, we put the Musahars and the Chamars, of the tanner caste; above these the Bauris, the Binds and the Karvas, who are fishermen; next the pastoral Goalas and the agricultural Kurmis; finally come to the Khatris and the Babhans, merchants and land-owners belonging to the highest classes. Let us now measure the nasal proportions of our subjects in order. We can incontestably establish that the Khatris have noses less broad than the Kurmis, the Kurmis than the Bauris, the Bauris than the Chamars, the Chamars than the Kols or the Mundas. In short it would appear that the anthropometric hierarchy is parallel to the social one and we can conclude that 'it is scarcely a paradox to lay down, as a law of the caste constitution, that the social status of the members of a particular group varies in inverse ratio to the mean relative width of their noses'.*[11]

Who could ask more? Our anthroposociologists can be satisfied. India generously gives them, petrified as it were by the caste system what Europe, confused by democracy denies them. Instead of the cephalic index, the nasal index allows them to note strangely precise correspondencies between physical and social differences.

However, what is this whole demonstration worth?

If it rested simply on the 'impressions' of travellers, or even on those of the inhabitants it would be all too easy to knock it down. First of all, since it is a matter of proving that truly biological differences are hidden beneath social differences one can only partially trust to the appearance, general aspect and the physiognomy of individuals. It is their manner which strikes us above all: but this manner, surely, tells us more about the idea they themselves have of their situation than it does about the constitution of their heredity? We note that observers pick on moral traits when they try to describe the exterior aspect of the Brahman. They are easily recognized, says the Abbé Dubois, from 'a certain detachment and liberty in their manner and posture'.[12] 'They walk', says Sherring, speaking of the Brahmans of Banares, 'with an air that I have never seen in any other human being: they give off a sense of their contentment with themselves, a sense of their own superiority, the conviction of their purity and essential holiness'.[13] Here we have a direct impression of soul rather than of body; it is tradition rather than race which is written on their faces. We might explain the martial appearance of the Rajput by an analogous phenomenon. By a thousand imperceptible touches, minds fashion bodies in their image: thus entirely moral differences can, in many cases, give us the illusion of physical differences.

How careful we must be over general impressions we can see when we remember that they are contradictory. Mr Risley, who has lived in India for a long time, tells us that a trained eye can

* See above p. 57.

tell a man's caste from his face. But Mr Nesfield has lived there for no lesser period and his opinion is quite different. He does not believe in the essential heterogeneity of the Hindu race, he tells us that the majority of Brahmans is neither more fair nor more finely made than the members of other castes; he challenges us to distinguish the road-sweepers from the students clustered outside the Sanskrit college in Banaras.[14]

Can one decide between these contradictory affirmations by an attentive comparison of complexions? Nothing empowers us on this point to adopt Mr Johnston's rash conclusions. How does he come to the idea that red is the distinctive colour of the Kshatriyas? They, as much as the Brahmans, claim to be descended from the white conquering race, and indeed very fine specimens of the Aryan type are said to have been recognized in Hindu warriors. In a general way the Banias of today correspond to the primitive Vaisyas: commerce is in their hands; they have, however, not a single trait of the yellow Mongol to whom Mr Johnston assigns the functions of commerce. Nor can we say that the black of the Dravidian type is only found among the artisan castes who correspond to the Sudras. On the contrary, it spreads in, admittedly diluted but continuous shades, across the Hindu world. And despite the old proverb which says: 'Never trust a fair Pariah nor a dark Brahman', it is not rare today to find Brahmans who are downright black, at least in lower Bengal and throughout the Peninsula. And even in the higher classes of the north-east the most widely spread colours are those of gingerbread, coffee bean, or, better, wheat grain.[15] The polychrome Hindu world is made up of an infinite number of nuances, and not as Mr Johnston would have it, of four clear-cut colours. His theory is more of a new legend rather than a confirmation based on observation of the ancient ones.

Mr Risley's imposing statistics are in another class. How can we reply to figures which come from so far? Certainly this coincidence of the two hierarchies, the social and the ethnic has something of the miraculous about it. 'Who among his readers would not be a little sceptical?' asks M. Senart.[16] But how can we justify our scepticism when we do not have documents with which to oppose those of Mr Risley?

Fortunately he has established a school of thought. Anthropometry has been followed up. New statistics enable us to limit the value of the general formulations which seemed possible in the light of the first measurements.

First of all we note that Bengal, where these first measurements were taken, is an exceptional area. 'Aryan immigration was never very dense there, as we can see from the language which is Sanskritic only in its vocabulary'.[17] It is possible that the races have not intermingled there for so long and racial types have been less blurred. But when we turn our inquiries to the south, we can establish that the mixing is now past history. 'The plains of India', writes Dr Cornish, 'have never supported a purely Aryan people'.[18] Either it has vanished or it has blended with the aborigines. Without travelling so far we find a mass of anthropometric data in the North-Western Province and in Oudh which contradict the theses of the anthroposociologists. Mr Crooke, adopting Mr Risley's method, has collected this material in a no less 'monumental' work.[19] He has measured 4,906 subjects. But his measurements in no way allow him to announce laws similar to those which earlier astonished us. The cephalic index of the 'twice-born' does not appreciably differ from that of the aborigines – which is not debated; but, much worse – their nasal index is not significantly lower. In a chart where subjects are ranged in ascending order of nasal size, if the Brahmans take second place (nasal index 59) after the Jats (55), the Dhanuks, people of undisputed Dravidian caste follow them closely (61), while the Rajputs (64) allow themselves to be shamefully outdone by the Banias (63) who are only merchants, and by the Gujass (62) who are only labourers. Other measurements were no more flattering to high-caste pride: in a chart ordering the subjects according to decreasing facial angle, the Brahmans and the Rajputs only reach sixth place with the same mean figure as the Chamars (65), five degrees below the Maujhis (70). If we add that in other charts the Kshatriyas and the Khatris, who equally claim descent from the warrior race find themselves one at the top, the other at the bottom of the scale, separated by labourers, dancers, liquor vendors as well as by priests, and finally that whatever measurements have been taken, all the lists of averages give a picture of the same disorder, it will be understood that the disorder is total: the findings in the north-west contradict those of the east.

In the last analysis have Mr Risley's findings the clarity which he supposes? When we look at his famous table of nasal indices, we are astonished to find that the Kayasths who, according to Brahmanic theory, are of Sudra race, have a higher place than the Brahmans, and yet more astonished to see the impure Chandalas ranking above the Rajbansis of royal blood. Examination of individual measurements raises more surprises. They show that a number of Brahmans tend, more than either Goalas or Chamars, towards a negroid profile.

In other tables, those of the cephalic indices for example, one can establish that the Brahman is close to the Bind as the Bābhan to the Bhar:[20] on that giving facial angles one finds the priest and the fisherman side by side, the farm labourer and the landowner – to such an extent that one might conclude with Mr C. J. O'Donnel that even in this exceptional region, the fusion of types has gone far: anthropometry has itself proved that it is henceforth impossible to discover function in race, or castes in skulls.

The melancholy conclusion at which M. Topinard has already arrived after analysing the anthropometric documents on Bengal is, then, indisputably confirmed: 'We have learnt one major fact: it is that India is far from being that land, dreamed of by the anthropologists, where types would emerge, simple and classical, reproducing those that legend and history going back 4,000 years and more made us expect. The populations are very intermixed, very confused and often contradictory, despite endogamy.'[21]

There is nothing about this result that should surprise us if we recall that the famous sacred codes whose selectionist regulations were so much admired by the anthropologists, express an ideal rather than a reality. The prescriptions are more dictated by the desires of the dominating caste, which drew them up, than by universally respected custom. It would be strange if anthropometric observations did confirm the Brahmanic theory of castes, since everything goes to prove – as we have seen[22] – that Brahmanic theory often conceals and distorts historical reality.

Just as castes are infinitely more numerous, so are they infinitely more mixed than we should be led to believe if we looked at India only through the eyes of Brahmans. The prohibitions of which their codes are full formulate high caste claims to purity; they are no kind of proof of purity itself. From ancient times there have been misalliances – even the sacred literature bears witness to many – and, despite the no doubt growing rigour of endogamous protectionism, they still occur before our eyes.[23] How then is it possible to show subsequently that to the differences and inequalities of castes there correspond differences and inequalities of races? Senart observes that 'So perfect an agreement, given the profound and quite accidental interminglings of so many elements – and Risley recognizes them himself – would certainly seem miraculous'.*[24]

We exaggerate the repelling force separating the primitive races if we believe it capable of dividing Hindu society into sections for all eternity. Here, as elsewhere, conquerors and conquered have come finally to embrace each other. Anthropo-sociology seeks its ideal land in vain. Let that spirit which is most opposed to egalitarianism dominate an entire civilization; let a concern for purity overrule all others and partition the society at its will: all is in vain. Sooner or later the highest barriers are surmounted, the most diverse elements are mixed and one can no longer demonstrate precise correlations between physical and social differences.

But if anthropometry has exaggerated the value of its measurements, we must not, in another direction, exaggerate the value of our criticisms. They show that, even in India, ethnic types have not stayed sufficiently clearly separated to enable us today to establish their differences objectively and evaluate them mathematically. But it still remains true, by common consent, that India is the country in the world in which the greatest efforts have been made to keep different groups of men separate; and if these efforts have not succeeded in preventing mixture altogether, that does not mean that they have had absolutely no effect.

* The complete quotation contains the parenthetical reference to Risley omitted by Bouglé.

For example if India no longer allows us to prove statistically a parallel between physical and social differences, perhaps it permits us a glimpse of a certain degree of harmony between these social differences and mental ones. We remind ourselves that India is the classic territory, not only of endogamy, but also of hereditary specialization. Through the centuries sons have necessarily inherited the occupation of their fathers: has this transmission of occupation, accompanying a transmission of blood, gradually adapted the qualities transmitted through blood to the qualities which the occupation demands? This coincidence of physical and social heredities has perhaps created, little by little, types which can be recognized if not by their exterior appearance, visible to the naked eye or measurable by compasses, then at least, by their internal configurations which the experienced eye can appreciate. How could such perpetually time-honoured practices not become printed in the brain in the form of innate faculties? The children of different castes would then have 'in the blood', as we say, an aptitude for meditation or a taste for war, here a gift for commerce and there, finally, an instinct for servility. The immobility of the Hindu world then preserves those specimens which anthroposociology vainly looks for in our own agitated world: the caste system is the appointed factory of constitutional specialization.

But how can we establish its existence precisely? Here we come up against new difficulties. The caste system has a vexatious nature. It hides its best effects and conceals its excellences from verification: it is like a famous armourer whose arms one cannot test; the hereditary qualities which it forges in the shadows are not allowed to shine in the sunlight, to be clearly seen and to prove themselves. *A priori*, children of different castes are specialized and consequently we cannot take the measure of their personal faculties. How can we claim that a child of servile caste is incapable of waging war or of interpreting the Vedas when in fact he has never been put to the test? Who knows how many wasted talents the caste system conceals in its low classes and inversely how many respected nonentities in its high classes? The hereditary distribution of functions conceals the natural distribution of faculties.

Could we, however, use a more indirect method to show that the two systems of distribution correspond exactly? Suppose that the society in which this hereditary specialization holds sway gives unimpeachable proofs of fecundity: a rich life, numerous and various works, marvellous civilization. Should we then not have the right to say that labour has been suitably divided in this society, and its functions justly distributed? The vitality of the whole would prove beyond doubt that each specialist group was at the height of its profession, and that the caste system creates, through the natural play of heredity, 'the right man in the right place'?*

But anyone can see that by adopting this method we should only stir up contradictory and arbitrary predilections. The partisan of hereditary specialization would set all the fine aspects of Hindu civilization in relief. For has it not astounded and in a way fascinated the west from the beginning? Its richness has attracted the world and the world has fought for the masterpieces of its weavers and goldsmiths. Its astronomical and mathematical discoveries have nourished our own science and the exuberance of its art astonishes our imagination. We recognize with stupefaction in its most ancient philosophy the profoundest reveries of our modern philosophers! The adversary, on the other hand, of the system might warn about thought which is wilfully obscure, and formulations which are merely hollow. It has been shown that the scientific contribution of ancient India does not finally amount to very much. The exuberance of its imagination only testifies to the impotence of its faculties of organization and unification. It has been able to create certain luxury industries but not true industry that can bring life to a people. It has lacked alike the intellectual power that can emancipate and the material power to protect. And all else apart, if it is true that its long past astonishes us, it must be accepted that for a long time now its creative force seems to have been exhausted. What has it produced in modern times which is original? It is a civilization marking time, or, rather, in retreat. What is there there to justify a eulogy of this 'systematic selection' whose instrument is caste? We could go on for a long time without any result,

* In English in the original.

exchanging remarks of this kind; they imply overall judgements on the value of civilizations; they in no way allow of precise demonstration.

Moreover if we could succeed in drawing up an exact balance-sheet of Hindu civilization and in measuring its true value, what would this prove, for or against, the theses of anthroposociology? How many other causes, other than the congenital qualities of individuals, have helped to turn the same wheel? It has often been shown how natural formations in India must shape the imagination and the will of the Hindus. And if we believe that social formation is even more powerful than natural formation, and that in this sense the caste system is truly 'the soul of Hindu civilization' let us recall that the moral effects of this system are singularly more in evidence than its physical effects. To understand the orientation which it has given to Indian civilization we do not need to seek for the obscure traces of its material operation. Does the cerebral make-up that a father passes on to his son really bear the imprint, the trade-mark so to speak, of his caste? Such equivocal hypotheses are useless. The truly social operations of caste – the twist that it gives to education, the limits that it imposes on imitation, the lines within which it confines ambition – sufficiently explain its power.

We are told about the Banyas,[25] a people of commercial caste, and very solicitous concerning a boy's future: they have their sons accompany them as often as possible, carefully teach them the rudiments of calculation and, as soon as they are able, involve them in the world of business affairs. If after that a young Banya proves himself a good tradesman, do we need to look for some innate aptitude which has predestined him for commerce? All the travellers have remarked on the dexterity of the Hindu artisan. Must we suppose that thanks to the caste system this dexterity is natural? Living with his father and familiarized from infancy with the instruments of his craft, he acquires his art unconsciously, by practice, without there being any need to suppose that he has received it mysteriously from his heredity. The son of a Rajput grows up with the idea that he is born for war: this idea is more responsible for his warlike tastes than is his temperament. In the same way the notions that young Brahmans have of the duties and rights of their caste, determine all their activity. Where psychological forces are so clearly evident, there is no need to invoke the virtues of race. The moral influences alone of the caste system sufficiently account for the degree of perfection to which India's civilization has developed just as they also explain the sort of petrification which it exemplifies. In fact, as a Hindu has rightly observed: 'It is the essence of the caste system that, through the mental habits which it imposes, it lifts men above savagery but halts them half-way on the road of progress'.[26] This halt and development can be explained without the intervention of constitutional specialization. The general development of Hindu civilization in no way, even indirectly, manifests the correlations sought by anthroposociology.

Perhaps, however, the intervention of British civilization performs an unexpected service in the discussion.

As we have seen it certainly does not prevent the caste mechanism from functioning.[27] The latter has victoriously resisted at more than one point, the direct and indirect pressures brought to bear upon it. Nevertheless the simple influence of European industry and administration cannot fail at least to increase the number of exceptions to the law of hereditary specialization. Certain openings are closed, but others open.

Thus in many castes while some hold to the primitive occupations and some turn to agriculture, others compete for the new occupations created by British civilization. A good number aspire to officialdom. This is one of the hopes that contribute to fill the daily increasing number of schools with a daily increasing and more motley crowd. If the British government does not throw open the higher ranges of the Civil Service as much as Hindus would like, at least in filling those posts which it does offer it takes no account of traditional distinctions. It claims to ignore differences of race as much as differences of religion. In that very society where the caste system but lately immobilized every element, a system of competition that mobilizes a large number is suddenly made available.[28] If now, after this mobilization, we examine the functions appropriated and the ranks reached by different castes, we shall, perhaps, obtain evidence of their specific qualities.

As regards military qualities, those who claim descent from the Kshatriya caste have them without a doubt: but have they a monopoly of them? On the contrary, it has been known for a long time that the Indian army is the meeting place for all castes, where the lowest, to quote Jacquemont 'rise up by taking the musket'. At least, if they were initially forbidden service in the army of Bengal, they freely took their place in the armies of Madras and Bombay. Today all receive into their ranks not only members of the lowest castes but also tribal people, 'outside caste'; and their officers express themselves very satisfied. Thus a Brahman cuts no less of a dash under arms than the Kshatriya, the Vaishya than the Brahman, the aborigine than the Aryan. Dressed in the same uniform, subject to the same discipline, infused with the same spirit, the various ethnic types blend into one social type, the sepoy.

But, in order to compare the different capacities of different castes it is, above all, important to analyse the distribution of intellectual functions. Would such an analysis give us, one way or the other, convincing results?

It is clear that the weight of tradition in this field hinders the play of individual vocation. Whatever their distinctive gifts some will be spontaneously carried towards the liberal professions: others will be fatally distracted from them. British observers tracing the curve of the development of public education in India, remind us of the obstacles which the traditional organization of castes places in the way of its extension. The number of illiterates does not decrease as fast as had been hoped. Only a certain number of castes appear to avail themselves sufficiently of the schools. It is because, in the memory of man, only certain groups had the habit and felt the need for instruction, those exactly for whom a certain minimum of culture was, in a manner of speaking, a professional obligation. Education enables the priest's son to read the sacred books, it helps the merchant's son to keep accounts. But the majority of castes enclosed in various manual occupations, have not acquired the sense that knowledge is a necessary thing: rather, they think of it as something reserved for others. It seems that it is not solely poverty but a sort of respect that prevents them from sending their children to school. In fact, when the idea does reach the lowest castes we find the higher protesting. In certain parts untouchable children, whose fathers follow degrading occupations, are only admitted as far as the threshold of the public schools: they are not allowed beyond the veranda.[29]

It is not surprising, given so many material and moral obstacles, that the members of low castes do not rise in the administrative scale as rapidly as might have been hoped. We are told that very few obtain posts which the government has opened to general competition. Among postal employees, teachers, *a fortiori* among judges, we find members of certain favoured castes, and always the same ones, in an immense majority. In Bengal, for example, out of 1,235 government appointments, 1,104 are monopolized by three castes: Brahmans, Baidyas and Kayasths. In the majority of provinces analogous proportions will be found.[30]

It is true then that the descendants of 'philosophers' still occupy today a privileged place in the liberal careers. Young Brahmans in pursuit of a future remember that study was the privilege of their caste. They turn in preference to intellectual occupations and many succeed in them. But is such success a proof of a hereditary intellectual superiority? One may legitimately doubt it when one finds that analogous successes are by no means denied to members of other castes. For a long time the Rajputs did not shine in situations calling for culture; many of them made it almost a point of honour not to be educated. But once they decided to leave their tents, we do not find that these descendants of the warrior race are fatally less apt for education. Two of the most famous 'Babus' of the Bengal High Court, Prasanna Chandra Roy and Saligram Sing are of the Rajput caste. In the judicial service of the same province the grandsons of Kasava Roy of Nakesipara, who was once the scourge of the land, shine in the highest rank. In the United Provinces it is the Khatris who occupy the highest offices.

Moreover, those who, in some provinces, compete with the Brahmans for places, often belong to castes to which tradition assigns a fairly low place. The Kayasths are not allowed among the 'twice-born' and are forbidden to wear the sacred thread. Nevertheless they are found at the highest levels of society. They succeed as well as the Brahmans in the universities; we are told that they even surpass them as authors, journalists and orators. Of the two eagles at the Bengal bar, one is a Brahman, the other a Kayasth. The Banyas, born-merchants, have nevertheless produced a number of distinguished writers. The Teli caste – a caste of Sudras, oil-pressers and grain merchants – today glory in the memory of Rai Kisto Das Pal Beador, one of India's greatest journalists. Srinath Pal, one of the most brilliant students of Calcutta University, who administers the vast estates of his aunt,* the Maharani Svarnamayi, is also a Teli. The Nayer of Malabar, who formerly were more of a tribe than a caste, while they have produced many domestic servants, can also claim a number of cultivated intellects. It was generally understood that members of the weaver caste were active people, but limited and unsuited to culture: nevertheless we see them, in their turn, winning distinction in the university and showing themselves not inferior, we are told, to the Brahmans and Kayasths.[31] The intellectual rise of the Shahas of Bengal, utterly despised as they were, has struck every observer. A great many members of 'inferior' castes have penetrated the 'superior' classes of Anglo-Indian society.

If all have not succeeded equally well are the cerebral structures of the constituent races to be blamed for it? Do not social circumstances weigh more heavily in the balance? The Napits, barbers, are rarely seen to rise in the scale of social function: is this because of a constitutional specialization in the barber race or rather because of the pressure of public opinion which, looking on barbers as beings at once impure and sacred, chains their sons to their traditional situations? In fact, where Christian missionaries have overcome caste prejudice they have also succeeded in bringing education to those lowest depths which seemed to be closed to it for ever.[32] It is therefore moral much more than physiological forces which decide the distribution of professions. The 'experiment' which British civilization has conducted on Hindu civilization does not reveal any hereditary marks, as it

* The text has *oncle* here.

113

were the specific weights, of different castes: there is nothing to show that their members carry a certain and determined vocation registered in their organisms.

Equally the British are at fault in claiming particular professional aptitudes for their own race. 'The Hindus' they sometimes say 'will never have the practical and scientific spirit necessary for running an industry.' To which the Hindus reply: 'If up to now we have not produced industrial goods, it is because we lacked technical instruction and sufficient capital. On the day that India has both, she will bring forth her engineers just as she has brought forth her advocates and her professors'.[33] And indeed the experiment which has begun justifies great hopes. With as much enthusiasm as other classes, Brahmans run to the industrial schools. Perhaps the grandsons of meditating Pandits will be, one day, the most practical of chemists or electricians. Do we have any right to set limits or to assign a single direction to the development of the Hindu spirit? Who can say that it will turn for ever in the same circle or always follow the same furrow? How can we believe in a mass specialization of the Hindus when despite the divisions of centuries, not one of its sections seems specialized in perpetuity?

This inquiry reminds us that it is imprudent to set limits upon the plasticity of the mind. Society can graft different plants upon the same nature. Only open new territories to races; bring new social forms to bear on organic forms; and you will see them blossom with unexpected flowers.

We have followed anthroposociology on soil that seemed prepared for it. All those resources that the western world, shaken not only by the creation of nations but also by the coming of democracy, unquestionably denied it, the Hindu world in its sacred immobility seemed to have saved for it. The earliest observers, trusting to the efficacy of the Brahmanic codes, believed that they were going to discover in India the precise formulation of the relations which unite bodily forms to mental faculties and social situations. A closer look was humbling – the precision of the first formulations was illusory.

Race

On the one hand anthropometric measurements, applied to subjects of different castes, do not allow us to conclude that the caste hierarchy corresponds exactly to a hierarchy of races. On the other hand, the transformation of Hindu society by British civilization does not allow us to conclude that hereditary specialization has deposited essentially different propensities in the sons of different castes.

In a word, correlations between physical differences, social differences and mental differences are still lacking. After this examination of the Hindu world, as before it, the guiding hypotheses of the philosophy of races, transformed into anthroposociology, remain undemonstrable, and unlikely.

2

Law

What are the general characteristics of Hindu law and to what extent does it bear the imprint of the caste system?

To find out we shall have recourse to the research of specialists, jurists and philologists. Such a survey provides one of the best opportunities to specify the tendencies of the social form with which we are concerned.

It will, in addition, allow us to test, on our way, certain recently formulated theories on the 'epochs' of law, on the original relation between civil and criminal law and between written and customary law.

For the purpose of the proposed analysis the code of Manu will be the basic text. This is not because it is, as was once believed, 'the code of India'. But it has been for centuries the best known and the most highly esteemed of all the Hindu texts which touch on questions of law. Many inscriptions name Manu as the leading law-giver and there is no revelation which has received more commentaries over a wider area. Further, the code of Manu appears to occupy an intermediary position in the series of these texts: if it is the first of the dharmashastras, manuals in verse earlier than the dharmabandha commentaries, it is later than the dharmasutras, the more or less sophisticated collections of Vedic aphorisms in prose. There is then the likelihood that the Manu-smriti will demonstrate the characteristics of the mean: we are told, for example, that it is less archaic than Gautama and less modern than Narada.[1]

What first of all strikes the European reader of the *Laws of Manu* is the multiplicity and variety of prescriptions which must seem to him quite alien to the legal sphere. 'The girdle of a

Law

Brahmana shall consist of a triple cord of Munga grass, smooth and soft; (that) of a Kshatriya, of a bowstring, made of Murva fibres; (that) of a Vaisya, of hempen threads (II, 42) – All the food must be very hot, and the (guests) shall eat in silence (III, 236) – Let him not step over a rope to which a calf is tied... Let him never wash his feet in a vessel of white brass... but let him not go to bed with wet feet (IV, 38, 65, 76). A Brahmana who does not invite his next neighbour...is liable to a fine...' (VIII, 392).*[2] Recipes for cooking, details of dress, rules of hygiene, advice on polite behaviour and rules of etiquette are found side by side and mixed together in this hotch-potch of precepts.

But however diverse the elements may be, the majority bear the same very clear mark: the stamp of religion. We soon realize that if there are absolute rules governing washing or eating in a certain way, about not touching certain objects or people, it is because otherwise one would suffer impurity or risk being at variance with divine powers. If certain ingredients are forbidden and others required, it is because the first are intrinsically impure, the others pure. From the auspicious or inauspicious properties of metals, the virtues of water or fire, the sanctity of the cow, arises this plethora of *tabus*, from which so many imperative duties are derived. In certain cases these rules seem quite simple: but let us be on our guard, for where we only see some hygienic precaution or rule of politeness, the Hindu may revere a ritual. And in other cases, if these duties strike us as unreasonable inventions, let us recall that religion has its own justifying reasons. The *Laws of Manu* is first and foremost a manual of pious conduct.

We shall not find law, then, in the Hindu codes other than mixed, or better, enveloped and penetrated by religion. This is not to say that it is impossible to distinguish some fragments, out of the heterogenous mass of ritual prescriptions, written in a style corresponding more closely to what we expect from a book of law. Fragments of this kind are more numerous and better concentrated in the *Laws of Manu* than in the earlier collections.

* Bouglé worked with the French translation of Loiseleur-Deslongchamps. I have cited the corresponding passages from Bühler's translation in the *Sacred Books of the East* series.

After detailing the many duties that make up a Brahman's life at its various stages, the Sage who is believed to be speaking comes to the duties of the king (vii): after the duty of defending his people that of dealing out justice is foremost. It is in this connection that the causes which the king may be called upon to decide are listed under eighteen heads (viii, 4–7). First come those relating to money and questions of property; debts, deposits, rescissions of sales and purchases, concerns among partners, disputes over wages and boundaries, etc. Next come assault, defamation, theft, robbery and violence and adultery. The duties of man and wife and the partition of inheritance find a place here also. A brief allusion to gambling and betting separates these prescriptions from the theory of mixed classes in which the various degrees of degradation resulting from a failure to observe rites or from illegitimate unions are expounded. A classification of the various punishments that attend the wicked in this world and the next, crowns the whole. It is a relatively vast construction, the enumeration of essentially juridical rules occupies more than a quarter of the entire work (713 verses out of 2,684). But vast as it is it is still far from resembling the body of our law. It is still essentially different in the distribution and respective proportions of its elements.

We do not allude here to the 'disorder' of the Hindu codes so vigorously ridiculed by the methodical mind of the late James Mill.[3] M. Jolly has shown that in the *Laws of Manu*, in particular, legal matters are ordered in a reasonable and quite rational manner, given the practical concerns underlying them. But it is exactly in this very organization that the preponderance given to certain parts surprises us. In the codes of western civilization to which we are accustomed the most numerous rules are those dealing with a return to the *status quo ante*. The law provides the individual who considers himself wronged with the means to prove his rights and obtain reparation for the damage done to him. If there is a sanction involved it is not a punitive one: it is not such as to make the guilty party expiate his offence; following the distinction proposed by M. Durkheim, it is 'restitutive' and not 'repressive'.[4] As compared with civil and commercial law, for example, both of which are governed by this spirit, truly penal law amongst us takes up little space. In the case we are analysing the relation is reversed. Not only are half of the juridical verses devoted to the repressive system but even when not expressly formulated, we feel the system's menacing dominance. The notion of a purely restitutive sanction does not emerge. There is no terminology to distinguish between civil delicts and crimes proper: it seems rather that all delicts are on the same level as offences, *aparādha*, calling for punishment, *danda*.[5] Indeed, despite the relative importance given to it in the *Laws of Manu*, civil and commercial law is still not separated from penal law. Both in cases which we would call civil and in criminal cases, the procedure is visibly the same. There are only some differences of detail: in the matter of admissible testimony, the competence of witnesses is not closely examined in cases of adultery, theft or violence (viii, 72). One can still feel at work the spirit of the ancient Sutras which requires expiation by punishment for all violations of all obligations whatsoever. It is not until we come to Brhaspati that we find the beginnings of a distinction.[6]

If further proof is needed that the authors of the *Laws of Manu* saw the role of law as essentially repressive we have only to recall their tragic lyricism as they hail the Genius of Punishment 'with black hue and red eyes'. 'Punishment governs all created beings, punishment alone protects them, punishment watches over them while they sleep; the wise declare punishment (to be identical) with the law... If the king did not, without tiring, inflict punishment on those worthy to be punished, the strong would roast the weaker, like a fish on a spit. The crow would eat the sacrificial cake and the dog would lick the sacrificial viands, and ownership would not remain with anyone, the lower ones would (usurp the place of) the higher ones... All castes, *varna*, would be corrupted (by intermixture), all barriers would be broken through, and all men would rage (against each other) in consequence of mistakes with respect to punishment' (vii, 18–25). A repressive law animated by such a spirit will not only be voluminous; it will fall heavily upon the guilty. Not only does it frequently threaten death, but also 'exacerbated' and 'qualified' death: by impalement, by fire, by the teeth of dogs, the feet of elephants, and by sharp razors. When it is not death, we have mutilations or brandings of all kinds devised with that fertile imagination which we admire in the production of the whole variety of magical acts. The majority of these inventions correspond to what M. Gunther has called the need for reprisals, in the widest sense of the word.[7] Sometimes the punishment is directed against the crime: the fingers of the thief and of the unchaste are chopped off, the tongue of the traducer is cut out. Sometimes the intention is to recall and symbolize the crime by branding: the adulterer* has the sign of female genitals stamped on his brow, the drinker of alcohol is branded with the distiller's sign. In addition to these punishments on the person we must add those which relate to goods: a complete system of heavy fines is worked out going as far as total confiscation. And should a criminal hope to escape these iron fetters, then his caste unites to reject him. He is denied fire and water and the village servants refuse to serve him. To touch him is to be polluted. He is as one dead among the living.

Moreover it is not only in this life but in the next life, or rather lives, that punishment with all these cruel inventions, attends upon the guilty. Sin stays with the sinner after death: he is reborn to suffer again. Here once more, through the cycle of rebirth, punishment reflects the crime or the circumstances of it, or the manner of its accomplishment. The stealer of clothes will be stamped by leprosy; the thief of grains will become a rat; the water stealer a marsh-bird. 'The violation of a Guru's bed (enters) a hundred times (the forms) of grasses, shrubs and creepers, likewise of carnivorous (animals) and of (beasts) with fangs and of those doing cruel deeds.' He who sheds a Brahman's blood remains in hell for so many thousands of years as there were particles of dust coagulated by that Brahman's blood.

The criminal has but one recourse if he would avoid such future torments and that is to bend voluntarily before the ordeals laid down by the Brahmans. Thus we find in the *Laws of Manu* a series of penances that resemble the penitential manuals of our own middle ages. If one does not want to go on paying for an offence for eternity, it must be redeemed in this world. The

---

* Bühler's *Manu* (ix, 237) reserves this punishment for the violation of a *guru's* bed.

penitent sinner must, in consequence sometimes mutilate himself, sometimes he will go so far as to commit suicide for his own salvation. At least he must accomplish some painful vow, sleeping on the bare earth, stay sitting in the sun's heat. He will fast for days on end, or subsist on water only, go without salt, eat only the five products of the cow. Above all, he will make amends in cash or kind to those whose power washes away every stain.

Hindu penal law uses many kinds of threat. In the codes, behind the series of temporal penalties we see a series of spiritual penalties and by the side of the punishments inflicted by the king or the gods, are those which the sinner can inflict upon himself. Sometimes it seems that these penalties substitute for each other; if a man has suffered the one he need not undergo the other. The sinner, once punished by the king, enters heaven as pure as the saint. Inversely he who accomplishes his penance is exempted from the fire that would have branded him and is only liable to a fine. Sometimes we see the two types of penalty blending as it were, in each other: the penance is to court punishment, to call it down on oneself so that it may wound and purify. The criminal is exhorted to redeem his fault by confessing it to the king, holding meanwhile the instrument of judicial punishment. As a general rule, especially for grave offences, the punishments are accumulated: a guilty person who has already been punished in his person or property must still perform some ritual penance before he is received back into his caste.[8]

Various as these penalties may be, they express the same juridical tendencies and obey the same preoccupations. There is respect for the same traditions, a concern for the same progressions. We see, for example, that in both the ritual and the secular series there is the same desire to extend punishment to the accomplices, the same proportional aggravation of guilt for recidivism, the same principles determining a legitimate defence. In both series even the culprit's presumed intentions are weighed in the same manner.[9]

In fact on this point, the system of penances proper seems to be less pliable than the other. We know that in primitive religions an involuntary stain is no less dangerous on that account and consequently calls for a no less severe purification. This mystical and partly material conception of sin is found in the Vedas; a notion of some sort of morbid fluid which adheres and which the patient must wash off at any price, even though he had nothing to do with the cause of his misfortune.[10] This conception survived for a long time, and in more or less concealed form, still operates in the codes. Some appear to argue that penances should be reserved for involuntary faults while only voluntary ones should suffer temporal penalties.[11] Manu preserves the memory of this priestly indecision when he says: ' (All) sages prescribe a penance for a sin unintentionally committed; some declare on the evidence of the revealed texts, (that it may be performed) even for an intentional offence' (xɪ, 45). In fact if we turn from principles to the details, we find that the system of penances itself takes account, more and more, of interior dispositions. Manu declares that if, to efface an unintentional offence, it is sufficient to recite certain verses, more severe mortifications are necessary when it is a matter of premeditated acts (xɪ, 46).[12] In other codes we note that in a more general manner, the rate of penance is doubled when the intention is perverse.[13] Here also the consideration of the *culpa* takes place side by side with that of the *dolus*. The parallelism of the two categories of punishment has been maintained even on this point.

Where, however, the unity of their preoccupations is most clear is in the precautions they take to maintain the hierarchy of caste by an ascending scale of punishments. It is striking that the greater part of the savage punishments we have listed do not touch the Brahman: his prestige disarms the rigour of the secular power. He can be condemned to banishment but not to death. Nobody may strike him, even with a blade of grass. More generally, the rate of punishment varies as a function of social situation: it reaches its maximum when the offended is of the highest caste and the offender of the lowest. A Brahman pays fifty *pannas* for insulting a Kshatriya; twenty-five for a Vaishya; twelve for a Sudra. But a Kshatriya who insults a Brahman must pay a hundred *pannas*; a Vaishya a hundred and fifty or two hundred; a Sudra will not escape a flogging. Analogous gradations, repeated in a hundred ways, are to be found in the calculation of penances, days of fasting or years of seclusion.[14] We must note one case in which the proportion is reversed: the Brahman thief is more heavily punished; no doubt the intention here is to prevent by this threat any abuse of that confidence which everyone is expected to repose in him (VIII, 338). But even this is a way of saying that all men are not of the same essence and that penalties, in their aggravations or attenuations, should before all else mark the degrees of the hierarchy. It is not for nothing that the apologists of Punishment give him as his most important mission the maintenance of rank and the prevention of miscegenation between the social species as much as between the animal species. The idea which is most repugnant to the law we are studying here is most certainly the idea of the equality of men before the law.

To sum up: from the codes Hindu law appears to us penetrated by religion and linked with inequality, less concerned with reparation than with punishment, and the most severe punishments at that. To what extent does the caste system account for these characteristics?

When this law works out in minute detail and with proportional variations according to rank, the number of strokes that must be suffered or the number of *pannas* that must be paid, it is directly translating, in its own way, the characteristic tendency of Hindu society. The majority of primitive bodies of law set up scales of a similar nature in fixing their rates of composition.[15] We find this among the Greeks as well as among the Germans. In the Gortyn Laws, for example, the tariff for fines in cases of adultery varies from five to two hundred staters; those variations are not only determined by the particular circumstances of the offence but by the social situation of the offender and the offended: on this score the truly free citizen is valued at ten times the worth of an inferior and forty times the worth of slave.[16] But nowhere have such discriminations been preserved for so long nor have they been spelled out in such detail, as in Hindu law.

This very insistence raises a doubt: such firmly drawn demarcations, such learnedly prescribed gradations are ordinarily the sign of a rigid will, but not perhaps of a docile reality. To what extent did these legal categories correspond to real ones?

The penetrating observations of M. Senart have warned philologists not to trust the illusions of Brahmanic tradition. Manu only distinguishes between Brahmans, Kshatriyas, Vaishyas and Sudras, whether discussing regulations of dress or the award of punishment: 'There are but the four castes, there are not five.' But we no longer need to demonstrate that this theory of the four castes, *chaturvarna*, is only a bold simplification. All the evidence indicates, as we have seen, that the Hindu world was not divided into four slices corresponding to the classical colours, but into an indefinite multiplicity of sections, no doubt derived from the primitive familial groups, *jāti*. This is what the authors of Manu are admitting when they enumerate the various 'mixed castes'. No doubt they explain the existence of these groups and their hierarchical distribution as divagations from the rules that they formulate: illegitimate unions, omission of rites, the relinquishing of custom or of ancestral occupation are so many causes of separation and degradation. But here we have, we are told, an explanation after the event which deceives no one and only betrays the embarrassment of the theoretician faced with facts that contradict his theory.[17]

Important as these facts are, it does not follow that the Brahmanic theory of punishment does not correspond, in its general tendency, to an ideal more or less clearly held by all the elementary groups of Hindu society. Divided as they may be they strive, in the spirit of the codes, to avoid the mixing of blood and the changing of occupation, and to respect the traditional rites. And all recognize the Brahman at their head. One thing among the proud decrees of Manu holds fast: the Brahman is like fire that needs no consecration to burn bright and remains pure whatever it consumes. Still today, after so many upheavals that have made for the most fluctuating distinctions, the one clear criterion that inquirers have for establishing caste precedence is, as we have more than once remarked, the opinion that the Brahman has of each one, which is registered in the acceptance or the refusal of the different kinds of food that they offer him. In addition we find that the offences condemned by Manu, the forsaking of hereditary customs, the omission of rites, illegitimate unions, are the cause of many degradations of rank.[18] A shadow can be more clear-cut and rigid than the body: Brahmanic law, in the broad lines of its anti-egalitarian system, is no less a projection of India's social structure.

That the plan behind this law is for the greater part drawn by religion need not surprise us when we think that scruples concerning purity are the keystone, or better the foundation stone, of all Hindu constructions, and that the parts are only ordered and kept in place by sentiments of pious respect and sacred horror. It has been claimed that caste is a 'matter of marriage'; others have said 'a matter of eating together'. The two propositions converge: originally the end of marriage was to ensure a continuity of officiants for the ancestral cult, and the meal, prepared under the protection of the supreme divine element, has all the characteristics of a ritual communion.[19] Which is to say in other terms, that caste is essentially a matter of religion.[20]

Some may hesitate to accept this definition. Hindus have changed their faith, converting to Islam, for example, or Christianity without having the strength, perhaps without having even the idea of rejecting the rule of caste. And again amongst those who remain Hindus, this rule co-exists with a diversity of doctrines. Beliefs differ or pass away, the practice remains identical.[21]

First of all, however, even if the practitioners have lost sight of the belief which generated their practice, this does not mean that it was not, in origin, instituted by religion. The tree bears leaves while knowing nothing of the roots.[22] And then, to require that caste refer in set terms to a certain mythology, before we can allow its religious character is, perhaps, to overstress the part of belief in the strict sense, in the religious sentiment. In matters of dogma the Brahman's tolerance is proverbial. He willingly accommodates the most heterogeneous products of imagination, even those that to us appear heterodox. Without more ado, he throws open his hospitable pantheon to the diverse divinities of his new clients. Because in his eyes the important, the essential thing about religion is that in respecting him one respects the rules of caste.[23] Every attempt to define Hinduism otherwise goes wide: to whatever sect he may belong, the Hindu knows himself by that instinctive fear of the supernatural which he experiences at the moment of violating traditional prohibitions governing bed and board.[24] So far from being one of its fruits, we would say that caste is the very kernel of Hindu religion.

Is it surprising after such an interpenetration of the sacred and the social that juridical prescriptions in India more than elsewhere, are impregnated with the religious imagination? Almost everywhere law is born and grows under the shadow of religion. Religion lends it its trust in the judgement of the gods, the constraining force of its imprecations, the magic virtue of its formulae and its gestures.[25] But the progress of law consists precisely in emancipating itself from this tutelage, to develop truly human resources. Human law, *jus* carves out a kingdom for itself apart from divine law, *fas*. It is because the Romans recognized this distinction early in their history that they are regarded in matters of law, as the teachers of the west.[26]

Even in Rome it would seem that the work of secularization proceeded more slowly than was once thought. We note the strong religious tone in the table of delicts amenable to the king's justice.[27] He acted in the name of a public vengeance, but this would appear to have been as executor of divine vengeance. Even in matters of civil justice, in the transmission of the *sacra*, which originally accompanied the devolution of goods, we now see a persisting religious pressure in the special protection given to property boundaries and in the clauses of all sorts that call the gods as witnesses.[28] To resist this pressure and to develop freely a 'bourgeois and profane' law, the considered expression of concerted wills, required all the organized power of a state, and that subject to the pressure of the people.[29] The 'laicization' of law could only occur in a civil polity reorganized according to the will of a self-conscious plebeian class.

But Indian castes were never able to come together to found such a polity and insist upon such a refashioning of the law. Persistent in their horror of contact and mixture the primitive familial groups never entered the way of concessions, compromises and reciprocal limitations. No plebeian class emerged to demand a recasting of the primitive structure. This is why among the Aryans in India not only is public law, so rich among their Greco-Italian brothers, reduced to its most simple expression, but also the distinction between divine and human law remains unexpressed.

It is not that the development of civilization did not force, here as elsewhere, a widening of the early juridical doctrine and obtain, for example, a place in the codes for the requirements of its more complicated economic organization. In this sense M. Dahlmann contrasts the age of *rita* with that of *dharma* which is less exclusively attached to the regulating virtues of sacrifice, and more preoccupied with the conditions and consequences of human activity. But the antithesis is indecisive, and its author must acknowledge that religion does not relax its grip upon *dharma*.[30] Hindu society never developed the necessary organs for the creation, or even the conception, of a laicized law.

The only organized force which emerges in the universal divisiveness, is precisely that which has charge of the maintenance, in the face of everything, of laws derived from a religious conception of life: the priestly body.

Such an expression is open to objection for even here the pride of blood, refractory to all unity, makes its isolating effects felt. We have seen that in reality Brahmanism is not a single body. As Sir Henry Maine observes, its originality lies in its independence of any organization.[31] Not only do numerous castes continue to proliferate within the Brahman class, but also each Brahman, superman by birth, since he has need of no investiture, does not recognize in principle any superior hierarch. This mass of born-priests has nothing in common with a Church.[32]

But it is nevertheless true that as representatives *par excellence* of the noble race and models of Aryan purity, performers of the same ritual operations and commentators of the same revelation, these born-priests represent the same ideal and enjoy the same prestige. Thus, without being unified themselves, they were able to imprint upon India the only kind of unity that it could support.

The development of schools was not lacking in the culture of this religious tradition. To merit the title of Brahman it is necessary but not sufficient to be born of Brahman blood. Initiation which is a second birth is also necessary. Then comes the study of the sacred books. And since there are many such books, and many more commentaries upon them, specialist traditions developed which became centres for Brahman students.

No doubt groups of this kind gave birth to the codes which we know. Should we therefore speak of veritable schools of law? Were *charana* as numerous as Colebrooke thought and were they university-like organizations, similar to the schools of our middle ages? Or did they not, rather, preserve the form of a familial organization? Their tradition, conforming to the general demands of the system, may have had more in common with the secrets which fathers pass on to their sons.[33] We constantly find that we are dealing with traditions transmitted and commented upon by a whole series of specialists, and this trait can itself explain some of the characteristics of the Hindu codes. In Manu, in particular, Bühler points out repetitions and even contradictions resulting from a series of rehandlings. It is possible that beneath the Sastra that we know we could discover a Sutra going back to the Vedic sect of the Mānavas. Traditions pondered for so long could scarcely fail to end up as a refined and complicated body of law. The pleasure that the writers of these codes seem to take in distinctions, proportions and classifications of all sorts, has often been noted. Are we to take this as simply an endemic trait of the Hindu genius? Or are we to think that if it is preserved and developed through so many generations, the social reality which they have before their eyes, divided and graded as it is, must be responsible in part. Be that as it may, the hot-house of the Brahmanic Schools must have been favourable to this exuberant growth of classifications.

The same professional milieu would lend itself to the discovery of those nuances that our historians of law admire, for example in the matter of assessing responsibilities in cases of recidivism or when there is a question of taking intentions into account.[34] Proof enough, as Thonissen said, 'that from far off times the banks of the Ganges were the scene of long juridical meditations'. Ordinarily the offended gods strike out blindly; to turn aside their vengeance people will, as indeed the Athenians did, prosecute inanimate objects. If despite its religious origins Hindu law is more supple and more subtle in these matters, it owes this perhaps to the reflections of specialists who were able to give it the benefit of the progress in their beliefs. In this connection the last book of Manu reveals a preoccupation which was already 'spiritual'. It is not surprising that they were willing to weigh the intentions of those who add to the number of sins the evil thoughts themselves, and to rise from considerations of an entirely material purity to an interior purity. We must add that the doctrine of transmigration while in intimate harmony with the caste system,[35] relates at the same time to a sense of the responsibilities of individuals. In telling man that his present situation depends upon his past acts just as his future situation will depend upon his present acts, it deprives him, no doubt, of the desire to protest against social inequalities, but it propagates the idea that at least within his own class, each should be judged according to his works; in this way it assists law to rid itself decisively of the doctrine of collective responsibility.

From this one can measure the great distance that the Brahmanic priesthood was able to carry Hindu law from its primitive stages. The most ancient form of justice is the vengeance inflicted by one group on another. At this period there is, properly speaking, no public crime; in killing a man, for example, or violating a woman, a member of one clan has damaged another clan; the latter will seek to rectify this damage by action directed not only at this member in particular, but at any member whatsoever of the offending clan. Other groups do not intervene.

To define this situation it has been proposed that these primitive delicts appear to be civil delicts rather than criminal ones. The justiciary which is also the offending group, caring little about an *animus delinquendi*, calls before all else for the reparation of a wrong, even an unintentional one. This assimilation lays itself open to ambiguity if it is true that the avengers feel obliged to act either because of the thirst for blood that they attribute to the menacing ghost of the victim, or as a result of a more complex feeling of solidarity which orders them to compensate at any price for the loss that the group has suffered; if, in other words, it is not only an instinctual cruelty, but an imperative of a religious nature which arms the familial, judiciary 'self'.[36] But at this period there is, above the conflicting clans, no sentiment of a public which could intervene to regulate and limit their vengeance, or to punish offences that they leave unpunished. Again, it is religion, but a wider religion going beyond familial limits which can shape this sentiment. It extends the net of its ritual interdictions. It attaches to the act of homicide, even committed within the family, the idea of a defilement that must, at all cost, be washed away. Its representatives, initially chosen as arbitrators, become advisers on law whose answers carry authority. Recently it has been shown that even in Greece, the land most opposed to theocracy, if there was no priestly power to monopolize the law, it was at least religion, calling down excommunication on violations of the divinely appointed order, which filled the gap between the period of family vengeance and that of prosecution by the state.[37] We see religion absorb the greater part of the familial *themis* to transmit it to the social *dike*: by disengaging the individual from the group it constitutes new delicts and at the same time new procedures. In the history of almost all civilizations, the same phenomenon is apparent; it has been maintained that not only among the Hebrews or among the Muslims, but even among the Germans and Romans, a priestly jurisprudence laid the base of all laws.[38]

At first sight it seems that this conquest of religious public law over religious familial law must come up against particular difficulties in India: caste is, after all, a sort of crystallization of the earlier family groupings and, on the other hand, the religion of the Brahmans was never able to organize itself as a public religion. But we have already seen how the attractive force of Brahmanism is powerful enough to take the place of the most efficient mechanisms. Under the influence of its doctrine of pollution it certainly seems that the family groups, however 'communistic' their tendencies, completely abandoned the notion of collective responsibility at the same time that they abdicated their right to vengeance. Nor is there any question, in India, of their not having exercised this right in primitive times: contrary to what was earlier thought, the Vedas have preserved a picture of *wergeld* instituted as always to halt the anger of groups while indemnifying them.[39] But it is true that very soon pecuniary compensations go to the Brahman. Just as he sits at the funeral feast in the place of the dead relatives whose shades are believed to stand behind him, so he substitutes himself for the offended family by collecting the reparation.[40] These are significant delegations: without breaking the family circles and without making them interpenetrate, Brahmanism found the way to make them all gravitate around itself. Thanks to the prestige of their priests, the Hindus had never to look for occasional arbitrators to settle their differences, as happened in other countries.[41] More divine than the Brehons of Ireland, and representatives of a tradition that they alone had the right to interpret, the Brahmans had all the necessary qualities to lift Hindu law to its second phase, and to establish, on the basis of religion alone, a kind of public vengeance in place of the private vengeance of the primitive collectivities.

Ordinarily, however, this is only a transitory phase. Religion, as M. Glotz has said, governs the interim. Soon we see it give way to the power of the state, which, having the law in its hands, then adapts it to its own needs and practices. In emancipating it, the state emancipates itself: nothing like this occurred in India. Of the evolution of its law we may repeat what has been said of the whole development of the civilization: thanks to the caste system it was lifted rapidly out of barbarism, but any further growth was soon prevented. It is the victim of an arrested development; it is petrified, as it were, in an attitude elsewhere abandoned. Hindu law was to preserve its religious colouring precisely because no political power rose up to counterbalance the power of the priestly caste, because, as M. Weber has said, the *sacerdotium* was never contained within an *imperium*.

We have frequently said: in India there are no rudiments of the state. Even the idea of public power is alien to it.[42] But as M. Fick observes, we must not take these expressions too literally.[43] All sorts of authorities have tried to rule over these immense masses: the people have seen empires succeed each other and principalities multiply in a disorder without equal.[44] The truth remains that all governments of whatever kind, have only rested on the surface of the Hindu world. None struck down into its depths to reorganize it. Precisely because the Hindus live isolated in the compartments of their castes, they seem made for subjugation by the entire world, without being assimilated or unified by anyone.

Incapable as they are of coalescing for active resistance, each of their groups offers the passive resistance of its traditions to pressures from above. In other words – and we always return to this – India lacks the city: the city which alone can institute methodical relations between peoples and governments and whose working has, in short, directly or indirectly, provided the models and the principles of all our western states. For lack of such a gestation, Hindu society was never granted a truly political organization, and the religious tradition was able to dominate the whole.

This religious tradition needed the collaboration of a secular power in order to impose its principles. However lively the primitive faith in supernatural sanctions might be, everywhere the need is quickly felt for a visible and weighty power, capable of assisting the will of the gods in making itself respected, and in establishing the order which they prescribe by making up for their errors and omissions. 'The Brahman's weapon is the word.' But however fearsome his menaces and imprecations, they are not sufficient of themselves to maintain public order: temporal penalties and a power physically capable of applying them, are necessary. It is from this, most likely, that we have the growing insistence with which the Brahmanic codes remind the king of his judicial mission. In fulfilling it he earns as much merit as if he had performed a permanent sacrifice; but if he leaves the guilty unpunished, may he be purified by fast. The renown of the scrupulous guardian of the law spreads far 'like a drop of sesame oil in water'. But the name of the negligent shrinks and congeals 'like a drop of clarified butter'. Manu in particular multiplies his recommendations to the king, whom he deifies – it has been supposed that the text was prepared for the education of a young *rāja* – and we have seen that he presents all his laws as so many royal duties. In later codes, going by the number of crimes of lese-majesty against which they defend royalty, we feel the ever growing importance of the king in matters of justice.[45]

But this development derogates nothing from the superior function of the Brahman. Not only does he remain the indispensable auxiliary magistrate of the king, but also the recognized

132

authority in legal matters. Here we must recall M. Lambert's remark on the necessity, when following the evolution of juridical institutions, of distinguishing between the shield of the law and the implement which forges it – between those who impose the law and those who formulate it.[46] It certainly seems that the secular power in India systematically left the task of enunciating the law to the spiritual power; either because it was little concerned with the juridical order or because it could not find the necessary authority in itself to modify it. Sir Henry Maine tells of a Sikh chief who had succeeded in establishing his power over the Punjab: he limited his ambition to raising taxes, he felt no need to enact one law.[47] Elsewhere, in Nepal, we hear that when the princes felt the need to organize their kingdom against the Muslim invasion, they called in a team of Brahman jurisconsults who immediately set about dividing the kingdom into its appropriate sacred categories.[48] Royal functions then, however they may develop here or there, do not trespass upon the functions of the priest. Throughout the long story of this civilization we do not find those conflicts over privilege developing between the two principles of authority which, elsewhere, have often made for the emancipation of the masses. The rivalry of Brahman and Kshatriya may have been long and eventful. We are familiar with all the signs of this that have been collected not only from Buddhist tales, but also from the epics and even philosophic writings.[49] But contrary to what occurred in the west, in India it was the force of religion which decisively tipped the balance. This is why it has sometimes been said that Brahmanism was able to realize the ambitions of our own medieval Church more fully than that Church itself, and that nowhere other than in India can one see so tight a grip of Church over state.[50] A lame enough analogy, if it is true – as the preceding discussion reminds us – that neither the term state nor the term Church, as we understand them in the west, is appropriate to Hindu institutions. The expression at least conveys the idea of what priestly omnipotence must have been like in matters of law.

We have yet to understand the nature of this power, the limitations it has come up against, and the way in which it was achieved.

The supremacy of the Brahmans in matters of law would be a veritable miracle if their wishes did not more or less directly correspond with the wishes, more or less consciously maintained, of the population recognizing that supremacy. If their strength was not contained from above it was because it was no doubt maintained from below. What we must be in a position to understand more precisely is the degree and form of the spontaneous collaboration of groups in the working of law. We shall see perhaps that here as everywhere the secret of Brahman power is its tolerance, suppleness and plasticity.

We have already noted the welcoming indifference of the Brahman in religious matters. Who knows if, in matters of custom, his policy was not the same and whether he was not content, often, to bless already established usage?

We must not forget that caste, as the descendant of the familial group, jealously preserves a certain number of judicial attributes. If the Hindus seem to have lost the custom of collective vengeance between group and group very early, at least they have kept within each group the practice of prosecuting and executing their own guilty members. If the primitive forms of intertribal justice have disappeared, tribal justice has on the contrary been solidly maintained. We know for how long in all civilizations the elementary collectivities kept the right to chastise those of their members who, by polluting them with disorder, threatened their very integrity. And no chastisement was more terrible than expulsion. Left to depend on their own resources, the outlaw, the *isgoï* of the ancient Russians, the *abrek* of the Osetians, the 'wolf' of the Greeks – is exposed to every peril.[51] No one to aid him, no one to avenge him; 'he is a withered pear that falls from the tree unnoticed'.[52] The Hindu who pollutes his caste is exposed to a comparable excommunication. We are told that still today nothing is more feared, or at least in the countryside, nothing is more terrible in its consequences than this solemn execution before the assembled caste.[53]

We have seen that the Brahmanic codes have not preserved a mere memory of these judicial attributes of caste; they take great account of them. The expressions which they use recall that it was in relation to the caste, ever ready to brandish the whip of excommunication over the sinner, that sins were originally defined: *pataniya, atipātaka, mahāpātaka, anupātaka* are so many faults which expose the sinner to exclusion from caste.[54] And further, the codes keep this very exclusion as a perpetually suspended threat. It is the supreme sanction and the prospect of it forces the wrong doer to bow to the application of yet others. To avoid this one sanction he must deliver himself to the rod, suffer hunger, pay fines. In the background of the jural scene behind the lifted finger of the Brahman we see not only the armed strength of the king, but the outraged tumult of the caste, ready to assemble and to rise up against the rebel and to reduce him to reason.

If Brahmanic law anticipates in this way the co-operation of the caste's judicial power we may suppose that it is very far from minimizing the decisions of this power, the precedents according to which it acts and the customs which it wishes to have respected. Sir Henry Maine compares the smallness and rigidity of caste with our own vast and vague classes. In the caste the sons systematically inherit their fathers' places and at the same time their beliefs, and are grouped around the *panchayat* which supervises them. He points out what a strong organ for the preservation of customary law such small bodies must be, and with what rigour they must cling to their immemorial traditions.[55]

In fact castes cling, as to a very condition of their existence, not only to the prohibitions which separate them but to the singularities which distinguish them. From this point of view the violation of some custom which seems insignificant to us, is in their eyes a vital matter.[56] And does the written law of the Brahmans deny the authority of this tenacious customary law? Quite the contrary, it makes a point of recognizing it. Manu in several places recalls that a king can not do better than instruct himself in the different received usages, in order that he may respect them himself and have them respected.[57] By this is not meant what we would call local usage for, properly speaking, the *lex loci* does not exist in India:[58] each individual wherever he may migrate, carries with him the law of his group. It is the traditions of these various groups that the Smritis intend to recognize and bless. In point of fact, where the Brahmans expressly decline all legal intervention is in matters having to do with guilds of artisans or merchants: here less than elsewhere their theories cannot supplement the multiplicity of practices elaborated under the pressure of this or that economic situation.[59] But in a general way and in more numerous cases, it is clear that the written law is ready to bend before the diversity of custom. One has no impression, as Mayne says, of 'an atom of dogmatism':[60] the Brahmans show themselves ready to lend the support of their authority to a number of laws that they have not themselves formulated.

As for those which they have formulated, are they of their own devising or has their chief merit been that they have acted as recorders? Brahmanic pride will not admit such docility with ease.[61] But as bit by bit we accumulate from sources other than the Brahmanic tradition, greater and more precise information about the customs of the different castes, we are led to think that for the broad outlines of the law – in the matter, for example, of the indivisibility of property and the procedures for dealing with this, the rules of succession and adoption – the differences are negligible, the spirit is the same. Here also it was possible to abstract the *koinous nomous* of the ancient familial groupings. The Brahmans were able to accomplish this work of generalization in their codes, by setting in relief the customs shared by the Aryan clans. Thereafter juridical thought would go further and recognize that on a number of points the customs of the non-Aryans coincided with those of the others.[62] The Brahmans would have energetically rejected some indigenous practices, such as polyandry, which were decidedly contrary to the ideal they represented. For the rest they had but to compose a *corpus* of traditions common to all the groups, Aryan and non-Aryan, juxtaposed on Hindu soil.

In the process of wrapping these customs in the cloak of religion and, to borrow the language of *Senchus Mor*, adjusting their 'law of the letter' to this 'law of nature', the Brahmans could not fail to modify in some way the existing law, to refine certain customs, and interpret others in a particular way in conformity with the suggestions of their own interests or the demands of their ideal. Thus they have been accused of more or less directly opposing the principle of indivisibility, encouraged by the hope of multiplying the number of separate domestic hearths which would give rise to greater demands for their sacrificial functions. Over the law of succession in determining the order of preferred heirs, they were to lay special insistence on the capacity of the latter to please the spirits of the ancestors by sacrifice.[63]

Nothing is more difficult to establish than the extent to which these truly Brahmanic prescriptions were accepted by the host of castes. Sometimes it has been noticed that they have adopted some Brahmanically conceived custom while at the same time stripping off and letting go the religious wrappings that the Brahmans had given it.[64] Elsewhere the Brahmans' prestige is so powerful that in order to resemble and approximate to them, castes take on some new restrictions, or practise some rites which do not appear to derive from their pre-existing traditions.[65] The most representative frame of mind is that expressed in the reply given to the English investigators when they asked about law: 'We follow the customs of our ancestors; when we cannot agree on custom we consult the Brahman'.[66] The Brahmans appear then as born arbitrators. No doubt they are so considered for their familiarity with the past and as the appointed guardians of both the general order and the particular traditions of each group. If their opinion is manifestly contrary to the ancient habits of castes would not the latter, disconcerted, hesitate to apply it? Be that as it may, if the Brahmanic codes are tacitly accepted in their broad outlines by the mass of castes from the Himalayas to Cape Comorin this dominance has no doubt been facilitated by the fact that they overlook customs peculiar to each, where they exist, while on the other hand they retain and consecrate those which are common to all.

Perhaps in this way we can solve the vexing question: what are the real imperatives, practical efficacity, real vitality of the Brahmanic codes? For too long we have been led to think of them as promulgated and applied in the manner of the Napoleonic code. Now we finally understand that for a code proper to come into existence and thrive there must necessarily be a combination of extremely complex political conditions, and precisely the conditions which were lacking in India. All that we have said about the way in which the Brahmanic codes must have been composed enables us to understand why, to use the words of M. Barth, they constitute a body of literature not of legislation. Private works, manuals for students, they describe perhaps the priestly ideal, but in no way guarantee to enfold reality. Following this line Mr Nelson is led to conclude that the least fault of 'Hindu law' is that, in truth, it only exists in the imagination of Brahmans and their dupes – the European philosophers.[67]

Closer attention to Hindu life allows us to move, today, towards a middle position. In fact, although the Brahmanic codes were never promulgated properly speaking, the majority of their prescriptions enjoyed an uncontested authority over the great mass of the Hindu population. Perhaps this authority is explained by precisely the method of tolerance and conciliation that we have stressed. Of this law also we can say that it leads to the extent that it has followed.

A recent theory, developed against the excesses of juridical romanticism, tries to show that wherever we are invited to admire some customary law, as springing from the unanimous and spontaneous practice of the people concerned, one can discover the patient work of religious jurisprudence.[68] It is not the slow and insensible labour of the collective consciousness, but rather the successive intuitions of inspired individuals that has evolved laws. Let us therefore, it is argued, stop opposing jurisprudence and custom: the latter is only the alluvion of the former. At first sight no case could have appeared more favourable to this theory than the one we have studied, if it is true that nowhere is there a more revered body of wise law-givers, than the Brahman castes. But if our latest observations are correct, even these demi-gods have acted more as depositaries than as creators. Innumerable collectivities, whose very constitution predisposed them to the maintenance of tradition, brought them their ready-made bundles of customs, that they, for their part, were most often content to accumulate and, in the process, consecrate.

The same analysis will perhaps help us to understand better why, generally, Hindu penal law speaks so firmly and strikes so hard.

Indeed it would seem that we have already furnished an explanation when we ran through the reasons why the whole of Hindu life is still hemmed in by religion. Can we not point to a constant relation between the preponderance of religious conceptions and the stringency of a penal code?[69] It is natural that where offences appear to be violations of the divine order they should evoke a sacred horror and that they should be repressed with unmitigated rigour.

But is this explanation sufficient? First of all could not religion keep her right hand on institutions and progressively employ less heavy threats? It is true that primitive beliefs 'react' with a sort of blind brutality, but since Hindu religion tended to a certain ethical evolution, since we can see a kind of progress in the tradition of its jurist-priests which is apparent in the refinement of certain concepts, we may wonder why this progress was not reflected in some attenuation of the punishments. We have yet to show what power was opposed to any such moderation.

Generally speaking it is not sufficient, when we are accounting for the characteristics of an institution, to show that it is enveloped by religion. Whence does it derive this halo that men see around it? What urges them to regard it as sacred? On these points we would like more light.

Besides, more complex explanations have been offered based on the volume and the severity of penal law. A constant relation between the harshness of penalties and the very structure of society itself has been indicated. The body of punishments is much more rich when societies are less complicated, less differentiated, less organized and when, at the same time we find a greater concentration of governmental force. On the one hand a very simple social type and on the other a central, absolute power, these are the two pillars of barbarian repressive systems. It is when these two conditions are united that the collective conscience is the most demanding; it demands a religious respect for the established social order and defends that order with the most cruel punishments.[70] To what extent does this theory accord with the respective situations of law and the caste system in India?

At first sight the discordance seems striking. Must we repeat that the very notion of state is absent in India, and that it has little conception of the power of a central government? Again, can we call Hindu society with its multiplicity of specialized, mutually repelling, superimposed groups, a simple and undifferentiated society?

But perhaps the objection rests upon a certain number of misunderstandings that we can now clarify. It is important to understand that when one speaks of a strong central power, as one of the causes of the ferocity of law, one does not have in mind a complex, extended government, with various and numerous functions operating at every point of the body social. Absence of limitation and counterbalance – that is the essence of absolutism. We have seen that precisely this condition was realized, better than anywhere else, in India. The very disunion to which castes condemned themselves left the field clear for any despot, large or small; the weight of their hand encountered no resistance.

Furthermore, to say strong government is not to think only of secular power. If it is true that this had little hold on Hindu society and leaves no profound mark, we have on the other hand measured the extent to which this society lends itself to the grip of religious power. All lacking in organization as it might be, the class of priests was able to impose upon the masses a respect never enjoyed by the best armed tyrant. All the *tabus* which in primitive society make a king at once adored and feared, a kind of man-god,[71] are concentrated on the sacrosanct person of the Brahman; no *mana* can rival that attributed to him. His prestige serves as a centre for the divided society which he dominates. The lines of power flowing from him order the myriad castes around him. And is it not a crime tantamount to blasphemy to violate the prescriptions sanctioned by such an authority, sufficient to call down the heaviest punishments? Against the severity of this absolutism there was no democracy in India which could raise the voice of 'philanthropy'.

That, on the contrary castes were ready to promote this severity, and the reasons for their voluntary co-operation with this rigorous repression, we can also understand. If the specialization of these closed groups has produced a form of division of labour in Hindu society, the phenomenon has nothing in common with that free and progressive differentiation that we see, for example, in our own societies.[72] Thanks to this, the independence of individuals has been born and the control of the collective has declined. This in no way resembles India where the specialized caste keeps its members immobile, locked close within the circle of hereditary custom and occupation. No more favourable milieu could be found for that unanimity of feeling, that intolerance of any divergence; which normally expresses itself in the sacrosanct character of custom and in the cruelty of punishments. The elementary collectivities whose juxtaposition forms the caste system belong in fact to a very simple social type. Their internal differentiation is minimal; it is not surprising that within each one the collective conscience is imperiously preponderant.

But when it is a matter of the relations between these elementary groups amongst themselves and the regulations which establish these relations, can we still speak of a collective conscience demanding a system of severe penalties to assure respect for these rules? If the constituent elements of the system strive to lie each one in its moral isolation and refuse any kind of unification, whence does the law which determines their relations derive its rigour? It is precisely because this multitude of circles meet at the same point. The distinct collective consciences have a certain number of common elements, and are agreed on certain sentiments. And they are those upon which their very separation rests. They all admit, more or less explicitly, that bloods should not be mixed, nor ranks confused. If it is true, in general, that a Hindu knows nothing of the customs of castes other than his own, at least it is for all an article of faith that there are and should be castes, and that before all else the order which keeps them distinct in their hierarchy should be respected.

No doubt this immobility is relative and on many points more apparent than real. Just as mixtures are not totally avoided, so distance is not always kept. We see more than one caste achieve, little by little, and with the strength of tenacious ambition, a higher rank in the hierarchy. But here we must repeat that there are some rules that continue to be respected even at the very moment of their violation. A misalliance is disguised, a rise in status is presented as a restoration to a tradition now better understood. Everything will be done, finally, to procure the absolution and the blessing of the Brahman, guardian of the whole system, the solid and living support of those sentiments which the system maintains and which maintain the system.[73]

The lack of the very notion of patriotism in Hindu society has frequently been noted. Everything that we have said about the normal effect of caste, 'the most active principle of disintegration that the world has ever known' helps us to understand this lack. But if our latest remarks are correct, a sort of substitute for national sentiment can be found in this same society: it is precisely the common attachment of these elementary groups to the traditional order which juxtaposes them. For this reason we have said that respect for the caste system is the patriotism of the Hindus. They enact a paradox in that they can only unite in the cult which divides them.

Within these limits it is permissible to speak of intense collective sentiments which emerge above the mass of castes. And we must not lose sight of these sentiments if we wish to understand why and to what point Brahmanic law, with the characteristics which we have recognized, plunges its roots into the centre of the Hindu soul.

3

Economic life: consumption

To what extent can the caste system work upon economic life? What forms do production, circulation and consumption assume in a society where men are divided and, so to speak, penned up in small groups which at the same time are hereditarily specialized and hierarchically superimposed the one on the other? If we want to answer this question from direct observation, we have only to look to Hindu civilization; there pre-eminently we have found, preserved or developed through the centuries, the hereditary differentiation, the reciprocal repulsion and sacred hierarchy which are the characteristics of the caste system.

In fact Sir Henry Maine pointed out a long time ago that we could see in India the tyrannical dominance of all sorts of influences that the economists are for the most part content to regard as negligible quantities and which they put down to 'friction'.*[1] According to Mr Ranade what is particularly instructive about the economic life of India is that it does not seem to realize a single one of the 'postulates' of western classical political economics.[2]

Unfortunately we know how jealously Hindu civilization preserves the secrets of its history, and particularly of its economic history. Already in the west, if for example we want to trace the evolution of a form or system of production, documents are often lacking; learned research has still not provided all the answers to sociological inquiries. Imagine the situation in the east, especially the Hindu east! Here for immense areas and indefinite periods we have, often, only such evidence as 'literature' provides: a literature whose offerings, already difficult to date, most

* See L. Dumont, 'The Village Community', in *Contributions to Indian Sociology*, IX, 1966, p. 81 fn.

probably – as everyone nowadays agrees – express a priestly ideal rather than a social reality. On a few, all too rare points, the reports of foreign visitors to India throw a still inadequate light. Inscriptions might give more precise details, but the classification of those which have so far been collected, is scarcely begun.

Despite this dearth of information it is perhaps possible, and not without value to offer some overall judgements upon the economic life of India. Here we would not pretend to precision as to the particular traits of different periods in its evolution, but to single out the most general, those, for example which, to the extent that they are opposed to types of economic organization with which we in the west are familiar, characterize the type of economic organization which has dominated Hindu civilization. Even if a certain number of questions which we shall be led to ask remain unanswered, the attempt will at least have this advantage that it will draw specialist attention to the gaps in knowledge which impede sociological induction.

The first generalization that one most of all encounters in this field, is an entirely pessimistic one. The economic life of the Hindus? It has been reduced, they would have us believe, to the beggar's portion, forever oppressed and restricted by the exuberance of religious life of which the caste system is only an off-shoot. The antithesis is classical. Since Max Müller, the activity of the Aryans of the west has frequently been compared with the apathy of their Hindu brothers.[3] Just as, they say, the life of a Greek, for example, was full of reality, for the Hindu it is a deceptive illusion.

Isolated in that great peninsula, softened and enervated by a climate too hot for his race, concern for positive action never counterbalances the adventurous vitality of his imagination. Victim of the phantoms he has himself created, he turns away from the soil. In a sort of lethargic passivity he lets the days run by; a stranger to that sense of reality which makes a race strong, he is incapable of thinking for himself and of manly action.[4] If Brahmanism did not create it, it inevitably maintained and exploited this incapacity.[5] The religious hypnosis under which the Hindu lives is the surest guardian of the bastion of caste when the Brahman is the born master. In the order of economic as much as political action, the same obsessions could not fail to retard the progress of Hindu civilization.

However, is there no appeal against this verdict? From various points of view it seems that opinion is turning decisively against such simplifying pessimism. It is a mistake – M. Sylvain Lévi makes the point – to think of Hindu society as a nation of meta-physicians. Here, once again, we have perhaps been the dupes of the literature of priestly thinkers. We must not let this curtain prevent us from touching the more varied and active reality which it conceals.

Let us not stop at the collections of liturgical songs, philo-sophical discussions, or juridical texts; let us rather try to reach out to active life through the epics: Mr Hopkins helps us to feel here a breath of sensuality, brutality and materialism that takes us far from the transcendental dreams in which India is sup-posedly wrapt.[6] The philosophy of the prevailing tone here, he says, is the philosophy of soldiers much more than a philosophy of priests. The scenes of the epics often lead us to think of the Teutonic warrior. What is true of military action may also be true of economic action.

In fact the age-long reputation of India, land of fabulous treasure and inimitable marvels is a sufficient proof that the activity of its peoples was far from completely lulled to sleep by the prestige of its priests. For centuries the peoples of the west have looked to India as to the source of all riches. The very conquests that she has suffered – from the Persians and the Greeks to the French and the British – are tributes to this reputation. 'India, commonly represented as sunk in a wonderful dream, detached from the rest of the world, is in reality the vulgar prey of the cupidity of a fascinated world.'[7] And even in normal times did it live in the disdainful isolation that we imagine? It would appear that no country has maintained a more widespread or more intense commerce. We know that Pliny estimated the balance of trade between India and Rome at a hundred million sesterces. Long before the Romans the Hebrews received from India not only precious stones, gold, silver and ivory but also cotton and tin. Later the small Italian republics thrived on the import not only of spices and aromatics, but also India muslin, silk and shawls. The hope of establishing more direct relations with her stimulated the ardour of Columbus and Vasco da Gama. The land of castes can boast not only of its ideas but of the goods supplied to the world. Formerly it was claimed that India was the cradle of all myths known to us from that of Dionysus to the myth of Wotan. No doubt an excessive claim, remarks Lassen, but he adds that India can claim other glories of a more material nature. Was it not for long years the granary where the world sought rice, sugar and cotton?[8]

No doubt credit must be given for this commercial importance not only to the situation of India, intermediary between the west and the Far East, but also to the resources of its soil and climate which ensured a great variety of products.[9] It is, says Mr Buckingham, more owing to its rare vegetable products than its mineral riches that 'India owes the advantage of being, through almost all time, the source of mercantile prosperity and the home of commercial enterprises.'[10] It remains to be said, nevertheless, that these natural riches could not achieve value, organization and exchange by themselves; there was still a need for the activity, patience, and ingenuity of the inhabitants. Mr Hunter, summing up all that they have done to achieve so lustrous a name in such distant countries, is not afraid to speak of the industrial and commercial genius they have shown.[11]

Independently of these external proofs, we have more direct traces of the economic vitality of the Hindus and these we find in the sacred codes themselves. No doubt Hindu law, as we have just seen is always, in principle, a law of a religious nature. 'Repressive' regulations take precedence of 'restitutive' ones. The very nature of the penalties proposed demonstrates the continuously tight hold of ancient traditions on the Hindu conscience. But beneath this primitive vegetation, stronger in India than elsewhere, commercial law did not stop growing. We have only to count the number of regulations relating to finance, the government of markets, customs, loans and interest to have proof that economic life was not as extinct in India as they imagine who believe that India only lived in and for its religion.[12] If we look closely at these rules we see that, on the contrary they pre-suppose a fairly strong dose of economic 'experience' in the society for which they are devised. Production must have been sufficiently intense and varied for commerce to have become, quite early, a separate occupation. Its representatives, used to travelling from one part of India to another and speculating on variations in prices, also show themselves capable of combining in common enterprises. Finally, the kings are particularly charged with the maintenance of a certain degree of equilibrium between the interests of vendors and consumers.[13] In matters of communal enterprise it is understood that profits will be divided proportionately to the amounts of capital invested, losses carried by the author of the loss in a case of grave error, unworthy people excluded from profit-making, incapable ones replaced. The king is not only to watch over 'weights and measures' and the quality of merchandise; he is called upon to regulate prices after consultation with the merchants: the legitimate profit of the latter is fixed at 5 per cent for local merchandise and 10 per cent for imported merchandise; fines penalize all coalitions for raising the market.

We must add that over and above these more or less precise rules, the codes usually carry a general prescription recommending the king to bend before the law and custom of corporations. It is a striking proof, among many, of the considerable place that these had achieved. The Hindu guild watches over the government of markets, organizes convoys, and gives its name to foundations. From very early on it emerges as one of the best established powers in society.

From all this we see that the caste system in no way stopped the economic life of the Hindus. Far from opposing the formation of the institutions which that life necessitates, it prepared for them. Far from raising dikes it opened up canals. Diodorus claimed that Egypt owed its prosperity to the organization of society into castes.[14] Would this not be still more true of India, where this same organization is found in more perfect form?

We must leave these generalities and, before balancing advantages and disadvantages, by a more analytic method take note first of all of the distinctive colouring of the different aspects of economic life in India under the caste system.

Effects of the system

The imprint of caste is most apparent on habits of consumption. In whatever quarter we look for the origin or origins of the caste system, we are agreed today that it is an essentially religious institution.[15] Sentiments of a religious nature sustain and maintain it: a kind of sacred horror, fear of committing a degrading sin, prevents the communion, mixing or contact of races, just as it hinders or delays changes of profession. The degrees of purity mark most clearly those of the social hierarchy: the greater or lesser degree of intimacy that their members have with the born-priest, establishes the rank of castes. We must not suppose that these sentiments arising from the small, closed, specialized and hierarchically organized groups that make up Hindu society are a consequence and, as it were, an epiphenomenon of religious life in India: they are rather its essence, they form the kernel of it. It has been noted frequently that however tolerant and fluid Hindu religion may be over questions of dogma, it is strict and definite over questions of practice, and the practices most close to its heart are precisely those that make for the survival of the caste system. What the Brahman teaches most clearly of all is respect for this system and the cult of his own superiority.[16]

If this interpenetration of a religious tradition and a social system does not at all predestine the Hindus to become a race of theologians speculating on the infinite, it must nevertheless encumber their daily life with all sorts of scruples. For this reason it is most likely that the influence of religious beliefs on modes of consumption, and, what one might call the 'commands' that they, directly or indirectly, lay on production itself, will be particularly in evidence in India.

In this sense it is permissible to maintain that, in India, all the arts, even the most industrial ones, have had to submit their products to the requirements of religion. It is not for nothing that Mr Birdwood opens his book, *The industrial arts of India*, with a brief resume of Hindu beliefs. 'In their traditional art', he writes:

There is nothing which does not have a practical end in view, nothing which does not have religious significance. A religious rule settles the material, the weight and colour of the different articles. A symbolism yet more obscure than that of colour and material is hidden in the forms of objects, even of those destined for the most common domestic use.[17]

148

Economic life: consumption

Recently we have discovered the meticulous symbolism which governs not only the general structure of our cathedrals but even the smallest detail of their decoration. In India, a more informed science might make analogous discoveries about the simplest and humblest objects: the Hindu religion is the most tyrannical and at the same time the most domestic of religions; it governs all the acts of daily life in the heart of every family.

It is in matters of food above all that the influence of caste is so striking. But it is not surprising when we recall that caste has been described as 'a matter of eating together'. Among very different races – among the Semites as well as the Aryans – we find in the very earliest time, the institution of 'sacrificial feasts'.[18] The meat is at once an offering to the ancestors and a confirmation of the kinship uniting the living: literally, it is a communion bringing together selected people who, by birth, have the right to eat certain foods prepared according to traditional rites. Caste in India retains and reinforces the exclusiveness of the primitive family. To avoid pollution at the time of eating is an important matter for the Hindu. To eat with, or even in the presence of, a stranger, or worse, to eat food which he has touched, are so many unpardonable sins.

From this fear of sins of the mouth are born all sorts of more or less complicated precautions, not only governing the eating but also the preparation of the meal, which is a kind of sacred act. We have already quoted the Hindu sayings: 'For twelve Rajputs – thirteen cooks.' 'For three Kanauja Brahmans, you need thirty hearths.' This concern for purity makes for a formidable consumption of earthenware vessels, from which derives the importance of the potter, the regular supplier to the community. Silvain Lévi here reports: 'The accumulated debris of pottery and the mass of clay pots drying in the sun, mark the entrance of every Hindu village'.[19] It is natural that rules governing purity in eating will be most strictly observed in the higher castes; they owe, after all, part of their prestige to their scrupulous observance of these rules. The decline of this or that group is often explained by the single fact that they have neglected them. A Brahman, guilty of such shortcomings, is the victim of bitter remorse. The Jatakas tell of a Brahman so appalled at learning that he had eaten food

tasted by a Chandala that after vomiting such nauseous nourish-
ment, he starved himself to death.[20]

But we must not suppose that scruples of this order were
limited to the Brahman caste. They are found sometimes even
amongst the lowest castes. For in that hierarchy which is the
Hindu world, mutual repulsion separates the elements. Even the
most universally despised jealously isolate themselves from those
who are universally recognized as superiors. Max Müller, in this
connection observes

There is a principle of reciprocity in caste. Do not believe that the rich can
visit the poor, nor the poor the rich, nor that a Brahman can invite a Sudra
to dine and not be invited in his turn. Nobody in India is humiliated by his
caste and the lowest *pariah* is as proud of his own and as anxious to preserve
it as the Brahman of highest rank. The Tunas (of the Sudra class) consider
their houses to be polluted and throw away their cooking utensils if a
Brahman enters.

Indeed during the famine of 1874, rather than accept food at the
hand of Brahmans, some Santals died of starvation at the door of
the relief kitchens.[21]

What is important in Hindu tradition is not only the quality of
the company but also the quality of the food itself. One cannot
eat indifferently with anyone and no more can one indifferently
eat anything. Some foods are *tabu* either for the population at
large, or more particularly for a certain class. We know that in
several countries certain foods are exclusively reserved and others
specially prohibited to certain sections of the population. It seems
that this regulation is most often linked with totemic beliefs:
a plant or an animal is sacred in the eyes of those who are believed
to be descended from it. Such people may not touch it, let alone
eat it on peril of death. Frazer has shown what influence such
beliefs can exercise, through eating habits, on the productive
system itself, on cultivation and rearing, by safeguarding some
species at the expense of others. In India it is apparently only
among the non-aryan tribes living on the confines of Hindu
civilization that we can find these beliefs in their pure state. But
we find traces of them among the Aryans also, both in the names
of Brahmanic *gotrā* and as in the cult objects of certain castes.[22]
May they not have influenced the nature of the foods forbidden
to the different castes?[23]

Indeed if we examine the scruples of this caste or that on this matter, we shall find, as so often, that a unifying current passes beneath the individualities, it flows from the universal prestige of the Brahmans, who still embody an ideal of Aryan purity. Following their example many castes at the same time that they adopt the cult of the cow – which together with respect for the Brahman is, we are told, the clearest characteristic of Hinduism – also limit themselves, in different degrees, to vegetarianism which the Brahmans, faithful to their doctrine of *ahimsa*, which forbids the taking of the smallest life, have made their own strict law. Thus religious beliefs have reduced the range of consumption more or less strictly for all castes. And they respect the traditional prohibitions in this matter with an obstinacy stronger than that of the family itself. From this point of view we can say that the scruples of the caste system contribute to diminish the resources of the population. Sir Henry Maine writes of that rejection of meat and drink which still limits the food supply of an over-populated country, and contributes to its periodical famines.[24] We should add that as Hindu beliefs elevate above all else the desire for posterity to ensure the performance of the essential cult of the ancestors, they favour the practice of infant marriage. Thus 'while it tends to increase the number of persons born, it limits the supply of food which might sustain life. Nobody can precisely say what is the capacity of the soil of India for supporting a great population, for the superstitions of the vast majority will not allow animals to be bred or killed for food.'[25] If we add (Maine's observation)* that the same system looks disfavourably on emigration, by which the surplus population might be drawn off, we must conclude that in fact this system, working as it does to increase the disproportion between the average quantity of subsistence and the population rate, is partially responsible for the economic rack on which India lives, shaken by the paroxysms of periodic famine.

But caste is not only a 'matter of eating together', it is also and more importantly, as we have seen, a 'matter of marriage'. Traditional beliefs not only encourage infant marriage – a good Hindu counts himself dishonoured if he keeps his children un-

---

* The passage from Maine concludes: 'Nor will the population emigrate.'

married for too long – they also impose the rule of endogamy upon marriage. A young Hindu must look for a wife outside his family but within his caste. Marriage is then, here more than elsewhere, a religious act in whose consummation the whole social order is concerned. On the occasion of marriage, a caste becomes conscious of its unity and rejoices in its continuity. This, no doubt, explains the ostentatious pomp with which these ceremonies are celebrated. Every traveller has been struck by the luxury which men of the humblest castes believe themselves obliged to display on these occasions;[26] there is, as we have seen, no caste so poor that it does not protect its collective self-respect and whose members would not wish to be well turned out on these holy days. We have here, we are told, a real social danger. 'Marriages are often the ruin of families.' The decennial reports of the Civil Service draw attention to this. 'The Hindu peasants incur excessive expenses for all family ceremonies. Vanity is involved in these demonstrations, and the more they are exaggerated, the more orthodox does a man believe himself to be'.[27]

Ostentatious expense must in a more general way, moreover, come quite high in the budget of the poorest families. Mr Monier Williams describes the dress of children that he saw in Bombay, the embroidered silks and satins that they wore, the jewels glittering at their wrists or ankles. Similarly the women wear a profusion of bracelets and rings of silver and gold; sometimes a small ornament in the nose of five or six pearls with an emerald in the centre. Seeing all this wealth which they carry on them it is difficult to believe, the author adds, in the poverty of India.*[28] In fact, most often it is the entire wealth of the family which is displayed in ornaments instead of being frozen in the vaults of a bank. This is, no doubt, why the goldsmith, even in the most modest villages, is almost as necessary a figure as the potter. Independently of the innate taste for finery common to some races, this special habit of luxury is maintained in India by the particular nature of the hierarchy which 'leaves almost everyone

* This astonishing statement must be treated with reserve. The observation was no more generally true of Bombay then than it is today and is a reflection upon Monier Williams' judgement.

some one else to despise' and which allows each group, however despised it may be by others, to preserve its own grain of vanity.

In other ways the play of vanity and its economic repercussions must encounter strict limits in India. In particular, what place has Hindu society for fashion and the variations which it naturally imposes on consumption? Where the innovation of the superior is soon adopted by the inferior, the superior seeks once more for distinguishing features. The widening movement of imitation makes the need for new originality more acute and there results a sort of spiral where appetite turns more and more rapidly in the pursuit of the novel. It goes without saying that in India the general fragmentation of society into opposed and superimposed groups would be particularly unfavourable to such a movement. Where the caste system reigns the empire of custom, which forces us to imitate our ancestors, opposes the inroads of fashion which invites us to imitate strangers. The entire society is immobilized, as much as a society could be, in a consecrated frame. It is not then surprising if laws and manners conspire to repress those who would change their positions and, by imitating their superiors too closely, expose the public to vexatious confusions over caste. The codes consecrate the numerous prescriptions on dress and insignia – belts, badges and buttons – of different castes. In practice great store is set by these exterior distinctions which have 'the invaluable advantage of preventing painful confusions'. Even wealth above the ordinary does not enable members of a despised caste to usurp certain reserved luxuries. In the south, the Shanars, despite their accumulated wealth, are excluded from the right to carry an umbrella, to wear gold ornaments, or to build houses of more than one storey.[29] The Abbé Dubois tells us what disputes and scuffles result when these rules are violated: 'Perhaps the sole cause of the conflict is the right to wear slippers or to ride through the streets in a palanquin or on horseback during marriage festivals.'[30] He describes the near riot which arose when a Chuckler, a cobbler, appeared with red flowers in his turban at a public ceremony.* Similarly in Nepal, M. Sylvain Lévi reports that the law forbade the Podhyas to wear

* The wearing of red flowers was objected to by the Pariahs as an exclusive privilege of the Right Hand faction.

the national headgear: jackets, shoes and gold ornaments were equally forbidden them. The Kasais were obliged to wear clothes without sleeves. Neither one nor the other, nor also the Kullus, was allowed a tiled roof.[31] Sumptuary *tabus* together with alimentary *tabus* have then been preserved in India longer than elsewhere: the social organization repudiates all that might favour the obliteration of degree, the mixture of blood and the confusion of groups.

We can easily gauge the importance of this system of preventive prohibitions when we recall the social causes connected with a phenomenon which in its turn produces an acceleration of industrial and commercial progress: the development and the refinement of demand at various levels of a population. To explain this it is not sufficient to take account, as does M. Durkheim of the pressure exercised by social density on the collectivity of individuals.[32] By obliging them to engage in a more active struggle for life, this pressure, he argues, over-excites their organisms which thus become more delicate and demand all sorts of new refinements. It is useful to add to this socio-physiological explanation a psycho-physiological one. M. Gurewitsch has rightly observed that it is difficult to account for the conversion of luxuries into needs, by the struggle for life alone.[33] The struggle for social power is much more responsible than the struggle for life pure and simple, in the way that it stimulates the superior to prove their superiority by all sorts of ostentatious consumption. It is thus that the greater part of the needs which distinguish the civilized are born: if these needs are universalized, if objects initially created for the benefit of the mighty become also objects of prime necessity for the masses, it is because the inferior, in their turn, set their self-respect to follow the example of their superiors.

This first phase of this process was not lacking in Hindu civilization. If its born-priests disdained the pomps of wealth, its *rājas* have a distinguished place in the history of luxury.[34] The reputation for luxury which Hindu society has, derives, no doubt, from the wonders amassed and proudly displayed in the courts of its princes on festival days. But if needs multiplied or became more refined in this way in the privacy of the court, the fragmentation of Hindu society prevented this movement from becoming general and from descending, bit by bit. The newly rich is not free here to rival the noble; India would not recognize the character of the parvenu. No doubt, despite all this, wealth here as elsewhere gave individuals a certain upwards movement; but here, more rapidly than elsewhere this movement is arrested by a mass of converging traditions. The prospect for personal ambition is soon cut short. Forbidden to hope that social distinction might be forgotten, ambition itself loses the purpose of its existence.

In other words the law of 'social capillarity'[35] cannot operate freely in this atmosphere: it lacks that perpetual mass effort towards 'distinguished' expenditure which, if it finally wears down and burns out the race, at least incites the greatest possible number of individuals to go to their limit and at once intensifies, as it diversifies, production by more numerous and more varied demand.

4

Economic life: production

What have been the effects of the caste system, not only on habits of consumption but on the system of production?

It is sometimes said that the division of labour is the very soul of caste organization: it is precisely because different races were early specialized according to their aptitudes, under the rule of *karmabheda*, that Hindu civilization was able to achieve so high a degree of industrial perfection.[1]

But what kind of division of labour are we talking about? What was the model and what were the pressures for the sharing out of tasks in India? In what direction and within what limits could its effects operate? In short, what are the distinctive forms, conditions and consequences of a division of labour that goes hand in hand with the parcelling out of society in little groups, jealously closed and at the same time rigorously hierarchized? What is the result of professional specialization thus reflected by a social differentiation?

Historians and theoreticians of political economy are nowadays agreed: we must first of all carefully distinguish the different forms of the division of labour that Adam Smith's analysis confuses when it heaps together manufactured pins, blacksmith's nails and the dress of the journeyman.[2] In addition to the phenomenon of the distinction of professions, or specialization, in the true sense – the example being that of a man who makes it his business to produce a single category of objects – we have to classify separately the *decomposition of operations* – here the product passes from hand to hand to receive its different forms within the same establishment – and finally, *the division of production* – where different enterprises collaborate not only to make but also to transport and market objects.

Economic life: production

From the definitions themselves we can easily see which form of the division of labour holds in India. It could not be the division of production which calls for a very complicated industrial and commercial organization, nor the decomposition of operations which requires the concentration of large numbers of workers in the same establishment. It is rather the distinction of professions, specialization in the true sense. In this area the Hindus seem to have pushed the divisions and sub-divisions as far as they could go. Occupations are differentiated not only according to the objects which they produce but also according to the instruments used to produce them: the slightest potentiality for monopoly is piously exploited. We find clear-cut distinctions already established in the most primitive occupations. The fishermen who use nets and creels, and those who use line and bait belong to two separate categories. Among hunters there are distinctions between those who hunt beasts, those who hunt birds and even those who hunt quail. The agriculturalists have long been separated from the pastoralists, despite the well-known advantages springing from the alliance of cultivation and animal rearing.[3] In the artisan groups, as might be expected, the instinct for sub-division is allowed yet greater play. Those who make turbans wish to have nothing in common with the makers of sashes; the caste that repairs shoes takes care not to make any.

There are sometimes specializations involving the decomposition of operations: we are told, for example, of three distinct operatives collaborating in the making of bows and arrows.[4] But, in classical India, we rarely come across a distribution of work in the hands of workers brought together by the same enterprise or a transmission of objects or materials from one enterprise to another. But are not these two phenomena those that one has principally in mind when one praises the economic benefits of the division of labour 'the creator of general affluence'? It is only where effort is broken up and the production divided that economies of all sorts occur – of time, space, industrial plant, technical apprenticeship – which allow the largest possible number of objects to come into the market at the least possible expense.

But if we look at this from the point of view of quality rather than that of quantity – from the point of view of antiquity, follow-

ing Marx's dictum, not from the point of view of modernity –
could it not be held at least that professional specialization, as it
is sanctified by the caste system, is well suited to use, reinforce
or refine by use the various aptitudes of races in the best interests
of all?

It is important to note at this point that one runs the risk of
serious misapprehension about the consequences and conditions
of the division of labour, if one continues to believe that wherever
it is found it models itself, in some way, on the given diversity of
natural aptitudes. According to this view, the principal *raison
d'être* and primary advantage of the division of labour would, in
fact be, according to John Stuart Mill, that it 'classifies individuals according to their capacities'. Experience is far from confirming this optimistic conjecture. Spencer himself is obliged to
recognize that the effects of what he calls 'the psychophysical
factor' (the sum of the mental and bodily dispositions of each
individual) are most often countered by the effects of other
factors:[5] in industrial organization the role of individual gifts is
practically indeterminable. Even when it is a matter of the
division of work between the sexes, it is notorious that it is
rarely calculated according to the natural differences that separate
them. The most fatiguing jobs are often confined to the weaker
sex.[6] We could agree with Mr Veblen that the majority of
employments under the head of industrial occupations were,
originally in primitive communities, feminine occupations.[7] It is
the strong who distribute jobs according to their own law; they
are obedient less to the wishes of nature than to their own
interests and tasks. The division of labour was originally 'forced'
rather than 'spontaneous'.

According to M. Gumplowicz, a similar constraint would be
the rule in the political society as well as in the conjugal society.[8]
Labour is never freely divided. In all states different races are
found: but their functions are determined less by their natural
aptitudes than by the inequality of their social situations. The
power-holding group reserves certain professions to itself,
leaving the remainder to subordinate groups or imposing them
upon them. Leisure rapidly becomes the most clear evidence of
superiority, to live the aristocratic life is to prove in every way

and with every luxury at one's disposition that one belongs to the leisure class. If then the powerful practise those activities which make for the achievement of prowess and the deployment of valour – preferably predatory activities – they will systematically leave to the oppressed the monotonous and fatiguing jobs lacking joy or honour – activities of an industrial nature. Dühring was in this sense right as against Engels: the division of labour does not produce the differentiation of society into classes: it is much more the pre-established differentiation of societies which determines the way in which labour is divided in them.*

If, indeed, one wishes to give an exact account of the motives governing the organization of labour in primitive societies, one should never forget to add, or even substitute ideas of a religious nature and *tabus* of different sorts, for calculations based more or less on interest. When it is a question of dividing tasks between the sexes, superstitious fears explain in some cases the abstention of men and in others the abstention of women. In the Lounda kingdom a man must not be present when nut-oil is being extracted; his presence compromises the success of the operation. Reciprocally, in Uganda a woman may never touch a cow's udder.[9] *Tabus* of the same order, no doubt, help to justify the general system of specialization, not only in domestic but also in political society. It is always in relation to 'men-gods', kings or priests, that there are a large number of things which their dignity forbids them to touch. The at once dangerous and beneficial electricity with which they are charged, strangely limits the area of their activity.[10] We remember the case of a certain Polynesian chief who preferred to die of starvation rather than use his hands to feed himself. The restrictions on the *Flamen Dialis* are still famous for their multiplicity and severity. But one rule analogous to that would suffice to forbid in principle a certain occupation to a descendant of a certain race; and in the religious distribution of functions, undoubtedly all the different sympathies or antipathies that primitive societies so willingly imagine must have played a more extensive role than we can easily understand.

---

* This seems to be an interestingly gratuitous interpolation. For Engels the categorical distinctions are simultaneously occupational. How labour is *subsequently* apportioned is a different matter. See *Anti-Dühring*, Pt III, §2.

Effects of the system

It is most likely that in India more than anywhere else, extrinsic factors were more important than intrinsic ones in the distribution of functions, since the belief in inequality has nowhere shown more vigour from the very beginning, in influencing all institutions. It is also most likely that among these external factors, religious ones have weighed heaviest since it seems that here especially power of a spiritual order has taken precedence over others and represents the summit and source of all social power. M. P. Lapie, inquiring into the general reasons determining the hierarchy of occupations indicates that a profession attracts esteem to the extent that it assures its members more power and independence.[11] It is important to add that these very notions of power and independence vary; they take on this or that nuance according to the general atmosphere of the sentiments prevailing in a society; they reflect the diverse 'scales of value'. In India, no value is superior, in principle, to that which a Brahman derives from his purity. By its power, without arms or wealth, with but a lifted finger he moves or halts things and men. His race possesses such spiritual affluence as to give him the power to impose on the elements of the Hindu masses which incessantly repel each other, the only order that they can universally accept. In a civilization so profoundly imbued with religion, it would be surprising if we did not find such a concern at the root of occupational distinctions.

It is by virtue of this singular dignity that we find the Brahman surrounded with a multiplicity of interdictions. They closely restrict, under pain of degradation, the number of occupations open to him. He is particularly forbidden not only to sell intoxicating liquor, alcohol or scent, but also meat, milk, salt, coloured fabrics, articles made of wool, of hemp or linen. The doctrine of *ahimsa* holds him back from the plough: in turning the soil he would risk killing living beings. We have said that many of these prescriptions were no doubt theoretical: the law of necessity forced many Brahmans to overstep the religious law. Even the codes allow them in times of 'distress' to practise agriculture and certain commercial activities. But on the whole they are no less a 'leisure class', connected by their nobility to activities of a spiritual order, sacrifice, prayer and study.

Economic life: production

What is true of the Brahmans may be true also of a number of other races to an unequal degree. In imitation of the Brahman they may, to prove their concern for purity, pride themselves on not being able to touch certain categories of beings or objects. If we could discover the *tabus* from which these aversions originate we might arrive at the ground of the specialization of clans which became immobilized in so many castes: the interplay of original incompatibilities would explain the vocations of groups and why certain professions are forbidden to some and reserved to or imposed upon others.

But even if this information is lacking, what we can see very clearly over and above the particular reasons for the specialization of each class are the broad lines of the hierarchic system which despite everything orders these closed groups and establishes a general parallelism between the racial distinction of noble and ignoble, and the distinction of occupations, pure or impure.

It is sometimes difficult to tell which of the two distinctions, race or profession, is the primary principle effecting respect or misprision. However the descent of the Aryans on India is represented – a succession of sudden and general invasions or a series of partial colonizations – we know with what horror the indigenous inhabitants inspired the new arrivals. The Vedic hymns resound with the insults hurled against the black, flat-nosed Dasyus who eat whatever comes to hand and offer no milk to the gods.[12] In the eyes of these Aryans, so proud of their civilization, how could it not seem that these barbarians must contaminate not only the objects that they touched but also the occupations that they practised?[13] No doubt this is one of the reasons why certain primitive occupations, and those that the aboriginal tribes must have practised before the advent of the Aryans – not only those of hunting and fishing but also those of the basket-maker and even the wheelwright – should continue to be especially despised: the occupations of the conquered, the work of savages. But it is important to add that here again religious beliefs continue to add their pressure to that of ethnic instincts. If hunters are held in low esteem this is not only because their occupation is a primitive one, but because it obliges them daily to commit the sin of killing animals.[14] Analogous scruples justify the degradation of curriers and tanners. It is the same for the *nāpit*, or barber, as for the washermen, of whatever race, on account of the impure contacts that the nature of their work imposes.[15]

This explains why it is so difficult to deduce the Hindu hierarchy, as Mr Nesfield has tried to do, from some sort of 'materialist' philosophy of history. He tells us that occupations are ranked more or less high accordingly as they have emerged after more or less complex inventions, at a more or less advanced stage of industrial progress. We have argued that if one wishes to explain the ranks of different castes, one must take into account many factors which do not belong in a 'natural history of industrial progress'.

Moreover, however the memory of such progress explains the superiority of artisan occupations, which in varying degrees use metallurgy, over those more open to the most savage races, it remains true that Hindu civilization, obsessed as it is with other criteria of prestige, assigns a very low place to activities of an industrial type. Mr Dutt has collected from different Hindu codes traces of the contempt in which industry was held.[16] It is among the impure castes and those who pollute the food they touch, with prostitutes, eunuchs, actors and drunkards, that Yajnavalkya classes not only curriers and washermen, but also weavers, dyers, oil-pressers, blacksmiths and goldsmiths. Elsewhere, in Manu, the superintendence of mines or factories and the execution of great mechanical works, are side by side with sins, *upapātaka* – between neglecting the sacred domestic fire and the dishonesty of those who fail to pay their debts. How could industrial skills develop in India, asks Mr Dutt, under the weight of such disparagement?[17] In this connection the general repugnance of the Aryans for manual labour has occasionally been referred to. But this repugnance is far from appearing with the same intensity and, above all, lasting so long in all the branches of the Aryan race. Among the Greeks, in particular, it seems that work was not held in so universal disfavour as, on the witness of philosophers, was for long supposed.[18] The truth of the matter is that where industrial work has been left to or imposed upon subjugated races, the inferiority of these races can extend to the occupations themselves.[19] This, amongst other things, is one of the economic crimes of which the institution of slavery stands accused. This institution had no preponderant place in India; functions were specialized and distances marked between different groups rather than within the same familial groups. But by the rigour with which these distances are marked and the disdain which weighs on the races deemed inferior and confined to occupations considered impure, India suffers as much and more than truly slave-based societies, the economic disadvantages of this sort of traditional depreciation of manual arts and occupations.

But at least, if it is true that the caste system, in organizing labour has taken more account of religious prejudices than of natural aptitudes, if it is true also that these prejudices have degraded skills which, had they been highly esteemed, would be useful to society at large, it could still be maintained that these difficulties are somewhat compensated by the professional talents that the same system has perfected in the bosom of the castes, each one linked to a trade passing from father to son.

Auguste Comte has rightly pointed out the universality and spontaneity of the practice of hereditary specialization. At a certain level of civilization, it seems at once inevitable and in-dispensable. Certainly nothing is more natural, initially, than the inheritance of professions as providing immediately, the easiest and most effective means of education by simple domestic imitation; the only feasible one at that time, since oral tradition still constituted the principal universal mode of transmission, either for lack of any other adequate procedure or, more im-portant, because of the lack of rationality in current conceptions.[20] Thus, as long as there were no organized techniques consolidated in manuals on the one hand, and so long as, on the other, there was nothing outside the familial group which resembled a public institution or school able to assemble children of different families, apprenticeship in the family is obligatory and the son will normally carry on the functions of his father. If this custom has continued in India longer than elsewhere, it is because India has grafted a religious obligation on to a material necessity. Even were the possibility open to him, a son would have scruples over abandoning the occupation of his ancestors. Must not this reinforcement of practice by belief in India have made for a tighter adaptation than elsewhere, of the qualities of race to the demands of occupation?

Do we mean by this that where hereditary specialization is the strict rule, professional qualities have more chance of being incorporated in the race and transmitted by heredity? The likelihood is problematical. Schmoller appears to accept that the skill, the technique of the father is, in a sense, transcribed into his muscles, nerves and brain so bequeathed to the son.[21] There is scarcely a need to add that this thesis is nowadays strongly contested. Not only is the theory of the inheritance of acquired characteristics open to objection, but even those who defend it hesitate, today, to include among heritable qualities, these, by definition unstable, combinations of complex practices which constitute a technical skill. Moreover, observations in India itself, following the innovations of the British administration which enabled the scions of different castes to 'compete' in making their way and showing their capacities, in no way allow us to conclude that the system has produced for different kinds of activity specially endowed races carrying innate treasures of ancient heredity.[22]

If, however, it is maintained simply that India, by closing off all other possibilities, has obtained a maximum yield from this domestic education which passes trade secrets from generation to generation, then nothing is more likely. The caste system is to be praised for the proverbial dexterity of Hindu artisans.

It is not only the gifts of its soil but also the work of its artisans which has perpetuated India's reputation through the centuries. From Megasthenes to Jacquemont, every traveller has been amazed by the wonderful results that they have achieved with so few resources. Jacquemont speaking of these workers in the towns reports: 'Each one works in the midst of his scanty goods, squatting like a monkey, and like a monkey no less adroit with his feet than with his hands. Their tools are wretched, and yet the most skilful worker in Europe, had he no others, would not be able to use them with anything approaching such adroitness.'[23] 'The Hindu goldsmith', writes another traveller, 'sets up his workshop wherever he is called. His furnace is a broken earthen pot, an iron pipe serves as a bellows. A pair of pincers, a hammer, a file and a small anvil are all his tools. He makes his crucibles on the spot with clay mixed with charcoal and cowdung which strengthen the crucibles and prevent them breaking in the fire.'[24] With such poor industrial equipment he nevertheless produces numerous little masterpieces. Truthfully, here there was never that gap between industry and art to which our mechanical civilization has accustomed us. In the meanest product we can recognize a 'crystallized tradition', worked out by an incomparable manual skill.[25]

We may conjecture what price is paid for such perfection. The instinct making for routine must here strengthen the respect for tradition. 'It is useless to show them (the Hindu carpenters) a swifter and easier way of sawing wood: they prefer to stick to the old methods they had learned from their fathers rather than adopt more suitable methods that were novel to them.'[26] So it is that under a system that gives a religious tinge to every act in life and in particular to professional acts, every innovation appears as some fatal sin against the ancestors. Even if one may feel the need one does not feel the right to innovate.

Hence a sort of social anchylosis which not only prevents an increase in efficiency within a caste by the perfection of techniques but also impedes the institution of new professions in which the too numerous members of the classical ones might earn a living. James Mill, preoccupied with the theories of Malthus, sees in this connection an evil influence of the caste system upon the movement of population.[27] By its rules governing the ancestor cult and infant marriage, it forces the population to unlimited growth while, at the same time its rules about occupational specialization divide it in advance into excessively rigid sections. If as a result of population pressure the section becomes too small, tradition will still not allow it to be broken. Thus it condemns to a rapid death those whom it has called into superfluous existence.

Clearly, when we praise in the division of labour the result of constraints developing from an increase in social density, we mean by division of labour the creation of new specializations:

we pre-suppose a sufficient degree of social mobility as to allow individuals, not hesitating to change their occupations, to turn towards the newly created specializations. It is just such innovation and mobility that the caste system prevents in principle. In fact, it may not prevent them totally: at least it is capable of hindering them quite considerably, and as a result it retards economic progress while at the same time limiting prosperity.

According to James Mill the system sets up a direct obstacle to prosperity and progress in another way: it is not only that it runs the risk of overpopulation in the occupational categories in which races are confined, but also that it positively prevents competition. After all, there is no proof, as we have seen, that the son will always be fitted by nature to take his father's place and fulfil his function. The surest way to get 'the right man in the right place'* would in fact be to allow the members of all castes to find their own careers and show what they are made of. This is precisely what the system opposes with all its might. As a result it risks depriving civilization of the hidden reserves of the infinite diversity of individual gifts. In any case it deprives it of all that individuals draw from themselves in their effort to rise in the social scale.

Some have praised the tranquil life of the artisan in a Hindu village, sheltered from the torment of competition: conditions eminently favourable to the pious cult of traditional techniques and the loving elaboration of humble masterpieces.[28] But also nothing to tax a man's ingenuity, to invent and, if his own faculties make it possible, to enable him to lift his head above his circle. 'Here', says Bernier 'each one's life glides gently on without an aspiration higher than his condition: for the embroiderer makes his son an embroiderer, the goldsmith makes his a goldsmith, the town doctor makes his a doctor also, and no-one marries except with people of the same profession'.[29] How then could the Hindus be spurred on to lead that life of incessant effort that Hesiod, for example, describes with so much sympathy? Can one not but think that a civilization that in advance discourages every kind of personal ambition has torn out the sinews of economic progress?

* In English in the original.

It is not only by direct action, by thus blessing incumbrance and frowning on innovation – that the caste system impedes production; in a more general way it is by opposing those changes in social organization which are the necessary conditions of economic progress.

No system could be conceived more suited to check the effects normally to be expected of the division of labour. Tied up in its own sacred threads it is incapable either of weaving a new solidarity out of the social segments that it has specialized, or of opening new fields for the scope of individuality.

We are told that the role of the division of labour is precisely to substitute an 'organic solidarity' which liberates the individual from the 'mechanical solidarity' which oppresses him.[30] Where a great variety of new occupations differentiates the ideas and the activities of men, the social totality no longer seems composed of homogeneous segments which, by virtue of the very uniformity of activities and ideas, remain fatally oppressive, exclusive of all heresy, all dissidence and all innovation. But it is still necessary not only if commerce is to develop between members of different clans but also for diversity to be tolerated within one clan – that primitive barriers be lowered and the politico-familial segments lend themselves to extension. The price of individual freedom is the obliteration of the segmentary structure of society.

It is precisely this structure that the caste system, so far from weakening, consolidates. When the division of labour is allied to such a system, it does not break it; on the contrary it takes over and flows into the moulds prepared by the clans. The arena of function is not clearly distinguished from the arena of birth. Everything is, on the contrary, devised to maintain their coincidence. The emergent occupational organization grounds itself in the pre-existing familial organization.[31] It is not surprising that consequently the distinction of occupations does not entail the liberation anticipated. Although we no longer have a multiplicity of clans properly so called, independent and equal, and although the elementary social groups are henceforth specialized and hierarchized, they remain in imitation of the primitive clans whose rule they prolong, exclusive and oppressive: each one of them in its isolation strives to govern the entire life of its members according to its own traditions. The organization of authority here leaves little place for the institutions of liberty, as Sir Henry Maine observed: *status* still repels *contract*.

Schmoller proposes a distinction between two types of specialization, each of which is founded in different conditions: those which are organized by order, under the authority, for example, of the family which distributes the various tasks between its members, and those which come into being freely, for example, by the agreement of two strangers who are both motivated by the prospect of the profits they hope to derive from the exchange.[32] The division of labour that we encounter in the caste system is intermediate between these two extreme types: here the work is divided between several groups and not within the family group. But this division is not organized by the liberty of the exchanging individuals in pursuit of the greatest profit. We are constantly confronted with a constrained division of labour – the specialized groups are subject to two pressures which reinforce each other, ethnic instinct and religious tradition.

Along these lines we return to the idea expressed by Mr Ranade – that in India above all, the realities correspond as little as could be to the postulates of western classical political economy. Our average man, says Mr Ranade, is at the antipodes of *homo economicus*.[33] It is not only religious tradition that deprives the majority of Hindus of that desire for the greatest gain by free exchange that the classical economist imputes to the normal individual: even should they think of 'the hunt for the dollar', their social organization does not allow them the means to pursue it. Here, more than elsewhere it appears that unlimited competition is only a myth. The economists can methodically set aside the factors inhibiting its free play in the west: but here the 'friction' seems stronger than the movement itself. The group in which a person is born fixes his social situation for life, the nature of his occupation and the circle of his relations. What does this mean if not that under this system everything is opposed to that diversity, variability and mobility which in our western societies corresponds to what we call individualism?

But, simultaneously, the caste system not only denies liberty to the individual, but also solidarity to the social whole. And this must entail, over and above the more obvious political consequences, new economic ones.

The closest solidarity rules within each caste. Observers have frequently admired the way in which caste members at once control each other with severity and fraternally support each other. But on the other hand, from one caste to another, Hindus remain strangers to each other and show, as Jacquemont says, 'the most abominable indifference'.[34] It has rightly been pointed out that sympathy is not fed solely by similitude:[35] diversity can also bring it about by the very fact that it is the condition of collaboration: 'Those who resemble assemble' but 'those who differ complement each other.' In this sense one may anticipate a drawing together due to the division of labour. But, once more, for this happy influence to be experienced it is necessary that it be not contradicted by the general current of the social system. If the latter works to deepen the trenches between the collaborating groups, the moral benefit of collaboration is lost. Which is precisely what has happened in India. Too many traditional scruples, too much instinctive disdain separates the members of the different castes for them to think of treating each other as collaborators. It seems as if the spirit of isolation animating castes, just like an electrical charge in elder-pith balls, forces them to repel each other at the very moment of contact. Hence the deepseated disunity of Hindu society, and these feelings of hostility or mutual indifference which have impressed all observers.[36] The scene reported by Megasthenes has often been the subject of comment: a Hindu peasant peacefully following his plough by the side of warring armies. Some have been pleased to see here proof of the warrior's respect for agriculture, the nurse of society; others have said that the fact is a symptom, among many others, of a grave social malady: penned up in their castes, Hindus are strangers 'to the best interests and ideals that are the basis of all healthy national life'.[37]

Certainly, throughout the centuries, what India has lacked more than anything is a national life. Only in our own days does it seem that British civilization, by its example, by the new milieux that it creates and the reactions it provokes, is beginning to inoculate the Babu with individualistic sentiments, and something resembling national sentiment. But under not one of the types of state that she has known hitherto, has India succeeded in making, has India ever considered herself, a motherland. Because of the divisiveness in which the caste system condemns them to live, the Indians have never been able to face up to the conqueror and have allowed empires, large and small, to weigh upon them. But the same system which has left the field open for these has also prevented their political action from sinking deeply into the social organization. They have succeeded one another across the surface of the Hindu world without breaking that surface. Consequently, there has never emerged that reciprocal activity between the high and the low, the parts and the centre which is necessary not only for political life but also for an intense economic life; the pillars of a true *Volkswirtschaft* were lacking.

One can better understand the significance of these lacunae if one recalls that India has never really had a body of towns large enough and numerous enough for the production and circulation of wealth and, at the same time, the production and circulation of ideas, the necessary centres of co-ordination. The real centres of life in India have always been the villages.[38] The majority of the Hindu population has always been a rural one.

The discussions of contemporary Hindu economists draw our attention to the grievous effects upon the economic level of the whole of this rural predominance combined with the pressures of the caste system.[39] Above all, they blame manufactured British imports. It is such competition, against which they have no resistance, that has snatched the tools from the hands of the last of the village artisans – driven them into the fields, which already, even without drought, are incapable of supporting an over-dense rural population. No doubt to compensate for this, British civilization created or developed centres of industrial production where the all too numerous Hindus could soon find employment as factory workers. But the development of such urban concentration has been slower than one might think. In the 1891 census Mr Baines estimated that 90 per cent of the population still lived more or less directly from agriculture.[40] With such a plethora how could a country's economy not be weighed down? It is very dangerous to be so much at the mercy of a single industry and that one the most hazardous of all. One of the Famine Commissions writes in its report:

The origin of the poverty of the people of India and the risk to which they are exposed in case of drought lies in the unhappy circumstance that agriculture is almost entirely the unique occupation of the mass of the population; the remedies for the present situation cannot be sufficient if they do not envisage progress in the diversification of occupations which will allow the surplus population to quit agriculture.[41]

But if today India complains of this faulty equilibrium of occupations, it is not only today that she suffers from it. The competition of British manufacturers by driving some weavers or cutters back to agriculture may have aggravated the sickness; it did not create it. 'From all time, towns have been the exception in India.' From all time, village life has been the rule, as unfavourable to the fusion of the different primitive groups as to the liberation of individuals.[42]

We remember the hypotheses of Sir Henry Maine. He described the village community still living in India such as it must have been in the early phases of our own western evolution. He found these traces of primitive Aryan communism: a body of consanguines held the land in common and cultivated it under the supervision of a sort of family council; apart from the agriculturalists a certain number of specialists served the needs of the whole.

Maine no doubt exaggerated the communistic character of this institution. More recent research has led observers to at least differentiate types of Hindu villages. According to Mr Baden-Powell one finds joint-villages in some regions either of manorial or aristocratic form or of a tribal or democratic form.[43] If common ownership proper is not found, at least the sense of common responsibilities is still alive; not only do members of the community have a right of preemption on land, but plots are periodically redistributed and non-cultivated land remains for the use of all. But this type of village – about which there is nothing specifically Aryan – is not the most widespread. In the severalty or *ryotwari* villages which are under the authority of a privileged chief who is not the sole owner, the land is divided into clearly separated lots. It can happen that these lots are redistributed, without this implying any sense of common ownership: solidarity perhaps, but not communism. The body of separate landowners forms the village fraternity in which the diverse artisan castes that serve it do not in any real sense participate.

However the variety of these types is defined, what is sure is that, in a general sense, the organization of village solidarity is unfavourable to the independent initiative of individuals, and in particular it opens few prospects for industrial and commercial progress.

Discussion continues over the place occupied by the village artisans. Sir Henry Maine appeared to incorporate them in the community, Baden-Powell excludes them. It seems that one must distinguish in each case: the place assigned, the dignity accorded varies according to the degree of impurity or the antiquity of the occupations in question. Sweepers and curriers are often forced to live outside the village limits. Elsewhere dealers in grain, money-lenders and tailors, while living within the village confines, take no part in festivals: these occupations are newly arrived. Carpenters, blacksmiths, potters and oil-pressers have been, on the contrary, long incorporated.[44] But the important aspect, from the economic point of view, is that whether kept at a distance or received within the village circle, these artisans are servants. They do not work for a market in which they would encounter competition and from which they would derive according to circumstances, high or low prices. They are most frequently paid with a certain quantity of grain according to a rate fixed by immemorial custom. We should add that ordinarily they are allotted a piece of land. They continue to be cultivators as well as artisans, and this accumulation of functions enables them, to a certain extent, to remedy difficulties resulting from the restricted number of their client-patrons. We can see that the type which modern economists called the 'closed economy' of small primitive communities still dominates here. One stage has, no doubt, been passed:[45] the various tasks are now divided among groups of different origin and no longer within the domestic groups, as is still the practice among the tribes who live on the confines of Hinduism. But still all work for the whole that they form without commerce in the proper sense.

A further stage is reached when we find a certain number of members of the same occupation concentrated in villages which serve the surrounding district: villages of potters, curriers, blacksmiths or even joiners. This phenomenon is also found in Russia and elsewhere.[46] Even in France, until recent times, we had villages where all the inhabitants, fathers and sons, were tinkers. It seems that this organization was the rule in India. The love of exclusiveness overcame the difficulties which distance must have imposed as much on purchases as on sales. The power of a tradition conformable with the tendency of the Hindu mind to classify and isolate cuts short, says M. Fick, the concerns of convenience.[47]

Later, towns assemble different artisan castes, each one inhabiting its separate quarter or street. Conditions are set for the development of commerce. But to see the limits that such a development encounters we must recall how the majority of these Hindu towns were born, and how they died. The literature describes their splendours with much complacency but they were for the most part initially no more than the settled camps of despots, large and small, collecting tax from a population unable to unite in its own defence. Camps became courts calling for a growing number of shops and workshops to minister to the glory of the prince and the needs of his following. Here more than anywhere arts and crafts are concentrated and organized manifestly for the service of the great. 'Nearly all the mobile capitals of empires' writes Sir Henry Maine,

have aspired to have a temporary centre which thus becomes the unique seat of the decorative arts and of those manufactures calling for delicate hand-work. Whoever might claim to belong to the class of superior artisans took his craft or his tools and followed the royal cortège. From this we have the splendour of the oriental capitals, the result of the multiplication of industrial forms in response to the wealth flowing into the court.[48]

Escorted caravans set out from and converged there; there not only did the artisan castes prosper and grow in social importance, but also the merchant castes, so many chambers of commerce which the prince was obliged to take into account, and whose leaders were sometimes persons of considerable position whom it was important to consult, we are told, before fixing the rate of duty. There were displayed those activities celebrated in the epics, there were applied the consecrated rules of the codes.[49]

These brilliant arenas had two drawbacks. Not only were they relatively rare, but also ordinarily ephemeral. The despotic power which illumined them, itself lacked stability. 'The capitals spring up, glitter and are extinguished: on the morrow the markets and warehouses, the ports of the town are deserted, empty and forgotten.'[50]

The conditions were lacking for the creation of that lasting and extensive urban network of which Ratzel speaks, whose channels of communication are the threads and of which the towns are the knots, and which is necessary for the organization of an intense interior commerce. Indeed, asks Mr Hunter, did the Hindus know real towns before the coming of British civilization? For their part the Hindus were only builders of temples; the Muslims, of palaces and tombs; the Marathas of ports; the Portuguese of churches. But the great *emporia* indispensable to trading activity, were never built.[51]

It is to be noted in this connection that despite the inroads commercial law made on religious law in India, it never gained that independence and *a fortiori*, that preponderance which it enjoyed in our civilizations. We know how much these owe to the law of markets in particular. As slowly but surely, the practices born of this type of periodic truce are generalized and regularized, a new law is formed, at once international and individualistic, laic and conventional, taking less account of traditional beliefs than of personal wishes. And it is precisely the mission of towns, guardians of markets, to imbue national organisms to the very heart with the spirit of this law.[52]

In India, there is nothing parallel to this slow and sure impregnation. Not that India lacked meeting places for the trade of merchandise. If it is a fact worthy of attention that markets properly so called are not mentioned in the Jatakas, we can conjecture that the pilgrims at the numerous and famous religious fairs, were also purchasers.[53] But the regulations emerging from the transactions in such gatherings do not achieve the ascendancy in Hindu society that they achieved elsewhere. Commerce had not the strength to call the tune, to substitute completely its own demands for those of religion, in the general evolution of law. And, again, this shows us that, compared with the rural life of the majority, urban life in this civilization was restricted within the narrowest limits.[54]

For urban life to flower and produce its normal fruits, more is needed than a collection of stones, walls, warehouses and markets; there must also be above all a municipal spirit. It is not the *town* that matters but the *city*.

Towns do not set their stamp on an entire civilization unless first of all they form autonomous centres capable of coordinating their activities: if in a word, their citizens have the unity necessary to safeguard their beneficial independence. But this is precisely what caste opposes: 'The strongest principle of disintegration to which humanity has ever been subjected, and which in India incessantly divides the people against itself.'[55]

From this we can understand how caste in a sense enhances the disadvantages of the guild. The two institutions are often called on to play the same role, to such a point that some have confused them. Like the corporation of our own middle ages, caste is not only an institution for mutual assistance – in its way, says Mr Hunter, it makes any poor law unnecessary, it is not only an organ of control to preserve technical traditions, it appears also sometimes to be an organ of defence capable, if necessary, of opposing a lowering of wages. But do these economic attributes explain its essence? They explain neither the consecrated hierarchy that superimposes castes, nor the mutual repulsion that opposes them. Here, as we have seen, we have to take into account the conspiracy of ethnic instinct with religious tradition. It is the activity of these antipathies and these scruples which condemns Hindu society to infinite divisions.

This one could not assert if caste were nothing more than a guild. 'The institution would have had less tendency', M. Senart observes 'to divisiveness and dislocation: the principle of its initial unification would have maintained its cohesion.' According to Mr Risley the excessive number of castes and their continued multiplication 'by fission' is a sufficient mark of their extra-professional origin.[56]

By reason of these characteristics, traditions and instincts, it goes without saying that caste is not only more profoundly given to routine than the guild and more severely hostile to all innovation but also, and especially, it is more closed, inward looking and exclusive. The corporation, just as it allows the mixing of bloods, admits the outsider by apprenticeship and allows coalitions between different corporations. Caste, repugnant to contacts as to admixture, is not only hostile to the adoption of new members, it also prevents or hinders relations between castes.

Here is perhaps the gravest disadvantage of the system: this intransigent spirit of divisiveness that makes any kind of higher organization in India impossible. In the western middle ages corporations, distinct as they were, nevertheless were able to coordinate to form the pillars of the township. And the townships were at once the fortresses of the burghers' independence, and the ports of commerce. We have only to think not only of the political but also the economic attributes of the councils composed of representatives of different guilds, and of how the 'municipal economies' by developing and organizing their relations, prepared the way for flourishing 'national economies'[57] – and we understand all that Hindu civilization has lost by allowing the seeds of the city to be buried under the massive weight of caste.

The caste system, by the very order which it imposes, no doubt serves to raise a society out of barbarism. But it runs the risk also of halting it rapidly and for a long time on the road to civilization. Its lustrations are those that petrify. In the area of economics also then, India presents a spectacle of a kind of arrested development.

5

Literature

To what extent are the races of India specialized? What is the structure of her law and through what channels does her economic life run? We have tried to answer these different questions. And in the course of this we have brought out the principal characteristics of Hindu civilization; and upon these characteristics we have observed the imprint, more or less clear according to the case, of that particular system which it has supported through the centuries, the caste system. Is it possible for us now to discern analogous impressions on the more subtle products of this civilization? It is said that literature expresses the state of society. It is not unlikely that relations exist between the literary and social forms which have predominated in India. It is worthwhile bringing them to light for our hypotheses on the effects of the system might receive a final and a striking confirmation.

Unfortunately, here more than ever, the task is difficult. To grasp this sort of subtle effluvium that rises from social forms to literary ones, two conditions seem at first equally necessary: a long familiarity with the details of these works, and a constant attention to the effects, direct or indirect, of relations between people. The first condition is most often lacking in the sociologist; the second in the specialists whom he is obliged to follow.

Nevertheless it seems possible, even here, if we take the trouble to collect and coordinate the observations of literary historians, to formulate provisional sociological explanations.

It goes without saying that we cannot claim to give single, total and exhaustive explanations. Particularly when we are dealing with the 'superstructure' of a civilization, it is clear that social forms are not the only ones at work. Forces of all sorts compete with them and the resulting involved action is most often so mysterious that here more than elsewhere, we must necessarily leave a wide margin for the inexplicable.

Moreover is not this what one is doing when one explains the characteristics of literatures by the *genius* of people? It is said, for example, that the Aryans in India are to be distinguished from their brothers in Greece by their innate love of the excessive. Compare the Mahabharata or the Ramayana with the *Iliad* or *Odyssey*, or the Upanishads with Plato's *Dialogues*. The Hindu genius is recognized by its amplifying imagination, not by an ordering intellect. Capable of subtlety in the detail it seems incapable of organizing wholes:[1] qualities and faults which but betray the aptitudes of the race.

M. Oldenberg has recourse to reasoning of this kind when, to explain the evolution of Hindu literature, he insists upon the effect of the mixing of bloods.[2] Little by little the Aryan conquerors allowed themselves to be conquered. The noble race was more and more contaminated. Then the intellectual level was lowered. A mysterious effeminacy and morbidity changed the tone of literature: the indigenous temperament had won.

It is possible that this chemistry of ethnic principles was not without influence. But who can fail to see, however, how obscure its operation must be? More generally, to hang the products of a civilization on the native tendencies of one or more races, is to classify rather than to explain. Out of the traits common to the masterpieces that a people admires one sets out to compose the physiognomy of its 'genius'. But why and how the literature of these people has taken a certain turn, that remains just as mysterious afterwards as it was before.[3]

One provides more substantial food for curiosity if, instead of being content to invoke race one evokes the milieu. It is not for nothing that the opening pages of histories of Hindu literature recall the distinctive aspects of India's soil and sky, flora and fauna. In that immense triangle, there are higher mountains and broader rivers than elsewhere; exuberant jungles where serpents swarm; following devastating floods, yet more terrible droughts; such natural surroundings must work profoundly on man's sensibility. Nature's forms must obsess him as her strength weighs him down. We remember Buckle's antithesis: 'In the West man dominates nature. In the East he is crushed by her.' Nowhere more than in India can the spectacle of things suggest to the mind the feeling of the power of life and the impotence of man. And this is why all Hindu literature must express at once the depression of the discouraged will and the sickly exaltation of unbridled imagination.

Such influences rising from the earth, falling from the sky, are by no means negligible. But here also it is clear that they do not explain everything; and that by attempting to explain too much by them one risks ending up in the play of analogies. Shall we limit our ambition, asks M. Ouvré, to symbolistic thinking: 'The immensity of India's territory is reflected in the length of Hindu poems, the Ramayana is long because the Ganges is not short, and apparently the auditors of the Mahabharata tolerated its many digressions and episodes because the tentacles of the Banian tree proliferate in the jungle.'[4] It is dangerous to seek solely in the nature of the milieu in which a civilization develops, the secret of its moral and intellectual orientation. Buckle, following his theory through, ends up with the conclusion that in India, where nature crushes the individual, those deifications supposed by eupherism* could not occur. Sir Alfred Lyall has, nevertheless, been able to show that such deifications are the rule rather than the exception and that eupherism is nowhere more clearly verified than in India.[5]

If then it seems to us that there is little place for the individual in Hindu literature, we must take care not to attribute this solely to the pressure of nature.

But the action of social forms is without a doubt even more all enveloping, at once more compelling and insinuating than natural forms. The relations that a poet, however much of a 'creator' he may be, has with other men open and close prospects to him. Whether he believes it or not, his imagination is, as it were, magnetized by the demands of his public.[6] His work serves the aims, flatters the passions and caresses the instincts produced in his contemporaries by their situation. Here also, through their

---

* 'The method of interpretation which regards myths as traditional accounts of real incidents in human history.' *O.E.D.*

unequal success, a sort of selection of literary attempts takes place and thus is explained the adaptation of style to the social milieu.

Without studying such concords in particular, historians of various literatures have often noted examples of them. Is it possible that we may find them in the literary history of India?

It has frequently been said, and we have already more than once encountered the proofs: India provides a magnificent example of what becomes of a civilization when it stays in the power of religion. Caste endures as essentially an institution rooted in religion and all the germs of secular institutions are as it were sterilized in its shade. It impedes the formation of those centres of intellectual curiosity and political activity which elsewhere organized resistance to primitive traditions. Through the scruples that it entertains it favours in a variety of ways the tight hold of the sacred on the social.

Hindu literature offers shining proof of this empire. It is no exaggeration to say that religion is the foundation stone of all the literary monuments of India. 'India possesses the biggest sacred literature, and one of the most ancient and interesting that we have, but even the term "profane literature", as we understand it, has no significance there and is only useful to us as providing a contrast.'[7]

This is not to say that all this literature can be reduced to mystical hymns or theological commentaries any more than the whole of life is exhausted by religion. In our study of the juridical system and the economic organization we found that Hindu reality at every point goes beyond the Brahmanic frame. The masses were not so 'hypnotized' as has been said. A medley of caravans ploughed across this immense peninsula. Courts displayed their luxuries for the admiration of envy. Interests other than spiritual ones preoccupied the Hindus. Other pleasures attracted them than those of theological speculation. Consequently India was not ignorant of popular tales and wordly poetry: she had, shall we say, a poetry of the caravanserai and a courtly poetry. There a temperament very different from the metaphysical temperament attributed to the Hindu nation reveals itself: ardent sensuality and sceptical irony, frivolity, wantonness, an immense power of fantasy united with finesse in observation.[8]

It is still no less true that for the greater part the literary monuments of Hindu civilization are built of stones dressed by religion. How many of them rest, directly or indirectly, on the Veda? The first poetry here is an invocation to the gods just as the first prose is an explanation of liturgy. The content of the four Vedas is almost all invocations and incantations, ritual formulae and magical spells. Later works are scarcely more than commentaries on this initial revelation.[9] The Brahmanas and accompanying Aranyakas claim to clarify the meaning of the cult. The Upanishads resemble rather more philosophical treatises: there is a greater freedom of speculation in them. Nevertheless it is not difficult to prove that speculation moves on the plane of the religious tradition. The Shastras are only various applications of this same tradition: their intention is to deduce from it laws for the conduct of life. Even in the periods when literature tends more to the terrestrial, its religious connections are visible for a long time. The theological tradition does not lose its rights even in eroticism...

Such survivals in India are most natural: the concern to lead the intellectual life, to know and to meditate was traditionally reserved to those who, by right of birth, were intimately related to the world of the sacred. The professional thinkers were the priests. It is not surprising that a system in principle committed to the labour of thought, the peculiar concern of the Brahman castes, should have produced first of all a characteristically priestly literature.

This characteristic is most apparent in the Brahmanas. As their name indicates, the Brahmanas are devoted to sacred science. Usually each is associated with an Aranyaka: 'Book of the Forest', that is to say a book for solitary meditation. Brahmana and Aranyaka are connected with a Veda which is taken as known and which they set out to explain. The declared intention of this literature of commentary is to explain to officiants the meaning of the formulae and practices which are necessary to the performance of the cult. The Brahmana is then a manual of theological techniques. The greater part of its speculation revolves around the idea of sacrifice which is as we have seen one of the pillars of Brahmanic prestige.

Sacrifice which assures the power of Brahmans is itself endowed by the Brahmans with omnipotence. If they are to be believed, it created the world. It constrains the gods. It becomes a god: theories in which it is permissible to see a reflection of very primitive notions. The essential religious act seems to be conceived here as a type of magical procedure. It is a sort of mechanical operation which, without the slightest moral intervention, puts good and evil in the hands of the sorcerer. 'So gross a religion', says M. Sylvain Lévi, 'presupposes a semi-savage people', but, he adds, 'the sorcerers, magicians or shamans of these tribes knew how to analyse their system, to take it to pieces, study its workings, observe its principles, establish its laws: they are the true fathers of Hindu philosophy'.[10] The Brahmans meditated and expatiated unceasingly upon these rites which it had become their monopoly to perform: an immense tree sprang from the humble seed, thanks to the powers of these professional thinkers.

Their speculation springs from the deepest roots. We find not only rites but also primitive myths at the base of the Brahmanas. We see once more the story of the floating egg from which everything was born, that of the man who dismembers himself to produce the world, and that of the animal species engendered from the metamorphoses of a divine couple. According to Mr Lang 'there is perhaps no myth which is widely spread in the lower races which does not have its counterpart in the Brahmanas'.[11] But here more than elsewhere this primitive material is worked over, drawn out and refined. Nowhere else are so many theological equations slipped in beneath tales of adventure. Nowhere are so many abstractions opposed for a final identification. Prajāpati is, from one point of view, an exalted man, a great concrete being: but he is at the same time the power of sacrifice, which the Brahman is pleased to follow with his dialectic in the various forms in which it appears.

It goes without saying that this dialectic frequently operates in obscurity, but we may venture to think that here obscurity is more sought after than eschewed. We are dealing with the literature of the initiated: we sense a concern to preserve the monopoly of an élite race rather than a desire for universal accessibility. No doubt we can find a love of enigma in the origins of all literature; but here the sibylline play on words appears to be a constant tactic.[12]

That this doctrine is finally inconsistent and stays, so to speak, in a fluid state need not surprise us. We know that the Brahmans had no councils and consequently no dogmas properly so called. There is no organ to formulate or impose a finished theology. All Brahmans are equally fit to comment on the revelation of the Vedas. Different schools were bound to develop and controversy to arise. Notions were refined and rarified but there was no authority that might close the debate. The Brahmanas have preserved for us the echoes of this free discussion among the born-priests: they are, after all, nothing but the 'collection of anonymous opinions, independent aphorisms and free observations grafted on to the explanation of rites'.[13] If we can discern a certain unity of tendency in them this is explained by the identity of the thinkers' situation which engendered the unity of pre-occupation: thus, little by little, the common treasure of the priestly clans was created. In the Brahmanas we do not have the work of a Church, but that of a priestly caste, keen to cultivate its faculties and at the same time to defend its privileges by justifying them.

But are these tendencies revealed only through the Brahmanas? Is there, in this matter, an unbridgeable gap between the Brahmanas and the Vedas? In the latter also we can find, if not the clear imprint of caste itself, at least traces left by the forces that worked to create it.

From its content we have seen that this collection of Vedic poetry does not reveal more than a very imperfect picture of the social organization that flourished when they were composed.[14] But their very form, their literary characteristics and their general tone can give us some valuable indications about this organisation.

For a long time scholars have been content to oppose the youthful poetry of the Vedic age to the entirely priestly literature of later times. To go back from the Brahmanas to the Rig Veda is also, they seemed to say, to go back not only from prose to verse but also from the abstract to the concrete, from scholasticism to life.[15] It is to see, freely running under the open sky, sentiments which appear but rarely in the later literature. Here at least the racial temperament has not been debilitated by the system. A number of authors have thus been pleased to feel, in the invocations to Indra, the fresh youth of Aryan vigour. Disdain is reserved for these Dasyus 'who narrowed our horizon' and betrayed the lively spirit of conquest.[16]

These warrior races reveal themselves to us with their faces lifted to heaven and one of their greatest complaints was the barbarous impiety of their enemies. At least this primitive Aryan devotion had nothing sickly about it. It did not separate man from action. The Vedic Rishis were not enclosed from the world. When they address the gods it is not a complicated tradition but rather entirely spontaneous feelings that inspire them. Nature itself speaks in their lyricism: the unique example, said Renouvier of 'intellectual primitiveness'.[17]

But a more profound study has turned the majority of specialists away from this first impression. It is observed that the process of devirilization begins from the Vedic period: scattered in the rich plains of India the invaders let themselves become soft. No doubt the climate saps their energy but at the same time we do not find any social phenomena developing which might temper character. We see nothing resembling a national life. It seems that already the weight of religious life had weighed down the balance to the great detriment of political life. With which goes not only a narrowing of horizon but also a sort of mutilation of personality.[18] It is notable that the heroes who pass through the Vedas are men of prayer rather than of war. Instead of an Achilles or a Siegfried, we have a Visvamitra taking pride of place whose 'austerities are his weapons'. Let us note further that when the warriors pray they do not directly address their gods in the manner of the Homeric heroes. Already another body is in the process of slipping in between gods and men. From the Vedas we can see the special preoccupations of these intermediaries, and, by the side of established professional practices, interests dictated by what M. Oldenberg calls their class interest.

In fact, sacrifice which later became the clearest assurance of Brahmanic power is also, for the Vedic Rishis, their dominant theme.

The Sama Veda is only a 'song book' for the use of priests singing during the celebration of the cult. The Yajur Veda, 'book of formulae', contains imprecations, blessings or exorcisms with which its users accompanied their manipulations. In the Rig Veda collection poetry itself figures as the 'auxiliary of sacrifice'. The hymn is most often only the servant of the rite. The praise of a god is only the prologue of an operation which by loading him with gifts, assures benefits to man.

How then can the Vedic poems have that spontaneity for so long attributed to them? It is pleasant to believe that in the hymns we can hear a tribal chief, surrounded by his fellows, letting his heart speak to summon up the dawn and avert the storm. But in reality we are faced with an officiant operating on behalf of some generous member of the laity. In the invocation that he makes to the gods there may be found an echo of impressions made on souls still easily surprised by the renewed miracles of nature, the works of sun and fire, air and water. In this way flashes of true poetry illuminate these litanies. None the less they are dictated by a spirit quite other than that of spontaneous adoration or naïve terror. Calculation is more in evidence than effusion. In the eyes of the officiant what is essential is that the ritual operation succeed and that it be connected with him. The broad outlines of the doctrine that the Brahmanas later adumbrate are already sketched out.[19] Sacrifice is not only an imitation of natural phenomena, it produced them. And as distinct from a truly magical operation it acts only through the intermediary of the gods. Sacrifice creates a sort of contract between men and gods which gives the performer a sort of constraining power. The idea of priestly omnipotence thus emerges from the Vedas, together with the warnings of danger to those who would dispense with his services, or would not reward him suitably.[20] Has not Bergaigne shown that the radiant chariot which so poetically opens the hymn to the dawn, in reality signifies reward? To this, the priests attribute all the effects of sacrifice; in their eyes it constitutes the essential element.[21] For this reason M. Oldenberg speaks of the interested aspect of Vedic poetry. A dual concern runs through it: to draw down on men the benefits of the gods and on the priests the rewards of men.

Poetry answering to such requirements must naturally have more of artifice than freedom in it. The hymns are redolent of craft. The authors boast of making a fine eulogy 'as a clever wheelwright makes a chariot'. Their dominating concern is not so much to express a personal emotion as to capture the gods in a well woven net. Technical preoccupations here over-rule poetic ones. Rather than express human sentiments in a language which is accessible to all, these priestly poets devote themselves to refinements of expression to dazzle the expert.[22]

In this way we can explain the puzzles, the plays on words, and the paradoxical identifications with which the Rig Veda swarms. There is something more here than that pleasure which all primitives have in asking riddles. Wonderful ambiguities are systematically accumulated. The most far fetched analogies are deliberately used to describe objects. The intention is evidently to obscure more than to clarify and to conceal at the very moment of revelation.

The Veda, moreover, has its own theory about this procedure: 'The gods are the friends of mystery', 'what is clearly expressed displeases them'. 'Sacred Things must only be partially unveiled.' Is this not to conceive of the gods on the model of priests, by virtue of that sort of professional anthropomorphism of which we find more than one example?[23] The priest gladly delights in enigmatic formulae: their obscurity is yet one more guarantee of his monopoly. For this reason, so far from gratuitously simplifying things – as did the first translators, obsessed with the 'naïvety' of the Vedas – we ought to respect the bizarre complications that are found there. For they were no doubt more or less intentional: the esoteric served the interest of those priestly families who were in the process of turning into castes.

At all events, to explain this growth of hyperbole and superlatives, we have to imagine a hot-house atmosphere where some qualities atrophy while others develop exuberantly, a 'milieu of mystical and verbal competition' where the virtuosi took pleasure in excelling in subtleties. 'We cannot conceive of the

birth of such poetry' says M. Oldenberg, 'outside organized
schools for sacrificial experts and priests, lovers of mystic
enigmas which, in play, they took turns to pose and to solve.'
Bergaigne had said earlier that what we find in the Rig Veda are
'the liturgical speculations of priestly families'. And where
Renouvier spoke of 'primitiveness', he speaks of 'Byzantinism'.
It can be seen how far we have come from those dreams of
primitive purity, pastoral innocence and spontaneous effusion
with which Max Müller deluded himself.[24]

Perhaps on this point we have only answered exaggeration
with exaggeration. Conceivably the 'artificialist' theory will be
modified in its turn.[25] From the observations which it has
accumulated, however, enough will remain to justify our conclusion: the most ancient poetry of India is, characteristically, the
work of a priestly class which, if not already formed was in
process of formation. From the time of the Vedic dawn we can
see the shadow of the Brahman interposing itself between nature
and soul. Sacrificial experts and professionals in the realms of
speculation had begun to monopolize intellectual life.

Do we find the same influences in the Upanishads? The word
Upanishad evokes, we are told, according to received etymology,
the picture of a circle of disciples sitting at the feet of the master
to receive confidential instruction. The Upanishad is intended to
be a secret lesson but the object of the lessons becomes truly
philosophical.[26] There are interminable discussions on being
and non-being, the self and the non-self, the various faculties of
the soul and the elements of the world. Speculation, which in the
Brahmanas only appears grafted to liturgy, here covers the whole
field.

It has been believed possible to see in this free speculation
proof that the circle of philosophers had widened well beyond
that of the born-priests and that castes other than the Brahman
took a preponderant part in intellectual life. Intellectual life must
have been singularly active in the courts where we see the
institution of thought-tournaments for which the prizes, given by
the kings, are cows with golden horns. The Satapatha Brahmana,
the Brahmana of a hundred paths, makes a Brahman woman, the

187

sage Gīrga, speak as follows:[27] 'As a son of the heroes of Kasi or of Vidēha bends his slackened bow, and with two deadly arrows, sets on his way, thus am I come to face you armed with two questions which you must resolve.' But it was not only women of the Brahmanic race, but also men of other castes who took part in these discussions. Kshatriyas must have shone in them. The Upanishads preserve the memory of the King Janaka, and his victorious arguments against the dialectic of the most famous Brahmans. Even more, we find traces of teaching 'going against the hair' *pratiloma*: we see sons of priests receiving instruction from a warrior's son.[28]

Elsewhere, it is said, the very orientation of thought reveals the existence of centres of intellectual attraction outside Brahmanism. Is it not apparent that in the Upanishads there is a systematic attempt to reduce the importance of sacrifice?[29] Intellectual effort is put above ritual operations. Access to the higher world is sought from knowledge. And this knowledge dissolves all the particularities of being, gods and men, in the ineffable reality of the unique being. Pantheistic metaphysics takes over from ritualistic commentary.

It is, in fact, very possible that at the higher social levels people were not satisfied with listening to the Brahmans. They had to debate with them. New sources of thought must have opened. But it is a massive self-deception to suppose that the philosophy of the Upanishads sprang fully armed from the minds of the Kshatriyas to combat the tradition of the Vedas and the Brahmanas. For it is clear that the former continues to derive its tendencies and methods from the latter. The Hindus are quite right, says M. Sylvain Lévi, to relate the Upanishads to the Brahmanas directly: 'A natural development has evolved the one out of the other.'[30] Pantheism, which spreads throughout the Upanishads is already in germ, as we have seen in the 'equations' of the Brahmanas. To repeat: 'This is that' is to be very close to showing that all is one. A world in which so many identifications are discovered is soon reduced to unity. The very fact, moreover, that here everything gravitates around sacrifice, must favour a monistic tendency. We read that Prajāpati, by sacrificing himself, produces all things. Phenomenal diversity is then presented as an emanation from a unique being, which is, at the same time, the universal substance.[31] Speculations about sacrifice, just as perhaps they suggested to the Hindu mind the idea of trans-migrations similar to the rebirth of the sacred fire, also incline it to recognize the existence of an unique being as a fundamental dogma.[32]

We should note, in addition, that the same propensity is observable in the Vedas. Tendencies embodied in the Upanishads are already apparent there: a critical tendency and, at the same time, a monistic one. It has frequently been said that in these so-called spontaneous hymns, somewhat sceptical reflections are more than once mixed in with poetic invocation.[33] The famous stanzas on the genesis of Being conclude as follows: 'Whence this creation came... if it was created or not created... he whose eye that watches over it from the highest heaven – knows, and yet, does he know?' In another hymn the question is repeated after each strophe: 'Who is this god whom we honour with sacrifices?' Here the singer is already a philosopher. Even though their existence is not put in doubt, the Vedic gods are never invested, in the hymns, with the precise and rigid forms which are contrary to the dissolving character of pantheism. Their features are shaded down just as their attributes are poorly differentiated. Vedic polytheism does not recognize the 'depart-mental' divisions of the classical polytheisms where each natural force is the province of one god. Perhaps such organization in the ideal world presupposes in the reality a degree of social organiza-tion to which India could not rise. It is always true that there is no city in its heaven.[34] It lacks order. We cannot even say that any one god is sovereign. All the gods become sovereign in turn.[35] Indeed, honoured with the same superlatives, they easily borrow each others' attributes. They couple, mix and melt the one into the other. They have no more distinct reality than have clouds.

Perhaps the lack is to be attributed, in part, to the preponder-ance of sacrifice. Can we be surprised if the gods are only vague and floating figures since they are here only the intermediaries, not to say accessories through which the power of the ritual operates on things? At all events it is in this power that all reality is absorbed. It can easily be seen that the Upanishads still conceive the supreme reality in terms of this power.

The Upanishads tell us that there is only one real being: that to which can be attributed no sensible quality and to which can only be attributed the quality of being. It is neither this nor that, but it is all, and alone it is. How do the philosophers conceive this universal substance? No doubt in terms of the self. They call it, then, *ātman*. It is possible to see in this notion of 'breath' a sort of spiritualized residue of primitive animism. But at the same time the real is presented in another aspect: in the aspect of cause rather than that of substance. In this aspect it is called *brahma*. And what is this *brahma* if not precisely the magic power which is at the disposal of the sacrificers? Prayer, formula, charm, ritual, *brahma* is essentially creative power.[36] In the hands of metaphysical speculation it becomes the active principle of the universe. But the metaphysical notion preserves the mark of its ritual origin. In this connection M. Oldenberg observes: 'There is not perhaps a more characteristic example of what is distinctive in the Indian mode of thought: this idea which does not originate from any contemplation of the sensible world but from meditation upon the power of the text of the Vedas and the task of the priest, grows by degrees until finally it gives its name to the highest conception that the mind can grasp.'[37]

The philosophy which was elaborated around this core exercised its attraction even upon those who most resolutely sought to shake Brahmanic domination and ritualistic servitude. We have seen that Buddhism did not escape.[38] If it uses popular tales for its propaganda, it remains faithful to its quasi-scholastic intellectual habits. Its dialectic follows the lines drawn by Brahmanic tradition for the Hindu mind. Under the grip of this tradition everything in India converges towards pantheism.

A very different pantheism, it has been frequently noted, from that which we find in the west.[39] Among us pantheism is, in a general sense, active and progressive. It says yes to life. It rejoices in the evolution of the rising spirit. It invites man to strive to assist this upward movement. There, on the contrary, it seems that effort is directed to the dissolution of this spirit in the ocean of being. Man's will is turned away from life. What he is made to fear more than anything is to live again.

Does this nihilistic idealism express, as has sometimes been pointed out, the impression that men must have of being crushed both by the cruel scourges of nature and the rigidity of their social organization? It is not unlikely. But another characteristic of the social organization is, no doubt, responsible for this tendency. Are not both the thirst for an unchanging unity and the disgust for ephemeral appearances born, more easily than elsewhere, in those circles of men withdrawn in a way from life, superior to wordly activity, and whose meditation was a game as well as an occupation?

If we would measure what such specialization of the intellectual life has given and denied Hindu civilization, we must compare India with Greece.

In Greece also we find priestly traditions at the origin of thought. They are nowhere lacking in the cradles of great civilizations. The historian of Greek thought observes: 'As far as historical knowledge allows us to say, the first steps in scientific research were never made except in countries where there was an organized class of priests or sages who combined the indispensable leisure with a no less indispensable stability of tradition'.[40] But he adds that 'there, the first steps were often the last because scientific doctrines acquired in this way, were too often crystallized in immovable dogmas, by amalgamation with religious beliefs... the leading string became a chain'.

It is precisely on this point that Greece enjoys a privileged position. She learned her first lessons from the Egyptians or the Babylonians. Colleges of alien priests gave her the point of departure. But on her own soil she had none to prescribe her route. Louis Ménard has emphasized this fortunate lacuna: the priests in Greece not only did not constitute a political body, a special class, but they did not in any degree have a monopoly of culture. Thus the 'crystallization of belief' which is ordinarily the work of priestly hierarchies could not occur in Greece.[41] Myths propagated by the poets were freely interpreted and criticized by the philosophers.[42] Instead of letting itself be frozen by tradition, human reason, increasing its inquiries and at the same time its scientific theories, turned freely towards reality.

How different was the situation in India! It was not that here either a Church emerged to modify tradition, as we have seen. Brahmanic religion remained, in the words of M. Barth, a religion of the *Book*.* The authority of the Vedas is not disputed. They embody a divine principle that gives birth to all.[43] It is important for the Brahman to communicate with this principle by the study of the sacred texts: this is a second birth for him. But at least, consecrated already by race, he is able to enter into direct communication with the sacred world. He holds the right to interpret revelation. He has to face no official body of guardians of the Book, whose decisions are law. This explains why India appears, as M. Henry said, at once so free and so conservative.

Nevertheless if these born-thinkers enjoyed a certain independence, this is precisely because they are the representatives of the sacred. They owe their prestige to their management of supernatural forces. Exactly because their kingdom is not of this world, we might say, their rule is not contested. And on this account the field of their meditation is, as it were, marked out in advance. They stay enclosed within the magic circle, the prisoners of their intellectual mobility. Their reflections, concerned with invisible realities, naturally turn away from appearances. Thus they can speculate *ad infinitum* without allowing sufficient place for observation.

For long it was fashionable to praise the scientific contribution of Hindu civilization. If the Hindus did not look at the earth, they did at least, it was claimed, observe the sky: their astronomy has won the admiration of centuries. In fact it seems that, even in this field, the scientific contribution of the Hindus amounts to very little.[44] Actually it is above all in the formal sciences that their genius, under the influence of the very system that governs their intellectual life, was to develop. One can, for example, easily connect the science of grammar to Brahmanic preoccupations. For the Brahman it was a cardinal duty to speak Sanskrit well. In addition, the words have in themselves a sort of sacred character.

* That is, unified by its literature; a sense quite different from the Koranic 'People of the Book'.

The success of ritual operations depends upon the way in which they are arranged and pronounced. It is not surprising, then, that they applied themselves to the science of words with that meticulous care to which Pānini's grammar bears witness.[45]

The presence of a revised religious tradition must, in a general way, have given the Hindu mind a taste for didactic literature. The privileged class who were the guardians of this tradition were

passionately concerned to ensure its perpetuation by meticulous teaching. As far back as we can go schools are very actively involved in the transmission and study of the sacred texts. The naturally subtle genius of the Hindus developed itself in meticulous observation and methodical classification. In acquiring the habit, they developed a taste for legislation. In religious matters, teaching and manuals took on some of the authority of their subject matter. Every branch of didactic activity acquired inestimable worth. In the field of profane literature, this activity preserved the habits it had acquired through its long concern with religious literature.[46]

This, no doubt, is why we find in Hindu literature something quite rare – technical treatises before works of art, theory before practice. The religious tradition contributed in this way to make formalism, in every field, one of India's intellectual habits.

But, this same tradition no doubt assisting, a sense of reality was lacking in India, and without love of action there was no concern for observation. This, more than anything, explains the distance separating the Hindu and Greek minds, although both light upon analogous expressions. Xenophanes who tends also to pantheism is, while still a poet, an observer. The thirst for knowledge drives him from town to town. While he amasses observations on geological strata, he notes political constitutions. In his indictment of anthropomorphism and its consequences, we may recognize the voice of a citizen anxious concerning the future of his fatherland. Thales' teaching has, through the intervention of poets, taken something from the religious tradition. They, in their way, already proclaimed that water was the principle of all things. But it is evident Thales drew his inspiration much more directly from observed facts. We see him draw a practical advantage from his inductions and establish an oil-press monopoly when his meteorological and astronomical findings enable him to foresee an abundant olive harvest. At the same time he is involved in political life and strove, we are told, to organize a federation of the Ionian cities. Astronomer and engineer, merchant and statesman – he was a stranger to no form of experience.[47] India has no such stories to tell. Her thinkers close their ears to the bustle of the dock-yards and the public squares. They stay enclosed in their castes, forever winding away the threads of their precious traditions.

It should go without saying that it would be a mistake to suppose that the Hindu soul in its entirety is revealed in the compositions of Brahmanic genius. This literature of initiates and professionals conceals more than it shows. Despite traditional specialization, these born-priests were not the only ones to think. Inevitably there must come a time when poetry and prose must express other hopes and habits than those peculiar to the priestly class.

First of all the religious life itself has other homes than the Brahmanic schools. We should grossly deceive ourselves if we believed that these imposed a ready-made faith upon the masses, one which they alone had elaborated. Outside their traditions and speculations, spontaneous beliefs incessantly proliferated. Around these beliefs, sects multiplied. More 'popular', they brought down to earth, so to speak, and gave personal form to gods who, in the hands of Brahmanic philosophy, had vanished in abstractions. On the other hand they established more credit for feeling, which is accessible to all, than for knowledge, for intuition than for dialectics. The day when these methods triumph marks the substitution of what is called Hinduism for Brahmanism.[48]

Here as almost everywhere in India it is difficult to discriminate periods. When we are dealing with Hindu civilization it is important to bear in mind the subjacent. Many forces do not emerge which, nevertheless, support all the rest. It is also necessary for the most part to speak of co-existence rather than of succession.[49] It is likely that there have always been independent sects side by side with the Brahmanic schools. But it is only from a certain period that literary monuments bear the mark of their activity.

As much must be said of feelings and ideas which are not related to religious life. We have seen that the Kshatriyas liked, sometimes, to follow the Brahman on to his own domain to fight him with his own weapons. But it is not unlikely that the majority of them felt other needs and sought after pleasures other than those of speculation. Relaxing in hunting after the battle and in the tournament after the hunt they led that high feudal life which is appropriate to a warlike aristocracy. A day would come when the feelings that such a life encourages and the representations which it suggests would carve their own place in the world of literature.

We feel these extra-Brahmanic sources of ideas and emotions running through the epics, but nevertheless we admire there once more the art with which Brahmanism channels and turns to its profit the very forces which it did not create.

Almost everywhere epic literature appears as a wife and hand-maid of warring aristocracy. In intervals between forays, they sing of glorious prowess to charm the leisured hour. Has a powerful family succeeded in its bid for domination? The bards then extol the great acts of its ancestors. Thus epic poetry maintains the respect of superior races as well as the love of adventure. It is a 'technique for domination and pride' as well as a feudal amusement.[50]

Such concerns were no doubt not lacking at the origin of the Hindu epic period. Here also we begin with the heroic chronicle, chanted by the hearths of princely houses. The recital of the conflict between the sons of Pandu and the sons of Kuru preserves, as it might be, a reflection of the wars of races and the battles of clans in primitive India. Whatever rehandling the early songs may have undergone before they entered the Mahabharata, we feel nevertheless, the rough breath of a bellicose society, ardent for play or war. We see the unending duel – distant prototype of the duel of Oliver and Roland – and ranged battles involving immense armies 'like the sea, like the Ganges', tournaments that bring together bowmen from every country in India, and gambling scenes where play is for a kingdom and even a wife. It is sometimes said that epic grandeur calls for exaggeration of action and of passion. It needs a background of violence and a trace of heroic savagery. At more than one point, this type of primitive heroism flowers in the Ramayana and in the Mahabharata. We sense in them the collaboration of races that live by war.[51]

But finally, how much more powerfully we feel the action of a class that lives by religion! The Mahabharata becomes in its final form, as has been said, a sort of encyclopedia of religious science. Speculation and prescription are heaped together pell-mell. The epic recitation has passed from the hands of the feudal bard into the hands of the Brahman – priest, jurist and philosopher.[52] In the famous episode of the Bhagavad Gita, Arjun about to throw himself into battle, stops his chariot; his driver, who is none other than the god Krishna, reveals to him, in the course of a long series of slokas, the most subtle reflections of the metaphysicians on the nothingness of beings. At every point traditions cultivated by professional thinkers surround and hide the primitive rock with their exuberant vegetation. The epic is no longer in the service of feudal memory but of the Brahmanic ideal.

No doubt we can discern progress in certain 'secular' tendencies. *Dharma* takes precedence over *rita*. The development of economic life develops rules which are not connected with things religious.[53] Similarly, it is clear that morality becomes 'humanized'. It seems to care less for the concern with ritual purity, and more for feelings of fraternity, generosity and pity. Nevertheless, while these virtues are highly praised, there is a constant concern for the prior respect of that body of scruples which assures the Brahman's superiority. The sins which are accounted more dreadful than any are still those which might pose a threat to his life or dignity, and disturb the caste system. No more than we see a clear distinction of *jus* and *fas*, do we find a frank laïcization of moral concern. Religious duties still take precedence over all. In essence they consist in respect for that sacred hierarchy of which the Brahman is both guardian and beneficiary.

It may be said that if religion throws its mantle over the epic, it is at least not the pure religion woven by Brahmanism. Threads of all sorts and of different origins are mixed in its web. This is true. The epics certainly bear the mark of sectarian activity. The ancient Vedic divinities step into the background. It is Vishnu and Krishna who are to the forefront of the scene. But such changes should in no way surprise us. They do not prove that Brahmanism has renounced its ambitions: on the contrary it continues to pursue them as it has always done by tolerance. Whether they are the innovations of sects or the traditions of races, Brahmanism finds a way to admit and assimilate all.[54] Precisely in the epic literature we see it using its useful *avatāra* theory. Thanks to this theory it is quite easy for the Brahman to find familiar gods beneath strange ones and ancient ones beneath new ones. Thus Brahmanism speaks to many publics at the same time and, with happily equivocal language, addresses an ever-growing crowd.

If we wish to judge with what art they have used outside forces to enlarge the circle of their action, we should remember how the Puranas were constructed. The Puranas are a kind of epic poem especially intended for those classes that could not read the Vedas. They are, as it were, novels about divine adventures. It is likely that the legends from which they are composed derive from the popular imagination itself. But Brahmanic speculation applying itself to these legends bends them to its own ends. It incorporates in these collections its cosmogonical theories, adapting them to the needs of the sects, and employs the tales to establish the supremacy of the Brahman caste.[55]

Thus in literature itself we find a new proof of the kind of opportunism that this caste of born-thinkers in India has shown in order to preserve its mastery.

As gradually literature draws away from its origins, the hold of the priests is less apparent. It is still possible to recognize the general imprint upon it of the system that divides and hierarchizes Hindu society.

Indian theatre was also born under the auspices of religion. For long it preserves the memory of this guardianship. Dramatic representations not only occur at the time of traditional solemnities, as for instance the feast of spring. Even the most frivolous of them take place under divine patronage. From Vedic times one can see, we are told, the efforts of priests to exploit the Aryan love of dance, song and spectacle for the benefit of their cult. Hinduism follows the same tactics. The divine figures of the epic period climb the stage. The adventures of Krishna, *avatār* of Vishnu, are favourite dramatic subjects. Siva, heir of Rudra, is recognized as the tutelary god of the theatrical profession.[56]

But whatever the influence of religion upon the development of the theatre, it was not to become, as in Greece, a kind of public institution, the centre of national life. Dramatic representations have always been occasional amusements in India, and most often they keep their private character. The majority of the pieces that have been preserved for us were no doubt played in the assembly hall of some *rāja*. They were limited to an élite public. They express in a variety of ways the aristocratic life of Hindu society more than the religious tradition.

The differences separating Hindu and Greek drama have often been noted. Aristotle's formulae have been used to define the opposition of the two. While Greek drama 'imitates an action' the *nātaka* 'imitates a condition'. 'Strong in body and intelligence' the Greek loves action to fever point: life itself cannot satiate him. The Indians, like all the barbarians of South Asia have strong and subtly vivacious minds, but no strength of body.[57] No doubt the effect of the climate, this apathy finds expression even in the nature of theatrical productions. But it is perhaps also in part the effect of the system, if it is true that caste, by limiting and restraining action, chokes the very love of activity itself.[58]

At the same time that they are not very active, the *dramatis personae* are poorly individualized. 'They are not individuals whose passions, loves and temperaments will develop freely in response to the incidents of life: they are unchanging types, placed in almost identical situations.' In the fixity of these characters we may see proof that the authors were less concerned to observe reality than to obey tradition. We have already discussed the way in which Hindu literature, born of religious seed, is essentially didactic. Practice is almost everywhere preceded by theory. Dramatic art is also dominated by traditional poetics, itself based on the authority of a god and a saint, Bharata, leader of the Apsaras. Indian theatre, we are told, provides us with the possibly unique spectacle of a theory accepted without dispute and applied with servile respect for fifteen centuries.[59] The authors' ideal seems to be to present us with the various classical types in a situation defined in advance and in conformity with the almost sacred laws of style. The fundamental traditionalism of the Hindus explains the conventional face of their theatre.

Reality itself, compartmentalized by the castes, only allows specific qualities to appear rather than the variety of individuals. Here the individual 'is effaced by and disappears in the species; the type triumphs over variety'.[60] Tell me your caste and I will tell you the bent of your mind, your habits and tendencies. Such a system is capable of determining not only the functions but the style of life, not only styles of life but character. It is natural that under such pressure men are less distinguished the one from the other, on the stage as in life, by their personal temperament than by their social status.

There is in addition a somewhat material proof of the pious concern of the theatre for the maintenance of caste distinctions. It is not only by a hundred pronouncements, *à propos* of everything and nothing, that drama, like the epics, preaches respect for the system. It renders it further homage by the diversity of languages which it allows to its different characters. It establishes a hierarchy of dialects. Technical treaties carefully define which is suitable for each condition. Sanskrit is reserved for people of high family. The others, according to their condition, speak the more or less vulgar Prakrits.[61]

We must add that people of inferior condition only have secondary roles in drama: 'The common people count as little in drama as in life.' The plot is most often confined within the palace. The protagonists are princes, alone worthy to retain the attention of the aristocratic audience foregathered in the assembly hall, with the spectacle of their amorous and warlike adventures.

The character of this audience explains not only the respect for hierarchy to which the theatre bears witness, not only the quality of the characters and the nature of the subjects treated but even the general tone of the works. It has been said that they are, in a sense, as little moving, or at least as little disturbing as possible. They seem to avoid on principle not only anything which might pollute but all that might over-excite. No doubt they are obliged before all else to respect the native purity and moral nobility of the audience. Therefore, they transport it gently, by means of a cunning prologue, into the ideal world of legends, which are, moreover, familiar to it. They will suggest only those emotions which are appropriate to its high social situation.[62]

If these various remarks are correct we may be permitted to conclude that the Hindu theatre also carries the imprint of caste. Dramatic productions which the *nātaka* most resembles, are those which will emerge in intellectual circles fashioned for the needs of an aristocracy. A whole world separates Hindu drama from our classical tragedy. The latter encloses the contest of ideas within the souls of its heroes, in the former it seems that nature rules all. This is, no doubt, one of the reasons why the romantics, in opposition to the classical theatre, extol the theatre of the Hindus. It is nevertheless possible to discover some traits common to both. The tragedy of Corneille and Racine, also destined for the royal court, separated by its choice of subjects from the masses 'prided itself on dignity and nobility; it turned away from real life and created a society of convention with invariable types that Aristotle would, no doubt, have refused to recognize but which Bharata would have willingly adopted'.[63]

Compare, on the contrary, Hindu and Greek theatre. There also religious emotion is the spring, but soon other streams widen the river and modify its course. Individual energy is exalted. National glories are praised. Social and moral questions are discussed. In a sense the effervescence of city life overflows onto the stage. But it is precisely this life that India lacks most of all. Her theatre, in its way, reveals all that she has lost by the sole fact that the Aryan clans instead of melting away in cities, have fixed themselves in the form of castes.

More generally because the caste system opposes the emancipation of individualities as much as the constitution of national unities, it condemns to atrophy the majority of literary genres which developed in western literature. Just as the system did not experience the combative eloquence of public men, nor history to record the great dates in collective life, so it is almost totally ignorant of personal lyricism, which expresses man's conflict or harmony with himself.

Literature

Thus literature in its turn has shown us those limitations to development which are the normal effect of the caste system. We said that it rapidly paralyses the vitality of the civilization which it has helped to bring out from barbarism. It cannot but mutilate the very spirit which it refines.

Endnotes

[The translator's remarks appear in square brackets]

To the readers of 'Année Sociologique'

1   This unity of views results from the general homogeneity which naturally established itself among those who collaborated in the Année as a result of working together for ten years; however *it leaves unqualified the liberty and responsibility of each author.*

Introduction

1   English translation by H. K. Beauchamp (Oxford, 1906), pp. 23–7.
2   *Chips from a German workshop*, II (London, 1867), p. 322.
3   *The tribes and castes of the N.W. Provinces and Oudh*, I (Calcutta, 1896), p. xvi.
4   W. J. Wilkins, *Modern Hinduism, religion and life of Hindus in North India* (London, 1887), pp. 163–4; De Lanoye, *L'Inde contemporaine* (Paris, 1855), p. 32.
5   English translation by Sir E. Denison Ross, *Caste in India* (London, 1930), p. 215. [All subsequent references are to this edition.]
6   *The tribes and castes of Bengal* (Calcutta, 1896), pp. xxi sqq.
7   *La civilisation en Europe* (Paris, 1882), p. 138.
8   *Comptes-rendus de l'Académie des Inscrip.* (Paris, 1848), quoted by Revillout, *Droit Egyptien* (Paris, 1884), I, pp. 132 sqq.
9   See article on 'Caste' in vol. II of *Supplement to the 4th, 5th and 6th editions of the Encyclopaedia Britannica.*
10 *Essai sur le Véda, ou étude sur les religions, la littérature et la constitution sociale de l'Inde* (Paris, 1863), p. 218.
11 *Caste in India*, p. 152.
12 Quoted by Schlagintweit, *Zeitschrift der Deutschen Morgenländischen Gesellschaft*, Bd. 33, p. 587. Sherring insists on the same point in *Hindu tribes and castes*, III (Calcutta, 1879), pp. 218, 235.
13 Karl Bücher, *Die Entstehung der Volkswirthschaft*, 2nd edition (Tübingen, 1898), pp. 338 sqq.
14 Several observers have offered evidence to show that these questions of class are not irrelevant to the 'crisis of secondary education'. See for example Langlois, 'La question de l'enseignement secondaire', *Revue de Paris*, 1 and 15 January 1900.
15 See Goblot, *Revue d'économie politique*, January, 1899. A good definition of class is still, however, difficult to find. When the social hierarchy is no longer blessed by the juridical system the difficulty is

that of finding the distinctive signs by which classes are recognized. Some attempts have been made to find the centres of class in the various professions. But if such a definition applies, at least in part, to castes it is decidedly too narrow for classes (see *L'Année Socio-logique*, VI, pp. 125–9, the criticism of A. Bauer's book *Classes sociales*, Paris, 1902). To understand the differentiation of classes it is obviously necessary to take into account as well as the professional specializations, the differences of economic levels. But these differences in turn need to be evaluated in different manners according to the case. If in the leisure classes more or less ostentatious expenditure is the mark of rank, at other levels it would appear that differences in salary are sufficient to classify people. (See in this connection *Revue de Meta-physique et de Morale*, 1905, pp. 890–905, the stimulating remarks of Halbwachs on 'La position du problème sociologique des classes'. There the author summarizes and criticizes the theories of Schmoller, Sombart and Bücher.)

16 In France, for example, the villages of Monistrol and Villedieu-les-Poêles.

17 Numerous examples are to be found in Auerbach, *Les Races et les nationalités en Autriche-Hongrie* (Paris, 1898), pp. 75, 119, 125, 209, 266.

18 There is an informative discussion of this subject in the *Revue de Sociologie* for the year 1900. It shows that the cases in which the father passes on his trade to the son are not rare but that they are difficult to classify and to enumerate.

19 We have tried to show this in the first part of our *Idées égalitaires*.

20 *Civilisation en Europe*, p. 138.

21 Cf. Fustel de Coulanges, *L'alleu et le domaine rural*, p. 299.

22 This expression is taken from Guizot's *Régime féodal*.

23 Thus the Eleusinian Eumolpides.

24 Schömann, *Griechische Altertümer*, I (Berlin, 1897), pp. 327 sqq.

25 Cf. von Müller, *Handbuch der klassischen Altertumswissenschaft* (Nordlingen, 1886), IV, p. 1.

26 No doubt one may find in Rome the *gentes minores* and the analogous *genē* of the labourers and artisans in Athens (cf. Wilbrandt, *Die politische und sociale Bedeutung der attischen Geschlechter vor Solon*). The *genos* was so essential to city law that the *plebs*, in order to enter the city, had to organize itself into *genē*. But at this time the collective inferiority of the *plebs* was not yet absolute and the plebians were beginning their campaign for equality of rights.

27 Herodotus, II, 164, 168, 37, 166.

28 Diodorus, I, 73; I, 74, sections 3, 8.

29 Cf. Revillout, *Cours de droit égyptien*, I, pp. 137, 138.

30 Cf. Maspero, *Histoire ancienne des peuples de l'Orient classique*, I (Paris, 1895), p. 305.

31 *Cours de droit egyptien*, ɪ, pp. 131, 136, 147.
32 Cf. Ampère, *Comptes-rendus de l'Académie des Inscrip.*
33 The expression used by Ampère.
34 We should be on our guard against confusing the actual facts with the law. Thus in many societies where polygamy is legally admitted, a large number of men remain monogamous – either due to their poverty or to the scarcity of women.
35 This information comes from Revillout himself, *Cours de droit egyptién*, ɪ, p. 165.
36 See Maspero, *Histoire ancienne*, ɪ, p. 290.
37 *Ibid.* p. 300 sq. Cf. Revillout, *Cours de droit egyptien*, ɪ, p. 145.
38 Leist, *Graeco-italienische Rechtsgeschichte* (Iena, 1884), p. 106.
39 As has happened in Germany. Cf. Bücher, *Die Entstehung der Volkswirthschaft*, p. 319.
40 Schlagintweit, *Zeitschrift der D.M.G.*, p. 578.
41 R. Fick, *Die social Gliederung im Nordöstlichen Indien zu Budda's Zeit mit besonderer Berücksichtigung der Kastenfrage* (Kiel, 1897), p. 194. Cf. English translation by S. Mitra (Calcutta, 1920), p. 302. [What our author writes is more literally true of the hunters, *ibid.*]
42 Sylvain Lévi, article 'Inde' in the *Grande Encyclopédie*.
43 Nesfield, *Brief view of the caste system of the N.W. Provinces and Oudh* (Allahabad, 1885), p. 19.
44 Numerous facts of this nature are to be found in Jacquemont's *Voyage dans l'Inde, pendant les années 1828 à 1832* (Paris, 1835–44).
45 *Ancienne relation des Indes et de la Chine*, 1728 edition, p. 40.
46 Fick, *Die sociale Gliederung*, pp. 178, 180, 181.
47 Strabo, xv, ɪ, 49.
48 Thus the word Mayara, which designates 'pastry-cook' is an altered form of the Sanskrit *modakakara* (pastry-cook); Tatwa and Tanti, which designate weavers, derive from *tantuvāya* (weaver); the name of the Kandus (grain-parchers) is said to come from the Sanskrit *kandu* (oven), etc. Nesfield (*Brief view of the caste system*, p. 84) says that 77 per cent of the names of castes are the ancient names of occupations. It is true that a certain number of the etymologies given by Nesfield have been contested, but a sufficient number remain uncontested to sustain his argument (see for example Lassen, *Indische Altertumskunde*, ɪ, pp. 795, 820, or the more recent work of Jogendranath Bhattacharya, *Hindu castes and sects* (Calcutta, 1896), pp. 236, 238, 252).
49 This last fact contradicts the supposed law that there is no return to agriculture once another occupation has been tried. See discussion referred to in *Revue de Sociologie*, 1900.
50 Senart, *Caste in India*, pp. 42 sq. Cf. Bhattacharya, *Hindu castes*, pp. 74, 112.
51 Dubois, *Hindu manners*, p. 292.

52 Crooke, *Tribes and castes of the N.W. Provinces*, I, p. cxlix.
53 Risley, *Tribes and castes of Bengal*, I, p. 49. Gait, *Bengal Report* (*Census of India*, 1901, vi), p. 351.
54 Risley, *Tribes and castes of Bengal*, I, p. 280.
55 Bhattacharya, *Hindu castes*, p. 309.
56 Risley, *Tribes and castes of Bengal*, I, p. lxxii.
57 Castes which are said to be agricultural only comprise 6½ million members but 34¾ million agriculturers were actually counted. Inversely 5½ million people belong to pastoral castes but no more than about 337,000 were actually found engaged in pastoral occupations. Cf. Crooke, *Tribes and castes of the N.W. Provinces*, p. cxlv.
58 Enthoven analysing the situation in the Bombay Province (*Census of India*, 1901, ix, pp. 209, 220) observes that only 22 per cent of the Brahmans were faithful to their traditional occupation. Despite the classical prohibition one finds that among them 47 per cent were in the administration and agriculture, 5 per cent were engaged in food services of one sort or another. Among the Vanis, who correspond fairly closely to the traditional Vaishya, 25 per cent were occupied in commerce, 39 per cent in food services, 10 per cent in manufacturing cloth or clothing, 3 per cent in agriculture, 2 per cent in the administration.
   Sylvain Lévi (*Le Nepal, étude historique d'un royaume hindou* (Paris, 1905), I, p. 246) points out that in many cases a caste 'reserves' an occupation for its members rather than 'imposes' one upon them – above all, let us add, if it occupies a sufficiently high rank in the hierarchy. Thus in Nepal the Buddhist caste, in every respect an imitation of a Hindu caste, has formed around occupation alone. It was created for the exploitation of a sort of legal monopoly accessible only to the descendants of the founders. 'The monopoly, it is true, is not always lucrative, as for example the privilege of painting the eyes of the image of Bhairava. The benefices from that are frequently insufficient to provide a livelihood for the growing number of interested parties. Fortunately the list of hereditary professions, long as it is, does not exhaust all the categories of livelihoods.' The caste freely allows its members 'to escape into the undefined area of occupations which do not belong to anyone'.
59 See however certain examples cited from the Jātakas, by C. Rhys Davids, *Notes on early economic conditions in northern India*, p. 868.
60 Steele, *Law and customs of Hindu castes* (London, 1868), p. xi. He considers fidelity to the ancestral occupation as one of the criteria of caste dignity.
61 Or by some fantastic etymology. Thus the Telis of Bengal who have given up oil-pressing for large scale commerce, claim that their name derives from *tula* (shop scales) and not from *taila* (oil), Bhattacharya, *Hindu castes*, p. 263.

62 *Ibid.* p. 228 fn.
63 Dubois, *Hindu manners*, pp. 49, 55, 61, 125–6, 128.
64 Pierre Sonnerat, *Voyages aux Indes orientales et à la Chine de 1774 à 1781*, 2 vols. (Paris, 1782), 2nd ed. in 4 vols with atlas, 1806. [Bougle gives no complete reference to Sonnerat and it is not therefore possible to say which edition he was using although it seems likely that it was the expanded edition of 1806.]
65 See Jacquemont. *Voyage*, I, p. 234.
66 Dubois, *Hindu manners*, p. 99.
67 Again certain exceptions. Cf. Dubois, *Hindu manners*, p. 23. Max Müller, *Chips from a German workshop*, II, pp. 334–8. But, 'apart from the fact that these exceptions are rare, they are generally based upon some definite motive' (Senart, *Caste in India*, p. 101).
68 According to Dubois questions of precedence sometimes gave rise to bloody battles (*Hindu manners*, p. 26). Since the recent census attention has been drawn to the emotion displayed by some castes in their fear that they were not classed according to their rank. The Khattris convened a meeting of protest at Bareilly and sent a memorandum to the census authorities, in order to insist upon their right to be classed as Kshatriyas. (*Census of India*, 1901. General Report by Risley and Gait, I, p. 539.)
69 Steele, *Law and customs of Hindu castes*, p. x.
70 In his enumeration of castes, Bhattacharya always begins by asking these questions (*Hindu castes*, first part). The English investigators for the most part arrived at the same criteria (*Census of India*, 1901, VI, p. 137; XVIII, p. 487; XXV, p. 133).
71 Weber, *Indische Studien*, X, pp. 20–4; Steele, *Law and customs of Hindu castes*, pp. 23, 28; Jolly, 'Recht und Sitte', in the *Grundriss der indo-arischen Philologie und Altertumskunde* of Bühler (Strasbourg, 1896), p. 127.
72 Jacquemont (*Voyage*, I, pp. 281–2) points out how difficult it is to make a sure classification of castes. Not only are the same names found in different provinces, but also in each province there is no universally recognized order of precedence. 'A man of very low caste will never put his caste in the very first rank but he will put it several ranks above that to which the other castes have agreed to assign it.'
73 When low castes improve their position they look for a genealogy which will exalt them; for their old name they invent a new etymology, or even try to change their name. But their rivals tolerate this rise with difficulty, whence the interminable disputes. Many examples could be given: the Kshettris claim to be Kshatriyas and observe the rites laid down for military castes, but others class them as Banias. The enriched Sunris have for long striven to be recognized as a pure caste. But only the degraded prophets of Hinduism flatter their ambition. Risley tells us that even those who work for the Sunris do

not like to touch their food. A Chandala would lose caste if he touched the seat upon which a Sunri was seated. See Risley, *Tribes and castes of Bengal*, ii, p. 279. Bhattacharya, *Hindu castes*, pp. 79, 190, 124, 138, 255, and Schlagintweit's article already cited, *Zeitschrift der D.M.G.*, 33, pp. 557, 566, 574.

74 Cf. Jacquemont, *Voyage*, i, p. 157; Sonnerat, *Voyages*, i, p. 110; De Lanoye, *L'Inde Contemporaine*, 1885, p. 128.

75 Christian missionaries despite the doctrines which they try to spread are obliged to take these repugnances into account. Fr Suau, *L'Inde Tamoule* (Paris, 1901), says that in many places the right hand side of the nave in the church is reserved for the Pariahs: they communicate only after the others. In Vadakenkoulam, a village composed of Sanars and Moudeliars, mutual hostility is so lively that they had to build for the Christian neophytes a church with two naves radiating from the common choir.

76 Schlagintweit, *Zeitschrift der D.M.G.*, 33, p. 581. Reports from Cochin State classify the impure castes according to the distance at which they pollute: some at 24 paces, some at 36, others at 48 and at 64. (Quoted by Vidal de la Blache, *Annales de Géographie*, juillet 1906. p. 440.)

77 R. Fick, *Die sociale Gliderung*.

78 *Ibid.* pp. 26, 28.

79 We have to distinguish amongst foods. The manner in which they are prepared makes them, if one may say so, more or less 'dangerous'. Brahmans will take food from certain castes which has been cooked with clarified butter (*pakki*) and not food cooked in other ways (*kachchi*). See Gait, *Bengal Report* (*Census of India*, 1901, vi, p. 367).

80 Sonnerat, *Voyages*, i, p. 108.

81 Jacquemont, *Voyage*, i, p. 255.

82 Bhattacharya, *Hindu castes*, p. 135.

83 Risley, *Tribes and castes of Bengal*, i, p. 157.

84 Risley remarks in this connection how important it is, when distributing succour in time of famine, to know the hierarchy of the castes and to know from whose hand each may receive food. The Chattar-Kais in Orissa are now among the 'lost castes' because they ate in the relief kitchens in 1866 (*Tribes and castes of Bengal*, i, p. viii).

85 Elliot, *Memoirs on the history, folklore and distribution of the races of the N.W. Provinces*, i, ed. Beames (London, 1869), p. 67 fn.

86 Risley, *Tribes and castes of Bengal*, i, p. xlii.

87 *Ibid.* pp. li sqq.

88 Hypergamy is the term proposed by Risley for this phenomenon.

89 Bhattacharya, *Hindu castes*, p. 41; Risley, *Tribes and castes of Bengal*, p. lxxxii.

90 Cited by Schlagintweit, *Zeitschrift der D.M.G.*, 33, p. 560.

91 Crooke, *Tribes and castes of the N.W. Province*, iii, p. 27.

92 Senart, *Caste in India*, Part II, ch. 2.
93 Cf. Senart, *Caste in India*, p. 115; Max Müller, *Chips from a German workshop*, pp. 343, 350; Jolly, *Zeitschrift der D.M.G.*, Bd. 50, p. 507.
94 Fick, *Die sociale Gliederung, passim*.
95 Jolly, *Zeitschrift der D.M.G.*, 50, p. 515.
96 Senart, *Caste in India*, p. 28. In the N.W. Provinces alone Nesfield distinguished forty Brahman castes, *Brief view of the caste system*, pp. 49, 115. The 1,500,000 Brahmans of Bombay Province are divided, according to Enthoven, into more than two hundred groups between which marriage is forbidden (*Census of India*, 1901, IX, p. 278).
97 Sir Alfred Lyall (*Asiatic Studies*, London, 1884, ch. v) shows how Rajputs are 'made' by the Brahmanization of aboriginal chiefs. Crooke (*Tribes and castes of the N.W. Province*, p. xxii) cites a certain number of Rajput 'septs' which clearly betray an aboriginal origin. Ibbetson (*Punjab Ethnogr.*, p. 421) believes so little in the purity of the blood of these claimants to Kshatriya descent that he goes so far as to say: 'The term Rajput is to my mind an occupational rather than an ethnographic expression.'
98 The disinclination of the different Rajput clans to eat together will be remembered. See above, p. 24.
99 Cf. Schröder, *Indiens Literatur und Cultur* (Leipzig, 1887), p. 419. Jolly (*Zeitschrift der D.M.G.*, 50, p. 614) proves by the names employed in the Smritis that their occupations attributed by the theory to the single caste of Vaishyas were in fact practised by very diverse groups. Cf. Fick, *Die Sociale Gliederung*, pp. 163 sq.
100 According to Fick there are no traces in Pali texts of a real caste corresponding to the theoretical Shudra caste. The officers of the modern Indian census declare almost unanimously that they have found nothing corresponding to the Vaishya caste and even less a caste of Shudras. (Cf. the results of the 1872 census summarized by Schlaginweit, *Zeitschrift der D.M.G.*) Cf. Beames, *The races of the North West Provinces*, p. 167, and Risley, *Tribes and castes of Bengal*, I, p. 271.
101 It was by the analysis of the distinctive case of the American democracies that Tocqueville brought to light the principal political, economic, moral, religious and even literary effects of the progress of the idea of human equality.

PART 1: THE ROOTS OF THE CASTE SYSTEM

Chapter 1: Caste specialization and the guild

1 Leopold von Schröder, *Indiens Literatur und Cultur*, pp. 152, 410.
2 Hermann Oldenberg, *Buddha: Sein Leben, seine Lehre, seine Gemeinde* (Berlin, 1897). [Bouglé used the 2nd edition of Foucher's translation

(Paris, 1903). Subsequent references are to Oldenberg's original text in the 3rd and enlarged edition (Berlin, 1897).] Sherring, *Natural history of caste*, quoted by Senart, *Caste in India*, p. 150.

3 Senart, *Caste in India*, pp. 148 sq.

4 *Das Altindische Volkstum und seine Bedeutung für die Gesellschaftskunde* (Cologne, 1889), p. 314.

5 The greater part of these expressions are used by Oldenberg *La religion du Véda* (Paris, 1903). Cf. *The Buddha, loc. cit.* [sic.]

6 This M. Dahlmann has tried to show in another work, *Das Mahābhārat als Epos und Rechtsbuch. Ein Problem aus Altindiens Cultur und Literaturgeschieffe* (Berlin, 1895).

7 Jhering, *Vorgeschichte der Indo-Europäer* (Leipzig, 1894), p. 225.

8 Dahlmann, *Das Mahabharat*, pp. 45 sq., 125 sq.; Jolly, *Zeitschrift der D.M.G.*, 50, pp. 26–44.

9 *Das Mahabharat*, pp. 69 sq.

10 *Ibid.* pp. 188 sq. Cf. Zimmer, *Altindisches Leben, Die Cultur der Vedischen Arier nach dem Samhita dargestellt* (Berlin, 1879), pp. 240–50.

11 Dahlmann, *Das Mahabharat*, p. 112.

12 *Ibid.* p. 112.

13 Doren, *Untersuchungen zur Geschichte der Kaufmannsgilden des Mittelalters...*, p. 5.

14 Dahlmann, *Das Mahabharat*, pp. 113–16.

15 *Ibid.* p. 24.

16 *A brief view of the caste system of the North-Western Provinces & Oudh* (Allahabad, 1885), p. 132.

17 *Ibid.* pp. 8–9.

18 *Ibid.* pp. 14, 19, 20, 27

19 *Ibid.* p. 80.

20 Dahlmann, *Das Mahabharat*, pp. 46, 72.

21 Nesfield, *Caste system*, p. 95.

22 See above, p. 18.

23 Thus the Peshirajis who have become quarriers are separated from the related Ahir who have remained shepherds: the Rajs, masons, distinguish themselves from the Sangtarash, stone cutters. The Bagdis are divided into Dulias, palanquin bearers, Machuas, fishermen and Matials, well-diggers. Cf. Nesfield, *Caste system*, p. 91. Risley, *Tribes and castes of Bengal*, I, p. lxxii.

24 Thus the Dogras are named after a valley in Kashmir, the Saruguparias after the river Saruju, the Saraswat Brahmans of the Punjab after the river Saraswati, etc. Bhattacharya, *Hindu castes*, pp. 49, 54, 55. Risley, *Tribes and castes of Bengal*, I, p. 47, cites the case of the Baidyas, divided into four sub-castes which correspond to the different parts of Bengal where their ancestors lived.

25 Cf. Lyall, *Asiatic Studies* (London, 1884), ch. VII, p. 173.

26 P. Foucart, *Des associations religieuses chez les grecs* (Paris, 1873), pp. 50 sq.
27 *Caste in India*, p. 166.
28 This is what we have tried to show at greater length in our *Idées égalitaires*, ch. II.
29 Cf. Gierke, *Das Deutsche Genossenschaftsrecht*; Prins, *L'organisation de la liberté* (Brussels, 1895), *passim*, Lalande, *La dissolution opposée à l'evolution* (Paris, 1899), ch. V.
30 W. J. Ashley, *An introduction to English economic history and theory*, 3rd edition (London, 1894), I, p. 76.
31 *Das Deutsche Genossenschaftsrecht*, pp. 225–30. Cf. Schönberg, *Handbuch der politischen Okonomie*, II, p. 484.
32 Ashley, *English economic history*, I, p. 71.
33 Gasquet, *Institutions politiques de l'ancienne France*, II, pp. 240–43.
34 Waltzing, *Les corporations professionnelles chez les Romains*, I, pp. 75, 166, 284, 329. Cf. Hearn *The Aryan household* (London, 1879), pp. 308–11; Brentano, *On gilds & trade unions*, p. 16.
35 Ashley, *English economic history*, I, pp. 77–8 rightly protests against the exaggeration in this hypothesis.
36 *Caste system*, p. 34.
37 *Cours de philosophie positive*, VI, ch. VII, quoted by Nesfield, *Caste system*, p. 95.
38 *Caste system*, pp. 96 sq.
39 See our *Democratie devant la science* (Paris, 1904), I.
40 Thus it is generally agreed today that the explanation of the origin of exogamy from a consciousness that man had of the evil effects of consanguineous marriages imputes too great a capacity for utilitarian reflection to primitive peoples. Cf. *Année Sociologique*, I, p. 33.
41 Oldenberg, *Buddha*, recalls what is said in the Satapatha Brāhmana of the land beyond the river Sadanira: 'Now it is an entirely good land for the Brahmans have made it habitable by the power of sacrifice.'
42 Nesfield, *Caste system*, p. 15.
43 For example the Tatwas of Bihar. Cf. Bhattacharya, *Hindu castes*, p. 232. [Bouglé's text confuses this caste with the Tantis of Bengal.]
44 Nesfield, *Caste system*, p. 29.
45 *Ibid.* p. 9.
46 Bhattacharya, *Hindu castes*, pp. 266 sq. Cf. Crooke, *Tribes and castes of the N.W. Provinces*, IV, p. 45.
47 *Caste system*, pp. 100 sq.

Chapter 2: The opposition of caste and family

1 *Caste in India*, pp. 188 sq. Cf. Lyall, *Asiatic studies*, ch. VII.
2 Zimmer, *Altindisches Leben*, pp. 185–90.

3 Senart, *Caste in India*, pp. 132 sq., cf. J. Athelstane Baines 'On certain features of social differentiation in India', *Journal of the Royal Asiatic Society of Great Britain and Ireland*, 26, pp. 657–75.

4 *Ibid*. p. 150.

5 Senart, *Caste in India*, pp. 129, 143 sq.

6 Barth. [There is no further reference. See note 9 below.] Cf. Jolly, *Zeitschrift der D.M.G.*, 1897, pp. 280 sq.

7 Zimmer, *Altindischer Leben*, p. 159. Cf. Senart, *Caste in India*, pp. 188 sq.

8 Oldenberg's objection to Senart's theory is principally this lack of precise information. Cf. *Zeitschrift der D.M.G.*, 1897, pp. 280 sq.

9 Senart, *Caste in India*, pp. 136 sq. See also Auguste Barth's remarks in his preface to *Religion of India* (London, 1882), p. xv. Cf. *Année Sociologique*, I, pp. 212, 219 on Crooke's *The popular religions and folklore of Northern India* (London, 1893).

10 Senart, *Caste in India*, p. 180.

11 The very names sometimes used to designate members of the family prove it: *homosipuoi, homokapnoi*. Cf. Aristotle *Politics* I, 2, 1252 b 13.

12 For example the feast of the Apaturies. Cf. Curtius, *Histoire grecque*, III, p. 494.

13 Senart, *Caste in India*, p. 182. Cf. Leist, *Altarisches Jus Civile*, pp. 200 sq.

14 *Ibid*. p. 178.

15 *Report on the Census of the Punjab*, 1881. Risley reproduces a part of this rare report in the *Ethnographic appendices* of the *Census of India 1901*, I (Calcutta, 1903).

16 Senart, *Caste in India*, p. 211.

17 Barth, Jolly, *Zeitschrift der D.M.G.*

18 Oldenberg, *Zeitschrift der D.M.G.*, 51, p. 279 fn.

19 W. Robertson Smith, *The religion of the Semites*, Gifford Lectures, 1890, pp. 159 sq.

20 *Ibid*. pp. 448–52.

21 *Ibid*. p. 269–75. Cf. Reinach, *Cultes, mythes et religions* (Paris, 1905), I, pp. 96–104.

22 *Année Sociologique*, I, p. 31. MacLennan recognized that exogamy was most often practised within the tribe. Nevertheless, in accordance with his theory, he regarded this interior exogamy as a late and derived form. Frazer notes that the Australian tribes in which the members can marry with the members of any other clan, seem to be an exception. Tribes are more often divided into exogamous phratries. Thus the Tlingit are divided into the Wolf and Crow phraties. The members of the Crow phratry must marry those of the Wolf phratry and vice versa. (Frazer, *Totemism*). J. W. Powell (*Sociology, or the science of institutions*, pp. 703–4) observes that facts which have emerged since MacLennan's time do not support the distinction

which he proposed: 'There is no people, tribal or national, which has not its *incest group*: all peoples are at once endogamous and exogamous'. It is therefore an error to suppose that endogamy is only finally established where inequality between groups is found.

23   A. C. Lyall, *Asiatic studies*, ed. 1899, pp. 254 sq.

24   Cf. W. Robertson Smith *Kinship & marriage in early arabia*, 1884.

25   It has been amply proved that totemic practices abound among the anaryan tribes. (Cf. Crooke, *The popular religion & folklore of Northern India* (London, 1896), ii, ch. 3). But traces of these practices have been found even among relatively high Hindu castes, for example the Pallivals of Rajputana (Bhattacharya, *Hindu castes*, p. 69), or among the Humkars of Orissa. Cf. Risley, *Tribes and castes of Bengal*, pp. xlv, sq.; Lang, *Myth, ritual & religion* (London, 1887), ch. viii. Still more, Oldenberg has succeeded in demonstrating the totemic origins of many Brahmanic *gotra*. (*Religion du Véda*, French trans. p. 71). Totemism is then not so alien to Hinduism as M. Senart appears to believe.

26   Cf. Durkheim *Année Sociologique*, i, p. 31, and Frazer, *Totemism*. Frazer even cites totemic groups within which sexual relations are obligatory. Cf. *Année Sociologique*, iii, p. 218.

27   In the Native States of Central India, says Sir Alfred Lyall (*Asiatic studies*, ch. vi, p. 176) we can roughly establish some sort of social scale, having as its simple base the aboriginal horde and for summit the pure Aryan clan: it would not even be difficult to show that these various classes are connected by a real link and that they have at some point a common origin. In different degrees Risley, Nesfield and Ibbetson are partisans of this common origin theory. On the relations between tribes and castes, see *Census of India*, 1901, i, *India*, pp. 514–23; vi, *Bengal*, p. 362; xvii, *Punjab*, p. 300; xviii, *Baroda*, pp. 434, 502; xix, *Central India*, pp. 198, 202; xxv, *Rajputana*, p. 124.

28   Cf. Baden Powell, *Village communities in India* (London, 1899), pp. 47, 63 sq.

29   Cf. Dareste *versus* Haxthausen, *Études d'histoire du droit*, pp. ix–xi.

30   G. Cohn, *Gemeindenschaft und Hausgenossenschaft*, 1899.

31   See Oldenberg (*La religion du Véda*, p. 32) on the links between Indianism and primitive religions. Crooke (*Tribes and castes of the N.W. Provinces*, i, p. 58) and Frazer (*Golden bough*, ii, pp. 342 sq.) both try to discern the traces of primitive practices in some Brahmanic ceremonies. Cf. Lang, *Myth, ritual & religion*, chs. iii, viii, xvi.

32   *Caste in India*, p. 172.

33   Durkheim has frequently drawn attention to these facts in *Année Sociologique*, i, pp. 307–32; ii, pp. 319–23.

34   See Nesfield, *Caste system*, pp. 92 sq.

35   [Bouglé's reference here is to p. 70 of Senart's work. The corresponding area of the English translation provides no discussion of

these matters. Senart's discussion of the relations between family and caste is in part III, chs. IV & V of the English version.] See also Hearn *The Aryan household*, pp. 121, 210, also Lyall, *Asiatic studies*, ch. VI: 'In the altering social conditions it becomes impossible for related groups to maintain connections with each other by descent from a common source. The masses turn to various occupations, establish themselves in different places, contract marriages with strangers, worship new gods; the play of chance in this more complicated existence, shatters genealogies, loosens the ties of blood and effaces the patronymic name.' [I have translated from the French. Bouglé's reference is untraceable but the reference to ch. VI which I have given runs much along these lines.]

36 *Das Altindische Volkstum*, pp. 56 sq.
37 *Caste in India*, p. 177.
38 *Ibid.* p. 189. The thesis is also maintained by Hearn, *The Aryan household* and by Leist, *Altarisches Jus Civile*.

Chapter 3: Caste hierarchy and the priesthood

1 This subordination has led to the mistaken belief that the feudal system was to be found in Scotland. Cf. Conrady, *Geschichte der Clanverfassung in den Schottischen Hochlanden* (Leipzig, 1898), pp. 12–21.
2 M. Buhl (*Die Socialen Verhaltnisse der Israeliten*, pp. 35–40) recalling these facts, concludes from them that the primitive organization of the Hebrews was fundamentally aristocratic. The conclusion is questionable. Cf. *Année Sociologique*, III, p. 347.
3 Albrecht Weber *Indische Studien*, x, p. 44. [Bouglé also refers to Auguste Barth, *Les religions de l'Inde*, p. 160. There is no p. 160 in the French edition of 1885. The reader may refer to the English edition of 1882, ch. II, section 1, pp. 39–63.]
4 See Caland, *Altindischer Ahnencult*, pp. 19, 144.
5 Jolly, *Recht und Sitte*, p. 127; Senart, *Caste in India*, p. 183.
6 Ibbetson, quoted by Senart, *Caste in India*, p. 85.
7 Cf. Maspero, *Histoire ancienne des peuples de l'Orient classique*, I, pp. 127, 304.
8 This leads Zimmer to say that the Brahmans have fully realized the ideal pursued by the Church in our middle ages, *Altindische Leben*, p. 139. Cf. Macdonell, *A history of Sanskrit literature* (London, 1900), pp. 159–60.
9 According to Weber, *Indische Studien*, x, pp. 26–32, it is easy to see that the two powers, which he calls the *sacerdotium* and the *imperium*, were not always amicable. Sometimes they helped each other, at other times they acted as mutual checks. Subtle formulae are employed to avoid giving predominance to one or the other. However, in the final analysis the Brahman is superior: he can exist without the Kshatriya, but the latter cannot exist without him.

10   Senart, *Caste in India*, pp. 138 sq.
11   See Regnaud, *Matériaux pour servir à l'histoire de la philosophie de l'Inde* (Paris, 1876), pp. 55–60. Fick, *Die sociale Gliederung*, p. 42. See above, pp. 66–8.
12   Quoted by Weber, *Indische Studien*, p. 30.
13   On the development of the importance of the *purohita*, see Oldenberg, *Religion du Véda* (French translation), pp. 319–26.
14   Cf. Deussen *Algemeine Geschichte der Philosophie, mit besonderer Berücksichtigung der Religionen* (Leipzig, 1894), I, p. 166.
15   *Caste in India*, p. 212.
16   M. de la Mazelière *Essai sur l'evolution de la civilization indienne*, 1903, see above pp. 66–7.
17   Sherring, *Hindu tribes and castes* (London, 1872), III, pp. 218, 235.
18   *Essai sur le Véda* (Paris, 1863), pp. 283–5.
19   *Philosophie des grecs* (French translation) I, p. 54.
20   *Ibid*. p. 282.
21   Thus the boar worshipped by certain aboriginal tribes becomes an avatar of Vishnu. Several examples of this 'Brahmanization of cults' are found in Crooke, Risley and Lyall (*op. cit.*). In this connection Barth comments on the convenience of the avatar theory: it allows the reconciliation of the aspiration towards a certain monotheism with an irresistible tendency towards multiple cults. (*Religions of India*, p. 101). Monier Williams (*Modern India and Indians* (London, 1891), 5th edition, p. 230) goes so far as to say, on the basis of these facts, that Hindu pantheism is only a facade for their polytheism. Cf. Hopkins, *Religions of India* (London, 1898), pp. 361 sq.
22   See Lyall, *Asiatic Studies*, ch. v, arguing against Max Müller. Cf. Schlagintweit, *Zeitschrift der D.M.G.*, 33, p. 568. Risley, *Tribes and castes of Bengal*, I, pp. xvi–xx.
23   See Bernier (*Voyages*, II, p. 138) 'When, on that matter, I told them that in a cold country it would be impossible to observe their law during the winter and this showed their law to be purely the invention of man, they gave me this pleasant reply: they did not claim that their law was universal, God had made it only for them and that it was for this reason that they could not receive foreigners into their religion and, in addition, that they did not think our Law to be false, it was quite possible that for us it was good.'
24   Cf. Sylvain Lévi, *La Science des religions de l'Inde*, p. 2: 'Indifferent to dogma as to rites, conveniently resting upon the pliable authority of the Vedas, the Brahman pursues with tenacity the ideal outlined by his legislators: his slowly victorious propaganda dreams of imposing the hierarchy of castes upon the whole of India, a hierarchy which lifts him above the gods.'
25   Senart, *Caste in India*, p. 105.
26   Quoted by A. Weber, *Indische Studien*, x, p. 71.

27 Senart, *Caste in India*.

28 Oldenberg, *Buddha*, p. 32.

29 Cf. Zimmer, *Altindisches Leben*, pp. 105–15.

30 *Tribes and castes of Bengal*, I, p. xxiv.

31 *Caste in India*, p. 169. [In *The people of India*, 1908, p. 28, Rislev modified the passage quoted by prefacing the clause: '*For those parts of India where there is an appreciable strain of Dravidian blood* it is scarcely a paradox etc.']

32 See above p. 105.

33 *Census of India* (Calcutta, 1903), I, *India* by Risley and Gait, p. 555; XIII *Central Provinces* by Russell, p. 193. Cf. Baines, *J.R.A.S.*, 26, p. 664; Risley, *Race basis in Indian politics*, pp. 751 sq.

34 Dubois, *Hindu manners*, p. 23. [The English translation has 'illustrious order'.] See also his detailed account of the detailed precautions taken by Brahmans to avoid pollution and their daily purifications. Cf. Vidal de la Blache, *Le peuple de l'Inde d'après la série des recensements* in *Annales de geographie*, 15 Nov. 1906, p. 437: 'It is not, as is often said, their purity of race but their ritual orthodoxy that establishes the idea of their social superiority.'

35 This is manifest in the zeal with which Brahmans are imitated. We see low castes adopting and scrupulously respecting some custom 'launched' by the Brahmans, in the hope of rising a degree in the scale of purity. In this way the practice of infant marriage and the interdiction on widow remarriage have been spread from caste to caste. Cf. Jolly, *Recht und Sitte*, p. 75. See above, p. 92.

36 *Sacrifice: its nature and function* by Mauss and Hubert, English translation by W. D. Halls (London, 1964).

37 The more so as these operations varied considerably in detail according to requirements. See S. Lévi, *La doctrine du sacrifice dans les Brahmanas* (Paris, 1898), p. 123. Many authors attribute decisive influence to these questions of technique in the formation of the priestly occupation. See, for example, Macdonell, *A history of Sanskrit literature*, 1900, p. 160; Deussen, *Allgemein. Gesch. der Philos.*, I, p. 169; Dutt, *Ancient civilisation of India*, I, p. 230; Baines, *J.R.A.S.*, 26, p. 663.

38 Oldenberg, *Religion du Véda*, p. 337.

39 On this subject see Oldenberg, *Zeitschrift der D.M.G.*, 1897, p. 274 fn.

40 Frazer lists the various consequences of this in *The golden bough*, I.

41 Proof that this consecration is a sort of normal condition for the Brahman, is the fact that he is not required to make any special preparation, except in unusual circumstances, before 'entering' the sacrifice. See Mauss & Hubert, *Sacrifice*.

42 See Bergaigne, *La religion Védique d'après les hymnes du Rig Véda* (Paris, 1878), I, Introduction. See above p. 185 sq.

43 *Année Sociologique*, II, Preface.

44 It is necessary, therefore, to generalize what Robertson Smith has to say about the relations between the Aryans and the Semites:

> The differences between the Semite and Aryan religions, for example, are not so primitive or fundamental as is often imagined. Not only in matters of worship, but in social organisation generally – and we have seen that ancient religion is but a part of the social order which embraces gods and men alike – the two races, Aryans and Semites, began on lines which are so much alike as to be almost indistinguishable, and the divergence between their paths, which becomes more and more apparent in the course of ages, was not altogether an affair of race and innate tendency, but depended in a great measure on the operation of special local and historical causes.
>
> In both races the first steps of social and religious development took place in small communities, which at the dawn of history had a political system based on the principle of kinship, and were mainly held together by the tie of blood, the only social bond which then had absolute and undisputed strength, being enforced by the law of blood revenge.

W. Robertson Smith, *The religion of the Semites*, 3rd ed. (London, 1927), p. 32. [Where Robertson Smith writes 'not altogether an affair of race', Bouglé translates 'nullement affaire de race'. In the final sentence Bouglé excises the role of blood revenge and concludes as follows: 'la cohesion n'est assure que par les liens du sang, les seuls qui aient une force absolue et indiscutée'.]

PART 2: THE VITALITY OF THE SYSTEM

Chapter 1: Caste and the Buddhist revolution

1 See Rai Bahadur Lala Baji Nath, *Hinduism: ancient and modern*, (Meerut, 1899), ch. 1; Dutt, *Ancient civilizations*, i, pp. 70, 104; iii, pp. 81, 153, 360, cf. Schröder, *Indiens Literatur*, p. 411.

2 M. de la Mazelière, *Essai*, ii, *passim*.

3 S. Levi, *Le Népal*, Introduction, p. 3.

4 This is what M. de la Mazelière has tried to bring out in the work cited above.

5 Lyall, *Asiatic studies*, ch. 1, 'Religion of an Indian province'.

6 See Barth, *The religions of India*, pp. 238–51; Monier Williams, *Hinduism*, pp. 136 sq.; Bhattacharya, *Hindu castes*, p. 395; Lyall, *Asiatic studies*, p. 34.

7 Barth, *The religions of India*, p. 143 observes that the Jains, while still refusing in principle to admit the existence of a sacerdotal caste, prefer to recruit their clergy from certain families, sometimes even, it seems, among Brahmans.

8 Bhattacharya, *Hindu castes*, pp. 440 sq. See his observations on the exclusiveness of the Ballhabites [Vallabhites], p. 456.

9 Lyall, *Asiatic studies*, pp. 193 sq.; Risley, *Tribes and castes*, p. lxxii.

10 *La Bible de l'humanité*, p. 75 fn.

11 *Nouveau essais de critique et d'histoire*, p. 344.

12 *Mythologie comparée* (French trans.), p. 396.
13 Barth, *The religions of India*, pp. 134 sq.
14 Burnouf, *Introduction à l'histoire du bouddhisme indien*, pp. 183 sq.
15 Oldenberg, *Buddha*, pp. 172–3.
16 *Ibid.* p. 170.
17 *Ibid.* pp. 202–23.
18 *Ibid.* p. 177. Fick also points out that there is rarely mention of the lower classes in the Buddhist orders. (*Die Sociale Gliederung*, p. 51.)
19 *Caste in India*, p. 205.
20 Burnouf, *Introduction*, p. 339.
21 Oldenberg, *Buddha*, pp. 360 sq.
22 Burnouf, *Introduction*, pp. 74, 328.
23 One of Oldenberg's criticisms (in *Aus Indien und Iran*) of Taine's *Essai* is that it exaggerates Buddhist pessimism.
24 Cf. Oldenberg *Buddha*, pp. 304 sq.; Barth, *The religions of India*, p. 114, Lehmann, in *Manuel d'histoire des religions*, Chantepie de Saussaye (French trans.), p. 387.
25 Cf. Kern, *Manual of Indian Buddhism* (Strasbourg, 1896), p. 12.
26 *Philosophie analytique de l'histoire*, ii, p. 143.
27 *Nouveaux essais*, p. 331.
28 Oldenberg, *Buddha*, p. 263.
29 Kern, *Indian Buddhism*, p. 49; Barth, *The religions of India*, p. 113.
30 *Année Philosophique*, 1868.

Chapter 2: Caste under British administration

1 This is the *Census of India*. For each Province there is a volume of statistics and a volume of reports. The general results for the whole of India are assembled into special volumes (edited for 1901 by Risley and Gait). May we be permitted at this point to thank Mr Risley who, once he knew that we were concerned with caste in India, most graciously sent us the entire collection for 1901.
2 See Piriou, *L'Inde contemporaine et le mouvement national* (Paris, 1905), chs. iv and xii; Métin, *L'Inde d'aujourd'hui* (Paris, 1903), ch. vii.
3 See above p. 30.
4 See Risley and Russell's criticisms of Nesfield's theory (*Census of India*, 1901, i, p. 550; xiii, p. 151). Cf. Hopkins, *India old and new*, pp. 180 sq.
5 Enthoven, *Census, 1901*, p. 521. Cf. Russell's report for the *Central Provinces*, xiii, p. 185.
6 Gait's report, *Census*, vi, p. 361.
7 Risley, after noting the obstacles confronting egalitarian reformers, concludes: 'Race dominates religion; the sect is weaker than the caste' *India*, p. 523.
8 *Central Provinces*, xiii, p. 156.
9 *India*, i, p. 524.

10 *India*, I, pp. 519, 531. Cf. *Central India*, XIX, p. 202; *Punjab*, XVII, p. 319; *Rajputana*, XXV, p. 124; *Baroda*, XVIII, p. 502.

11 See for example: Luard, *Central India*, XIX, p. 193; Russell, *Central Provinces*, XIII, p. 142; Gait, *Bengal*, VI, p. 351.

12 *Rajputana*, XXV, p. 130.

13 *India*, I, p. 539.

14 See Gait, *Bengal*, VI, pp. 366 sq.

15 *Central Provinces*, XIII, p. 164.

16 See Risley's conclusions, *India*, I, pp. 555–6.

17 *Bombay*, IV, p. 183.

18 *India*, I, p. 425. Cf. *Central India*, pp. 193 sq.

19 *India*, I, pp. 425 sq.

20 *Ibid.* p. 429.

21 *Rajputana*, XXV, p. 129.

22 *India*, I, p. 430.

23 See F. Chalaye's reflections upon *l'Européanisation du Japon* in *Revue de Paris*, I February 1904 and our own articles, 'Orientalisme et sociologie' and 'Les consequences sociologiques de la victoire Japonaise' in *Revue Bleue*, 26 January and 13 April 1907.

PART 3: THE EFFECTS

Chapter 1: Race

1 Topinard, 'L'Anthropologie du Bengale' in *Anthropologie*, March–June 1892, no. 3, p. 282.

2 See Reibmayr, *Inzucht und Vermischung beim Menschen* (Leipzig, 1897), pp. 94 sq.

3 Risley, *Tribes and castes of Bengal*, I, p. 26.

4 *Voyage*, I, p. 153.

5 Quoted by Schlagintweit, *Zeitschrift der D.M.G.*, 33, p. 307.

6 Risley, *Tribes and castes of Bengal*, I, p. 39.

7 *Ibid.* II, p. 110.

8 *Ibid.* I, p. 30.

9 'Races et castes de l'Inde' in *Anthropologie*, 185, VI, pp. 176–81.

10 Published in the *Ethnographical glossary* which accompanies the two volumes cited above on the tribes and castes of Bengal.

11 *Tribes and castes of Bengal*, I, p. 34.

12 Dubois, *Hindu manners*, p. 322.

13 M. A. Sherring, *Sacred city of the Hindus*, p. 14, quoted by Crooke, *Tribes and castes of the North-Western Provinces and Oudh*, II, p. 160.

14 *Brief view of the caste system*, p. 75.

15 See the observations of the officials in charge of the census collected in Schlagintweit, *Zeitschrift fur D.M.G.*, 33, pp. 572–99.

16 Senart, *Caste in India*, p. 169.

17 Barth, 'Bulletin des Religions de l'Inde' in *Revue de l'Histoire des Religions*, XXIX, p. 58.
18 *Madras Census Report*, I, pp. 116–75.
19 Crooke, *Tribes and castes of the N.W. Provinces.*
20 *Ibid.* p. 137.
21 *Anthropologie*, Mar.–June, 1892, p. 310.
22 See above p. 25.
23 Schlagintweit, *Zeitschrift fur D.M.G.*, 33, pp. 560–75.
24 Senart, *Caste in India*, p. 170.
25 Crooke, *Tribes and castes of the N.W. Provinces*, p. 174.
26 Pramatha Nath Bose, *History of Hindu civilisation during British rule*, I, pp. 30 sq.
27 See above p. 83.
28 Pramatha Nath Bose, *Hindu civilisation, passim.*
29 *Census of India 1901. India*, I, pp. 162 sq.
30 *Ibid.* pp. 217, 220.
31 The bulk of these examples is derived from Bhattacharya, *Hindu castes.*
32 *India*, I, p. 163.
33 See Pramatha Nath Bose, *Hindu civilisation*, III.

Chapter 2: Law

1 Jolly, *Recht und Sitte* (*Grundriss der Indo-arischen Philologie*, Bd II, 8 Heft), pp. 14–19.
2 *The laws of Manu*, in *Sacred Books of the East*, ed. G. Bühler, 1886.
3 *History of India*, 3rd ed. (London, 1826), pp. 192 sq. Cf. Jolly, *Recht und sitte*, p. 17 and *Zeitschrift für vergleich. Rechtswissenschaft*, 1878, pp. 234–60 (*Über die Systematik des indischen Rechts*).
4 *The division of labour in society* (English translation) Free Press, 1964, p. 69.
5 Oldenberg in *Zum ältesten Strafrecht der Kulturvölker* (Leipzig, 1905), p. 73.
6 Jolly, *Recht und Sitte*, p. 138; Dareste, *Études d'histoire du droit*, p. 78; Oldenberg, *Zum Strafrecht*, p. 74.
7 *Die Idee der Wiedervergeltung in der Geschichte und Philosophie des Strafrechtes* (Blasing, 1895).
8 Jolly, *Rechte und Sitte*, p. 123. Oldenberg, *Zum Strafrecht*, p. 25, cf. *Manu*, IX, 236, 240; XI, 53.
9 Jolly, *Recht und Sitte*, p. 121.
10 Oldenberg, *Religion du Véda* (French trans.), pp. 243, 271.
11 *Yajnavalkya*, quoted by Oldenberg, *Zum Strafrecht*, p. 76.
12 The different degrees of false witness are remarkable, VIII, 120, 121. See other examples in Thonissen, *Histoire du droit criminel des peuples ancien* (Brussels, 1869), p. 58.
13 Jolly, *Recht und Sitte*, p. 122.
14 Jolly, *ZVVR*, 1903, pp. 112–15.

15 Westermarck (*The origin and development of moral ideas* (London, 1906), p. 434) has collected several examples.

16 See Glotz, *La solidarité de la famille dans le droit criminel en Grèce* (Paris, 1905), pp. 383 sq.

17 See above p. 25.

18 *Census, 1901*, VI, *Bengal*, p. 361; I, *India*, p. 528. We have already suggested that, on more than one point, the English enquirers seem disposed to react against the excessive suspicion inspired by Senart's criticism of the theory found in Manu.

19 Senart, *Caste in India*, pp. 21 sq., 180.

20 If we have not devoted a special chapter to religious phenomena this is because in every chapter, whether we are dealing with law, economics or literature, we perpetually see religious beliefs and scruples at work.

21 See Schlagintweit, *Zeitschrift der D.M.G.*, 33, p. 583. See *Census 1901*, I, *India*, p. 523.

22 In this connection see what Marillier has to say on Melanesian *tabu* in *Études de critique et d'histoire*, 2nd series (Bibl. de l'École des Hautes Études), p. 42.

23 Barth, *The religions of India*, p. xvii; Monier Williams, *Modern India*, p. 228; Irving, *Theory and practice of caste* (London, 1853), pp. 134, 137. Mayne, *Treatise of Hindu law*, on the Census of 1891 (*N.W. Provinces report*, p. 192 and and *Assam report*, p. 84).

24 M. A. Sherring, *Hindu tribes and castes*, III, p. 276.

25 Kohler, 'Rechtsgeschichte und Weltentwicklung', *ZVVR*, 1885, p. 323.

26 Ihering, *Esprit du droit romain*, I, pp. 268–307.

27 Girard, *Histoire de l'organisation judiciaire des Romains*, I, pp. 32–5.

28 Lambert, *La fonction du droit civil comparé*, pp. 639 sq.

29 Cuq, *Les institutions juridiques chez les Romains*, I, p. 23.

30 *Das Mahabharata als Epos und Rechtsbuch*, p. 290.

31 Maine, *Études sur l'histoire de droit* (Paris, 1889), p. 283. [This is a collection made by a French editor of various separate articles.]

32 Schröder, *Indiens Literatur und Kultur*, p. 412.

33 See West and Bühler, *A digest of Hindu law*, 4th ed. (London, 1919), pp. 31–2; J. C. Ghose, *Principles of the Hindu law* (Calcutta, 1906); Mayne, *Treatise*, p. 38; Maine, *Early law and custom* (London, 1891), pp. 12 sq.

34 See Kohler, *ZVVR*, 1903, pp. 184 sq.; Thonissen, *Histoire du droit*, p. 61.

35 See above p. 78.

36 Kovalewsky, *Coutume contemporaine et loi ancienne. Droit coutumier ossétien* (Paris, 1899), pp. 287 sq.; Steinmetz, *Ethnologische Studien zur ersten Entwicklung der Strafe* (Leyden and Leipzig, 1894). Cf. Mauss, *Revue de l'Histoire des Religions*, 1897, pp. 50–8.

37 Glotz, *La solidarité de la famille*, pp. 232 sq.
38 Lambert, *La fonction du droit civile*, pp. 231–804.
39 Roth, 'Wergeld im Veda' in *Zeitschrift der D.M.G.*, 41, pp. 672–6; Jolly, *Recht und Sitte*, p. 131; Oldenberg, *Zum Strafsrecht*, p. 72; Kohler, *ZVVR*, 1903, p. 180.
40 Jolly, *Recht und Sitte*, p. 127; Caland, *Altind. Ahnencult*, p. 144; Senart, *Caste in India*, p. 182.
41 Kovalewsky, *Coutume contemporaire*, pp. 315 sq.
42 Senart, *Caste in India*, p. 219.
43 *Die sociale Gliederung*, p. 75 fn.
44 See Sylvain Lévi, *Le Népal*, ɪ, Introduction, p. 4.
45 Jolly, *Recht und Sitte*, pp. 16, 127, 132; Kohler, *ZVVR*, 1903, p. 188.
46 *La fonction du droit civile*, p. 730.
47 Sumner Maine, *Lectures on the early history of institutions* (London, 1885), p. 382; cf. Lyall's review published in the French translation of *Dissertations on early law and custom*.
48 Sylvain Lévi, *Le Népal*, ɪ, pp. 15, 229.
49 Fick, *Die sociale gliederung*, ch. ɪv; Weber, *Indische Studien*, x, pp. 26–30.
50 Macdonell, *Sanskrit literature*, p. 160; cf. Zimmer, *Alt. Leben*, p. 192.
51 See Glotz, *La solidarite de la famille*, p. 23; Kovalewsky, *Coutume contemporaire*, p. 197.
52 Daghestan proverb quoted by Kovalewsky.
53 Jolly, *Recht und Sitte*, p. 119; Senart, *Caste in India*, part ɪ, ch. 6; Dubois, *Hindu manners*, p. 38.
54 Jolly, *Richt und Sitte*, p. 115.
55 Main, *Etudes*, p. ɛ¹
56 Senart, *Caste in India*, p. 69.
57 See the passages noted by Sorg, *Introduction à l'étude du droit hindou*, pp. 40–5.
58 Mayne, *Treatise*, p. 54; Ghose, *Principles*, p. 726; cf. Maine, *Early history of institutions*, p. 7.
59 Ghose, *Principles*, p. 722.
60 *Treatise*, p. 5.
61 Ghose, *Principles*, pp. 1, 3, 720.
62 This is Mayne's opinion in the above cited work; cf. Jolly, *Recht und Sitte*, p. 48; Hunter, *Imperial gazetteer of India*, vɪ, p. 116.
63 Mayne, *Treatise*, p. 4; Ghose, *Principles*, *passim*.
64 Mayne, *Treatise*, p. 10.
65 The custom of marrying children very young and particularly that of preventing widow remarriage can be explained in this way. See above p. 92.
66 Arthur Steele, *The law and custom of Hindu castes* (London, 1868), xɪɪɪ, p. 122.
67 J. H. Nelson, *A view of the Hindu law as administered by the high court of judicature at Madras* (Madras 1877) and *A prospectus of the scientific*

study of the Hindu law (London and Madras, 1881). Criticized by Barth in *Revue critique*, 1878, i, p. 417; 1882, ii, p. 109.

68 Lambert, *La fonction du droit civile, passim.*
69 Westermarck, *Moral ideas*, pp. 193–8.
70 See Durkheim, 'Deux lois de l'évolution penale', *Année Sociologique*, iv, pp. 65–95. Cf. his *The division of labour*, part i, chs. 3 and 4.
71 This is the organizing theme of Frazer's observations in *The golden bough.*
72 James Mill in his article 'Caste' in the *Encyclopaedia Britannica*, shows how the division of labour between castes blocks the progressive effects of a division of labour in the economic order. We must say that the same is true *a fortiori* of the effects of the division of labour in the social order. See above p. 156.
73 See the conclusions which emerge from Risley's enquiries concerning the hierarchy effectively recognized. *Census of India*, i, *India*, pp. 539 sq.; vi, *Bengal*, pp. 366 sq.; xiii, *Central Provinces*, p. 164.

Chapter 3: Economic life: consumption

1 Maine, *Études*, pp. 306, 358.
2 *Essays on Indian economics* (Bombay, 1898), p. 8.
3 *Ancient Sanskrit literature*, p. 18.
4 Oldenberg, *Buddha*, p. 12; *Die Literatur des alten Indiens* (Berlin, 1903).
5 Sherring, *Hindu tribes and castes*, iii, pp. 225–35.
6 'The social and military position of the ruling caste in ancient India, as represented by the sanskrit epic' in *Journal of the American Oriental Society*, xiii, pp. 180–90. On the early vitality of the Aryans in India see Romesh Chunder Dutt, *A History of civilisation in ancient India, based on sanskrit literature* (Calcutta, 1899), pp. 6–10.
7 Sylvain Lévi, *Le Népal*, p. 4.
8 Crawfurd, *Researches on ancient and modern India* (London, 1817), i, pp. 287–303; Lassen, *Indische Alterthumskunde* (Leipzig and London, 1867), i, p. 341; ii, p. 557; iii, pp. 5–11; iv, p. 880. Cf. Hunter, *Imperial gazetteer of India*, vi, ch. xix.
9 Lassen, *Indische Alt.* i, p. 343.
10 *Tableau historique de l'Inde*, 1833.
11 [In Bouglé's original text there is confusion here. Two passages are annotated as 1 and the third as 2. There are however only two references at the foot of the page. The first 'Op. cit. vi, p. 555, 91 [sic]' must relate to the 1881 or the 1885–7 editions of the *Imperial gazetteer*.]
12 See Dahlmann, *Das altindische Volkstum und seine Bedeutung fur die Gesellschaftskunde*. Cf. *Das Mahābhārata als Epos und Rechtsbuch.*
13 Lassen 'Ueber die altindische Handelsverfassung' in *Zeitschrift der D.M.G.*, 16, pp. 427–38. Cf. Dareste, *Études d'histoire du droit* (Paris, 1899), ch. iv.

Endnotes to pages 147–157

14 Quoted by Reveillout, *Le droit égyptien*, I, p. 150.
15 See above p. 125.
16 Monier Williams, *Modern India and the Indians*, pp. 157–62; Irving, *Theory and practice of caste*, pp. 134–7.
17 G. Birdwood, *The industrial arts of India* (London, 1880), p. 2.
18 Robertson Smith, *The religion of the Semites*, pp. 255–314.
19 *Le Népal*, I, p. 234; cf. *Industrial arts*, p. 311.
20 Quoted by Fick, *Die sociale Gliederung*.
21 *Comparative mythology* (London, 1881). Cf. Sherring, *Hindu tribes and castes*, III, p. 335; Monier Williams, *Modern India*, p. 49.
22 *Totemism and exogamy* (London, 1910).
23 See Dalton, *Ethnology of Bengal*, p. 56. Risley, *Tribes and castes*, I, xliv; rice, for example, is *tabu* for the Dhan section of the Chota Nagpur Mundas. They are obliged to eat millet. On prohibitions connected with totemism and the connection between them and caste traditions, see Crooke, *The popular-religion and folklore of northern India* (London, 1896), II, p. 159.
24 Maine, *Early law and custom* (ed. 1891), p. 48.
25 Maine, *Études*, p. 616.
26 De Lanoye, *L.Inde contemporaine*. Cf. Sonnerat, *Voyage*.
27 Quoted in *Journal des Savants*, 1895, p. 271; Vidal de la Blache, *Annales de géographie*, July, 1906, p. 241.
28 *Modern India*, pp. 29–61. [This astonishing statement is one of those rare examples which indicates that Bouglé had no first hand experience of India. It was no more generally true of Bombay in his day than it is now.]
29 Bhattacharya, *Hindu castes*, pp. 26–7.
30 Dubois, *Hindu manners*, pp. 26–7. [The wearing of red flowers in this manner was objected to by the Pariahs as a privilege exclusive to the Right-Hand faction.]
31 *Le Népal*, I, 372.
32 *Division of labour* (English trans.), pp. 272–3.
33 *Die Entwicklung der menschlichen Bedürfniss und die sociale Gliederung der Gesellschaft* (Leipzig, 1901).
34 See Baudrillart, *Histoire du luxe*, 1878, II, ch. VI.
35 A phrase used by Dumont in *Dépopulation et civilisation* (Paris, 1890).

Chapter 4: Economic life: production

1 Dahlmann, *Altind. Volkstum*, pp. 65, 112.
2 See our 'Revue générale des théories récentes sur la division du travail' in *Année Sociologique*, VI, pp. 73–122.
3 Fick, *Die sociale Gliederung*, p. 194. Nesfield, *Brief view of the caste system*, p. 19. Risley, *Tribes and castes*, II, p. 183.

4 Rhys Davids, 'Notes on early economic conditions in northern India' in *Journal of the Royal Asiatic Society*, October 1901, p. 868.

5 The reference here is to a French translation *Les institutions professionnelles et industrielles* (Paris, 1898), p. 305. See *Principles of sociology*, II and III.

6 V. K. Bücher, *Die Entstehung der Volkswirthschaft*, ch. II.

7 Th. Veblen, *The theory of the leisure class* (New York and London, 1899), p. 5.

8 *La lutte des races*, pp. 204, 216, 235.

9 Bücher, *Die Entstehung der Volkswirthschaft*, pp. 30–5.

10 See the many examples given by Frazer in *The golden bough.*

11 'La hiérarchie des professions', in *Revue de Paris*, 15 September 1905, pp. 390–417.

12 Zimmer, *Altindisches Leben*, pp. 105–15.

13 Fick, *Die sociale Gliederung*, pp. 205–10.

14 *Ibid.* p. 204.

15 Bhattacharya, *Hindu castes*, p. 306. Cf. Crooke, *Tribes and castes of the North West Provinces*, IV, p. 45.

16 R. C. Dutt, *History of civilization in ancient India*, III, pp. 197, 318.

17 *Ibid.* Cf. *D.M.G.*, 37, p. 586.

18 See Guiraud, *La main-d'œuvre industrielle dans l'ancienne Grèce* (Paris, 1900).

19 On the consequences following even today upon analogous contagion phenomena, see Aubert, 'Maîtrise du Pacifique', *Revue de Paris*, February 1907, p. 877: 'In the eyes of these whites the Asiatic lowers and pollutes any trade that he follows.'

20 *Cours de philosophie positive*, V, p. 183.

21 See *Principes d'économie politique* (French trans.), II, p. 442.

22 See above p. 111 sq.

23 Jacquemont, *Voyages*, I, p. 321.

24 Sonnerat, *Voyage*, I, p. 186.

25 Birdwood, *Industrial arts*, pp. 130–6.

26 Sonnerat, *Voyage*, I, p. 184.

27 Article 'Caste', *Encyclopaedia Britannica* (1824 supplement).

28 Birdwood, *Industrial arts*, pp. 315–20.

29 Bernier, *Voyages*, II, p. 37.

30 Durkheim, *Division of labour.*

31 *Ibid.* p. 199.

32 *Principes d'economie politique*, II, pp. 250 sq.

33 *Indian economics*, pp. 8, 122.

34 *Voyages*, I, 272.

35 Durkheim, *Division of labour*, part I, ch. 1.

36 See Sherring, *Hindu tribes and castes*; de la Mazelière, *Essai sur l'evolution de la civilisation indienne*, *passim.*

37 Oldenberg, *Buddha*, p. 11. Cf. Ratzel, *Politische Geographie*, p. 24.

38 'The social organization of India is essentially anti-urban' Baines, *Report on the census*, 1881, I, p. 274. Cf. Vidal de la Blache, *Annales de Géographie*, 15 July 1906, p. 374.

39 See Métin, *L'Inde d'aujourd'hui* (Paris, 1903), ch. VII. Cf. Piriou, *L'inde contemporaine*, ch. IV.

40 *General report on the Census of India*, 1891, p. 97.

41 Ranade, *Indian economics*, p. 120 *et passim*.

42 Senart, *Caste in India*, pp. 194 sq. Hunter, *Imperial gazetteer*, VI, p. 46. Piriou, *L'inde contemporaine*, 'Caste helps us to understand the village, as the latter helps us to explain the former.'

43 *The Indian village community* (London, 1896); *The origin and growth of village communities in India* (London, 1899). Cf. *Année Sociologique*, I, pp. 359–63, IV, pp. 334–7. See also Abdullah Yusuf-Ali, *Life and labour of the people of India* (London, 1907), pp. 77, 220.

44 Baines, *General report on the census of India*, pp. 93 sq.

45 See Hunter, *Imperial gazetteer*, VI, p. 599.

46 Senart, *Caste in India*, p. 167; Hearn, *The Aryan household*, p. 241.

47 Fick, *Die sociale Gliederung*, p. 182.

48 Maine, *Études*, p. 157.

49 Hopkins, *India old and new*, pp. 203 sq.; Fick, *Die sociale Gliederung*, chs. IX and X.

50 Silvain Lévi, *Le Népal*, I, p. 4.

51 Hunter, *Imperial gazeteer*, p. 557.

52 Huvelin, *Essai historique sur le droit des marchés et foires*, 1897; 'L'histoire du droit commercial', *Revue de synthèse historique*, 1904.

53 Rhys Davids, 'Notes on Early Economics', *J.R.A.S.*, October 1901, p. 874.

54 Abdullah Yusuf-Ali in his recent *Life and labour of the people of India* to which we have already referred, insists upon the importance of the fact that while the villages in India are distinct unities and the centres of a communal life, the towns were, for the most part, no more than 'geographical expressions without such a life', p. 3.

55 Sherring, *Hindu tribes and castes*, III, p. 218; *Census of India*, 1901, *Central Provinces* (report by Russell), p. 194.

56 *Census of India*, 1901, I, pp. 553 sq.

57 Schmoller, *Principes*, II, chs. II, III.

Chapter 5: Literature

1 Senart, *Caste in India*, pp. 218–19.

2 *Die Literatur des alten Indiens* (Berlin, 1903), pp. 11, 132.

3 Lacombe has frequently emphasized this point. See *De l'histoire considerée comme science* (Paris, 1894), ch. XVIII and, above all, *La psychologie des individus et des societés chez Taine, historien des littératures* (Paris, 1906).

4 Ouvré, *Les formes littéraires de la pensée greque* (Paris, 1900), p. 7.

5   Lyall, *Asiatic studies*, ch. II.
6   On this subject see Lanson, 'L'Histoire littéraire et la sociologie', *Revue de métaphysique et de morale*, 1904, pp. 266 sq.
7   Henry, *Les littératures de l'Inde* (Paris, 1904), p. 1.
8   Hopkins, 'The religions of India' in *Handbook of the history of religions*, ed. Jastrow (Boston and London, 1898), p. 2.
9   See Lehmann's preliminary observations in Chantepie de la Saussaie's *Manuel d'histoire des religions* (French trans:) Paris, p. 317.
10   Silvain Lévi, *La doctrine du sacrifice dans les Brahmanas* (*Bibl. de l'École des hautes études*, XI) (Paris, 1898), p. 10.
11   Lang, *Myth, ritual and religion*. On the relation between Brahmanic rites and popular practices, compare Hillebrandt: *Ritual-Litteratur, Vedische Opfer und Zauber* (in Bühler's *Grundriss*, 1897, p. 2).
12   Oldenberg, *Die Literatur des alten Indiens*, p. 25.
13   Silvain Lévi, *Doctrine du sacrifice*, p. 7.
14   See above p. 42.
15   Winternitz (*Geschichte der indischen Literatur* (Leipzig, 1904), I, pp. 64 sq.) instances and discusses the opinions of the partisans of 'spontaneous poetry' in the Vedas. Cf. Macdonell, *Sanskrit literature*, p. 65.
16   See Dutt, *Ancient India*, I, p. 95.
17   *Introduction à la philosophie analytique de l'histoire* (Paris, 1896), pp. 304, 311. Cf. Deussen, *Allgemeine Geschichte der Philosophie mit besonderer Berücksichtigung der Religionen* (Leipzig, 1894), I, p. 74.
18   Oldenberg, *Die Literatur des alten Indiens*, pp. 23, 51.
19   Oldenberg, *La religion du Véda* (French trans.), pp. 260 sq.; Silvain Lévi, *Doctrine du sacrifice*, Introduction, p. 9.
20   Oldenberg, *Religion du Véda*, pp. 313, 337. Cf. Macdonell, *Sanskrit literature*, p. 73.
21   Bergaigne, *La religion védique d'après les hymnes du Rig-Véda*, III, p. 319.
22   Oldenberg, *Religion du Véda*, p. 373. Bergaigne, *La religion Védique*, III, p. 320.
23   Oldenberg, *Religion du Véda*, p. 37. This notion is emphasized by Schröder, *Indiens Literatur*, p. 145.
24   Silvain Lévi, *Revue Critique*, 1892, p. 3.
25   See Henry's criticism of Silvain Lévi's thesis in his Preface to Oldenberg's *Religion du Véda* (French trans.). Cf. Hopkings, *Religions of India*, pp. 17 sq.
26   Regnaud, *Matériaux pour servir à l'histoire de la philosophie de l'Inde*, I, p. 9. Cf. Deussen, *Allgemein. Geschichte*, I, part 2, p. 17.
27   Oldenberg, *Buddha*, p. 50.
28   Regnaud, *Matériaux*, p. 63. Cf. Hopkins, *Religions of India*, p. 226.
29   Deussen, *Allgemein. Geschichte*, part II, p. 58.
30   Silvain Lévi, *Doctrine du sacrifice*. p. 10.
31   Deussen, *Allgemein. Geschichte*, part I, p. 174.

32 Silvain Lévi, *Doctrine du sacrifice.*
33 See for example Deussen, *Allgemein Geschichte*, p. 97. Oldenberg, *Buddha*, p. 36.
34 Oldenberg, *Religion du Véda*, p. 29.
35 For this reason Max Müller insists that, in connection with vedic religion, we should not speak of monotheism nor polytheism but *henotheism*. See Schröder, *Indiens Literatur*, p. 77.
36 Deussen, *Allgemein. Geschichte*, part II, Theologie. Cf. *Das System des Vedanta* (Leipzig, 1883), part I; Hopkins, *Religions of India*, x; Mauss and Hubert, 'Theorie genérale de la magie', *Année Sociologique*, VII, p. 117.
37 *Buddha*, p. 47.
38 See above, pp. 76–8.
39 See for example Regnaud, *Matériaux*, II, p. 202.
40 Gomperz, *Les penseurs grecs* (French trans.), I, p. 48.
41 Louis Ménard, *Du polythéisme hellénique* (Paris, 1863), III and p. xiv.
42 Decharme, *La critique des traditions religieuses chez les grecs, des origines au temps de Plutarque* (Paris, 1904).
43 See Lehmann, *Manuel*, p. 322.
44 Early on Bernier remarked (*Voyages* (Amsterdam, 1710), II, p. 150), recalling the peculiar astronomical theories of the Brahmans with whom he had talked: 'All these enormous irrelevancies made me often think to myself that if these were the famous sciences of the ancient Indian Brahmans a lot of people were deceived in their notions about them.' Cf. Milhaud, *Leçons sur les origines de la science grecque* (Paris, 1893), p. 144.
45 Oldenberg, *Literatur*, pp. 139–45.
46 Senart, 'Le théâtre indien', *Revue des Deux Mondes*, 13 May 1891, p. 109.
47 See Gomperz, *Les penseurs grecs*, I, pp. 53, 170, 177.
48 Barth, *The religions of India*, ch. v. Cf. Hopkins, *The religions of India*, chs. XIV, XV.
49 Hopkins, *The religions of India*, p. 169.
50 Ouvré, *Les formes littéraires de la pensée grecque*, p. 60.
51 Hopkins (*Journal of the American Oriental Society*, XII, pp. 181, 190) insists on this warlike characteristic. See Lehman's remarks in *Manuel*, p. 316.
52 Oldenberg, *Literatur*, p. 157. Cf. Burnouf, *Le Bhagavata Purana*, p. 15.
53 Dahlmann, *Das Mahābhārata als Epos und Rechtsbuch*, part II, section 2.
54 Barth, *The religions of India*, pp. 169, 222 sq. Cf. Crooke, *The popular religion and folklore of northern India* (London, 1898), pp. 107, 110, 132.
55 Burnouf, *Le Bhagavata*, Introduction, p. 35, lii. Cf. V. Henry, *Les littératures de l'Inde*, p. 190.

56 Sylvain Lévi, *Le théâtre indien* (Paris, 1890). See Senart, 'Le Théâtre
    indien', *Revue des Deux Mondes*, 1 May 1891. [The earlier reference
    to Senart's article gives 13 May in the same *Revue.*]
57 Silvain Lévi, *Le théâtre indien*, p. 474.
58 Senart, *Caste in India*, p. 121.
59 Silvain Lévi, *Le théâtre indien*, p. 153.
60 *Ibid.* p. 420.
61 Senart, *Caste in India*, p. 89; Silvain Lévi, *Le théâtre indien*, p. 423.
62 Silvain Lévi, *Le théâtre indien*, pp. 417 sq.
63 *Ibid.* p. 425.